Beyond Chrismukkah

SAMIRA K. MEHTA

Beyond Chrismukkah

The Christian-Jewish Interfaith Family
in the United States

The University of North Carolina Press *Chapel Hill*

Set in Arno Pro by Westchester Publishing Services

Manufactured in the United States of America

The University of North Carolina Press has been a member of the
Green Press Initiative since 2003.

Library of Congress Cataloging-in-Publication Data
Names: Mehta, Samira K., author.
Title: Beyond Chrismukkah : the Christian-Jewish interfaith family in the
    United States / Samira K. Mehta.
Description: Chapel Hill : University of North Carolina Press, [2018] |
    Includes bibliographical references and index.
Identifiers: LCCN 2017020958 | ISBN 9781469636351 (cloth : alk. paper) |
    ISBN 9781469636368 (pbk : alk. paper) | ISBN 9781469636375 (ebook)
Subjects: LCSH: Interfaith marriage—United States. | Children of interfaith
    marriage—United States. | Interfaith families—United States. |
    Jews—United States—Identity.
Classification: LCC HQ1031 .M445 2018 | DDC 306.84/30973—dc23
    LC record available at https://lccn.loc.gov/2017020958

Cover illustration: *Multi-Ethnic Holiday Foliage* © 2016 Michael Gale.
Used with permission.

Chapter 5 was previously published in a different form as "Chrismukkah:
Millennial Multiculturalism," *Religion and American Culture: A Journal
of Interpretation* 25:1 (Winter 2015): 82–109. Used here with permission.

Contents

Acknowledgments ix

INTRODUCTION 1

CHAPTER ONE
To Stem a Rising Tide: Interfaith Marriage and Religious Institutions 15

CHAPTER TWO
Blended or Transcended: Interfaith Families in
Popular Culture, 1970–1980 51

CHAPTER THREE
One Roof, One Religion: The Campaign for a
Jewish (Interfaith) Family 78

CHAPTER FOUR
They Sure Will Be of Minority Groups: Interreligious, Interracial,
Multiethnic Jewish Families 112

CHAPTER FIVE
Chrismukkah: Millennial Multiculturalism 136

CHAPTER SIX
Living the Interfaith Family Life: Dual Religious Heritages
Shaping Family Cultures 161

CONCLUSION
For the Sake of the Children: Identity, Practice, and the
Adult Children of Intermarriage 201

Notes 221

Bibliography 239

Index 249

Figures

1. *Bridget Loves Bernie* 60
2. Unitarian-Jewish *chuppah* 83
3. African-American story-quilt *chuppah* 123
4. Chrismukkah card #1 157
5. Chrismukkah card #2 158
6. Bridal couple with rabbi and Franciscan friar 163
7. Bar mitzvah invitation 190
8. Chelsea Clinton's wedding 202

Acknowledgments

I have always been a communal learner, and so more people than I can possibly thank have helped develop this project. I alone am responsible for the shortcomings in *Beyond Chrismukkah*, but its contributions to our field and to the study of interfaith family life in the United States were created in collaboration with the colleagues, friends, and informants who have given of their time and expertise throughout my writing and research. Most importantly, I must offer my most profound thanks to the people who opened their lives to me. Most of them remain unnamed in this monograph, but I am beyond grateful for their trust.

Gary Laderman has believed in me and my work since the beginning, even at the moments when I did not believe in myself. I am grateful for his mentorship, his generosity, the pride that he shows in me, and his incisive and constructive criticism. Elizabeth Bounds and Eric Goldstein have always been available for critical feedback and wise counsel. Don Seeman answered phone calls from the field to brainstorm and troubleshoot ethnographic encounters. Tisa Wenger has read more than one complete draft of this project, and her feedback has sharpened both my thinking and my language. Dianne Stewart, Judith Weisenfeld, Rebecca Davis, and Laura Levitt have been unstinting with their friendship and their mentorship. Wallace Best was my advisor early on, and he has never truly given up the role. Julie Byrne, Amy DeRogotis, Sylvester Johnson, Pamela Klassen, and Kathryn Lofton have been very generous with their support. I am the scholar that I am because of the teaching, mentorship, and scholarship of Bob Orsi, David Hall, Ann Braude, Mark Wallace, Ellen Ross, and Yvonne Chireau.

I have received feedback on drafts and chapters of this project at seminars and workshops of the Sloan Foundation's Center for Myth and Ritual in American Life (MARIAL), the Tam Center for Jewish Studies, and the program in Religious Practices and Practical Theology, all at Emory University. I thank Courtney Bender and the Religion in America Seminar at Columbia University for the opportunity to present an early draft of chapter 4. An earlier version of chapter 5 appeared in the Winter 2015 issue of the journal *Religion and American Culture*. I thank Phil Goff, the editorial board, and the anonymous reviewers for their contributions to that chapter. The Religion,

Food, and Eating Seminar of the American Academy of Religion; the Unitarian Universalist Scholars and Friends; and the Donner Institute's Symposium on Religion and Food have all offered important space for honing ideas. I have received valuable feedback on my work at many conferences including the American Academy of Religion, the Association for Jewish Studies, and the Scholars Conference of the American Jewish Historical Society.

My work would not be possible without archives and the people who maintain them. I am grateful to the staffs of the American Jewish Archives, the University of Notre Dame, the Catholic University of America archives and the Stuart A. Rose Manuscript, Archive, and Rare Books Library at Emory University. I firmly believe that behind every scholar stands an army of reference librarians. In particular, I would like to thank Erica Bruchko, of the Robert W. Woodruff Library at Emory University; and Gloria Korsman and Renata Kalnins, both of the Andover Theological Library at Harvard Divinity School.

At the University of North Carolina Press, Elaine Maisner not only saw the potential in my work, but also has been a patient editor who has guided me to more careful and accurate uses of language and, therefore, more precise thought. Becki Reibman has answered my endless questions about process. Thank you also to Stephen Barichko, Dino Battista, and their respective teams.

I benefited from the financial generosity of a number of organizations. Emory University funded large portions of this work and attendance at conferences to share it. The Tam Institute for Jewish Studies at Emory University and the Bernard Radar Marcus Center of the American Jewish Archives provided me with funding for summer research. The University Seminars of Columbia University provided subvention funds to create an index. The Northeastern Consortium for Faculty Diversity gave me the opportunity to spend a year at Allegheny College, developing as a teacher and a scholar. The MARIAL Center granted both a year of funding and a generous research budget, and I completed the book while on fellowship at the Library of Congress's John W. Kluge Center.

Throughout the process, many colleagues and friends have been supportive and challenging interlocutors. Feminist conventional wisdom says that one should never be the only woman in a writing group. That advice might apply generally, but not when one has the luck to write with David King, Brian Campbell, and Lerone Martin. They, and Ben Brazil, have critiqued many drafts. Over the years many colleagues have read drafts, offered feedback, and let me know when interfaith families appeared in popular culture or in the news. My deepest appreciation to Brandon Bayne, Joanna Brooks,

Letitia Campbell, Jenny Caplan, Jodi Eichler-Levine, Thomas Fabisak, Gillian Frank, Shreena Gandhi, Rachel Gross, Ryan Harper, Rachel Kranson, Adrienne Krone, Jenny Wiley Legath, Rachel Lindsay, Emily Mace, Mandy McMichael, Sara Moslener, Donna Mote, Nora Rubel, John Senior, Emily Sigalow, Josef Sorett, Angela Tarango, Jennifer Thompson, Heather White, and Ben Zeller. Amy Caldwell often shared insights about the publishing process and I have appreciated them.

I have had a number of institutional homes. Thank you to the communities of Emory University, Allegheny College, the Museum of Jewish Heritage, and the John W. Kluge Center of the Library of Congress. In particular, thank you to my current institutional home, Albright College. Victor Forte, Jennifer Koosed, Mary McGee, and Robert Seesengood are unparalleled departmental colleagues. Trudy Prutzman has lightened many a load. I have been similarly lucky in my writing support group: Bridget Hearon, Heidi Mau, Shreeyash Palshikar, and Carrie Skulley. Thank you also to the Bridge Club for making me welcome.

My life is rich in friends who are what anthropologists call a "fictive kinship network." They have enhanced this book in a myriad of ways. Every woman should have such friends as Susannah Laramee Kidd, Yoshimi Azuma, Rachel Gordan, Amy Robertson, Almeda Wright, Soledad Caballero, Angela Tarango, Chaos Golubitsky, and Adrienne Krone. They are my laughter and my support. Terry Egdal and the Podhorzers, Joshua Lesser, and the Ben Yoar clan form the basis of my Atlanta family. Wherever I am living, Gloria Korsman and Kerrie Harthan provide my home away from home. Jeremy Melvin changed my life when he asked me to be godmother to Matilda, a great gift. Anthony Petro has shared my joy in professional and personal success and has stalwartly stood by me in more difficult moments. The past decade of near constant conversation has hugely enriched my life and I look forward to decades to come. For more than twenty years, Cameron McGlothlin's friendship has given my life a bedrock of unconditional love and support. I thank him for both, most recently expressed by his willingness to read the penultimate draft of this manuscript.

In her edited volume *Half/Life: Jew-ish Tales from Interfaith Homes*, Laurel Snyder refers to her "muddled mishpocha." I would like to thank mine for never questioning (at least to my face) my choice to become a scholar of religious studies. I would particularly like to thank my mother, Linda Hotchkiss Mehta. She is an editor, and I have benefited immensely, from not only her parenting and support, but also her professional expertise. (I particularly appreciate the help with permissions and footnotes.)

In his translation of the eleventh century Irish poem "A Monk and His Cat," W. H. Auden talks about the wonderful parallel work and play of scholar and pet, as they, alone together, share their separate pursuits. Though Greta is a dog with a bone, rather than a cat chasing a mouse, she has always been my Pangur. It is to her that I dedicate this work, for surely, without her companionship and the more recent addition of a second canine companion, Maggie Mae, its creation would have been a lonely thing.

Beyond Chrismukkah

When Jewish Barbara Zeitler married Catholic Jeffrey Kendall in 1988, they agreed that any children of the marriage would be raised as Jews.[1] At the time, she was a member of the Reform movement, frequently described as one of the most liberal branches of Judaism. He was not particularly engaged in Catholic life. In 1991, however, Mr. Kendall joined the Boston Church of Christ, a movement with its roots in the Church of Christ but with more authoritarian tendencies.[2] He came to believe that those who did not accept both Jesus Christ as their Lord and Savior and the particular teachings of the Boston Church of Christ were "damned to go to Hell," a place characterized by "weeping and gnashing of teeth."[3] Apparently, this did not cause major disruption to the marriage until 1994, when Mrs. Kendall and the children adopted Orthodox Judaism.[4]

Shortly thereafter, Mrs. Kendall filed for divorce as a result of the irreversible breakdown of the marriage, and in 1995 the court became involved in navigating the religious training of the children. In court, Mr. Kendall declared that he could no longer support raising his children as Jews and would do anything in his power to keep them from damnation to hell by bringing them to Christ. Ultimately, Judge Christina Harms of the Supreme Court of Massachusetts ruled to restrict how Mr. Kendall could present his religion to his children. While the parents were allowed to share their own beliefs with the children as long as those beliefs did not alienate the children from the other parent, the court ruled that "the [defendant] shall not take the children to his church (whether to church services or Sunday School or church educational programs); nor engage them in prayer or bible study if it promotes rejection rather than acceptance, of their mother or their own Jewish self-identity. The [defendant] shall not share his religious beliefs with the children if those beliefs cause the children significant emotional distress or worry about their mother or about themselves."[5] Practically, this ruling meant that while Mr. Kendall could hang pictures of Jesus Christ on his walls, despite the fact that his children would visit, he was not allowed to "take the children to religious services where they receive the message that adults or children who do not accept Jesus Christ as their lord and savior are destined to burn in hell."[6] He was allowed to share family traditions like Christmas and Easter, but not to use them as opportunities to teach his children about their truth claims.

Embedded in Judge Harms's rulings in the Kendall divorce case are a number of assumptions about what constitutes "religion" and what constitutes "family traditions." She insisted that Mr. Kendall must respect his children's religious identity, but she also defined Christmas and Easter as family traditions, rather than as religious practices. Thus, the Massachusetts judge's decision was a natural outgrowth of discussions about interfaith families throughout the 1980s and 1990s, as religious leaders, family members, and the media moved from conversations about the phenomenon of interfaith marriage to questions about how interfaith families would formulate a religious identity. There were two broad approaches—one camp argued that children must have a single religious identity, which was more in line with arguments from the previous decades; while another opinion argued that there were innovative ways to combine Christian and Jewish traditions in the home without confusing or damaging children. Like the aforementioned court case, both of these positions implicitly turned on definitions of key terms and concepts like "religion," "culture," and "ethnicity."

In *Beyond Chrismukkah*, I explore marriages between Christians and Jews in the United States during the second half of the twentieth century and the beginning of the twenty-first. Interfaith marriage can be defined in any number of ways, including viewing marriages between members of similar Protestant denominations as "interfaith" because of real differences in class, theology, or polity, or because of strong historical tensions between the traditions. Polling organizations such as the Pew Forum on Religion and Public Life and scholars such as Robert Putnam and David Campbell, however, have recently defined interfaith marriage as marriages occurring across large "family groupings," so marriages between Catholics and Hindus are interfaith, but so are marriages between mainline and evangelical Protestants. Using these definitions of interfaith marriage, in the 1990s 50 percent of all American marriages began as interfaith marriages, with 30 percent of the marriages remaining mixed and 20 percent becoming religiously homogeneous through conversion or the selection of a third religion.[7] American Catholics intermarried at a rate of between 40 and 50 percent. In 2016, the Pew Forum on Religion and Public Life released a study demonstrating that a full 20 percent of American adults grew up in interfaith homes.[7] Interfaith family life, then, is a major and formative piece of the American religious landscape.

These numbers reflect many kinds of religious blends beyond the Christian-Jewish marriage (including marriages across Protestant family groups), but they indicate that Americans are finding spouses from across the diverse

American religious landscape and finding ways to create homes and families that bring any number of traditions into contact with each other, not just in the public square, but in the most intimate spaces of life. Moreover, while these decisions may be highly personal, the negotiations that they entail on the family and communal level speak not only to how these families view themselves religiously, but also to how they define themselves in the distinctly American sphere.

While there are many kinds of interfaith marriage, and while in earlier eras, marriages between Catholics and Protestants or within Protestant groups were considerably more socially complicated than they often are today, I have chosen to focus on Christian-Jewish interfaith, heterosexual marriage, and the families that those marriages create. Why, though, study interfaith marriage between Christians and Jews? After all, American Jews make up a comparatively small portion of the American population—approximately 1.7 percent in 2007.[8] Somewhere between 40 to 50 percent of new Jewish marriages are interfaith. Why, then, study a group of families that make up less than 1 percent of the population of the United States? First, in the contemporary United States, Christian-Jewish interfaith marriage provides the archetype for interfaith marriage in the United States. These are the mixed marriages that dominate the American imagination in a variety of ways, from literature to film to television and other forms of popular culture. They also provide an important model for how Americans define the ever-shifting terms of "religion," "culture," and "ethnicity" in families formed in our increasingly pluralistic society. And, to be clear, when I say that the Christian-Jewish model provides an example for how interfaith families navigate these categories, I do not mean that they simply provide a model for scholars. American families that combine other religious traditions are inundated with Christian-Jewish examples, throughout popular culture, but also in advice literature and other resources outlining how to make such families work. The Christian-Jewish interfaith family is not the most common kind of interfaith family in the United States, but it is the archetypal kind.

In *Beyond Chrismukkah*, I analyze the shifting distinctions that various actors draw between religion and culture in the lives of interfaith families and the strategic purposes that those distinctions serve. Thinking about religion and culture as strategic terms provides a new paradigm for understanding interfaith families, but it also advances our understanding of how American society defines and uses those concepts and encourages scholars to continue to explore and question how we draw those boundaries. I use practices to investigate the drawing and redrawing of the lines between religion and culture.

Specifically, I track how Christian-Jewish blended families have found ways to bring religious practice into their homes: how they have been allowed to; how they have wanted to; how they are imagined; and what they have done. These investigations place interfaith marriage within the American religious and secular landscape and use them to examine the ways in which Americans navigate the meanings of "religion" and "culture" in their daily lives.

Beyond Chrismukkah traces the ramifications of these distinctions, and how it is that multicultural interfaith families transgress these very areas of taboo, recasting practices, goods, and events in order to consume across traditionally demarcated boundaries, to create new hybrid family practices and religious cultures. I move through eras of response to interfaith family life, moving from the late 1960s and 1970s, when religious leaders found themselves confronted with a newly rising rate of interfaith marriage, to the early years of the twenty-first century, when interfaith marriage had been part of the landscape for a full generation. I carve out a new space that situates interfaith marriage—and the interfaith family—as a distinctly American, always blended, and potentially multicultural phenomenon. Such terms allow an exploration of these families on their own varied terms, free from the structures of a particular religious movement and its stakes.

Which boundaries any given person or community chose to police around plural religious identities were deeply tied to questions of what identity requires protection—a religious identity or a cultural one. These terms were defined and deployed in debates about how to determine the religious lives of interfaith families, used strategically to describe a constellation of Jewish and Christian practices and beliefs according to whether those arguing sought to restrict a family to one religious identity and to define which religion should "win out" and become the family's sole tradition, or whether it was possible, potentially even preferable, to combine multiple practices in a family home. In part, *Beyond Chrismukkah* demonstrates that popular culture, in various permutations, framed elements of Jewish and Christian as "ethnic" or "cultural," while clergy and other religious leaders focused on aspects of Judaism and Christianity that they could define as "religious" and control within institutional life. For Jewish leaders, the terms of their discussion were influenced by their attempts to redefine Judaism as an American "religion," over and above an ethnically oriented self-understanding. Similarly, these definitions traded on shifting definitions of Christianity that waffled between distilling Christian identity down to its creedal terms, framing many noncreedal practices as cultural and therefore either safe to include in Jewish family life or inessential, such that Christians could unproblematically sacrifice them.

I also unpack the implications of framing interfaith marriage in the opposing terms of religion and culture. When defined as culture, interfaith marriage can serve as a mode of assimilating into a dominant Protestant society, as Jewish spouses adapt to their Protestant partners' world, or as, together, Catholic and Jewish spouses "meet in the middle" in the neutral territory of the self-defined individual, free from the constraints of family and heritage. Alternatively, cultural definitions can allow the interfaith couple to move into the space of multiculturalism. Multiculturalism has its own logics, and chapter 5 will explore those understandings of what culture entails. In this world, religious practices, already heavily shaped by the logic of the marketplace, are framed as equivalent and consumed in parallel (or in combination) to create new blended (and yet optional) religious identities. Particularities of meaning and understanding may have been lost in this multicultural understanding of these traditions, but a new moral framework has been enacted around practices previously the sole domain of Christian or Jewish experience.

As in the Kendall divorce, arguments for Judaism and Christianity as religions tend to privilege theology over practice. In looking at the relationship between Christianity and Judaism, for instance, these conversations resulted in assertions that Christians could subscribe to everything that occurred in Judaism because Christianity was Judaism "plus Christ." This attitude thus made the decision of religious affiliation easy, precisely because it discounted both worship practices and any understanding of a Jewish culture to which the Christian partner could not seamlessly convert (and which Reform authorities could neither easily define nor, in point of fact, completely discount).

These challenges demonstrate why, throughout *Beyond Chrismukkah*, I have paid close attention to the very concepts of "Christian" and "Jew," because, depending on the source in question, they hold a multiplicity of meanings: from affiliation with a specific Christian or Jewish organization to an individual's nebulous connection to a sketchily understood identity that is, in that person's framing, identified with anyone from her grandmother to Woody Allen to the Archbishop of Canterbury. In conversations about interfaith family life, traits are characterized as Christian or Jewish without regard for the range of practices in each tradition and sometimes based on stereotypes only loosely connected to historical reality. I have explored how people have used the terms with an eye toward understanding what is at stake in typifying characteristics as being inherently tied to Christian and Jewish identity.

Pluralism in American public life has often traded on three realities. First, all of the religious traditions in question shape themselves, as much as possible, to a Protestant norm, for instance, by fitting appropriate readings or prayers into the format of a Protestant worship service. Second, truth claims are kept out of the public square—religious groups seek common ground, for example, by agreeing to work together at a soup kitchen, but also by not discussing real differences in underlying value systems or core beliefs. These compromises in public are considered acceptable because, third, it is understood that each group can retreat to its own private space, be it family or religious home, where its members will no longer need to compromise. Interfaith family life removes that private space, forcing people to negotiate competing practices and truth claims in their most private space. Families need to decide how to interact with their distinct traditions, and religious organizations have to decide how to treat inter-religiously blended families.

I have aimed to produce an investigation of interfaith family life that is dedicated to lived religion—that seriously considers the institutions and structures that shape the options available to interfaith families, while also considering how those families work within and push against those structures to create their own practices, traditions, and meanings. To that end, I have pulled my research material from a wide array of sources, some institutional, others popular. I have also done limited ethnographic field work and extensive oral history interviews.

In analyzing Christian and Jewish institutional responses, I have limited the scope of my discussions of religious institutions and leadership. In the Jewish context, I have concentrated on the responses of the Central Conference of American Rabbis, the rabbinical arm of the Reform movement, and the leadership of the Union for American Hebrew Congregations, the congregational arm of the Reform movement, in terms of their internal conversations, their external statements, and the publications they sponsored. As both the largest American Jewish movement and one of the most liberal, the Reform movement was on the forefront of struggling to respond to interfaith marriage and has, since 1978, made outreach to those in interfaith marriages one of its primary goals. In considering Catholic thought, I have looked specifically at policies on and theologies of marriage that have a direct impact on interfaith couples in the United States, whether they originated in Rome or with the American Church.

Tracking Protestant thought, even once limited to the Protestant mainline, poses a particular challenge because the various denominations operated (and continue to operate) independently, as demonstrated in the contemporary moment by their range of reactions to gay marriage. While the Protestant mainline was starting to lose some of its public status to evangelicals in the 1970s, in the 1960s and 1970s these more liberal voices were still, largely, the

voice of public Protestantism. Additionally, while evangelicals were more iso-
lationist in their approach to Christian identity, during this period, the Protestant mainline was deeply interested in ecumenicism, including in forging
relationships with Catholics and Jews, and therefore had more of a stake in
navigating the somewhat rocky shoals of interfaith marriage. As a result, I focused my archival research primarily on the formal reactions of the Protestant
mainline.

Because I was interested in broad conversations about interfaith marriage and most interested in taking an average of the Protestant position
on the subject rather than focusing on individual denominations, I turned to
the magazine *The Christian Century*. While the denominations have very different perspectives on the relationship between the individual believer or
individual clergy member and the religious hierarchy, and others have no
religious hierarchy, but rather denominational structures that serve as coor-
dinating bodies, the magazine allows a broad view of how the Protestant
mainline understood the problem. Although this publication does not give
the fine-grade distinctions of whether an individual minister was primarily
responsible to his congregation (and therefore to their views on interfaith
marriage) or to his bishop, it presents the public conversation on religion.
It also highlights the importance of the individual believer as a moral agent
in Protestant thought and the ways in which the mainline was considering
fears about the institution of marriage. It is in this context that the magazine
presents the public Protestant voices on interfaith marriage—the voices to
which the American Catholic hierarchy and the Reform leadership would
be responding.

I thought primarily about straight families because this work is largely a
cultural history that examines resources for and depictions of interfaith families produced before the gay marriage movement built up steam in the early
twenty-first century. While gay marriage is part of the landscape in which we
currently live, for the bulk of the time considered by this monograph, gay
marriage was not a primary goal of the gay rights movement, and the families
that gay people created were not the targets of the "interfaith marriage industry." Certainly, cultural depictions of interfaith gay couples from this period
exist, including Jewish Louis Ironson's relationships with Protestant Prior
Walter and Mormon Joe Pitt in *Angels in America*. Like the interfaith relationships in *Angels in America*, most of these depictions centered on childless
couples, and as I was primarily interested in how interfaith nuclear families
are imagined, policed, and innovated, these examples were less helpful to my
central questions than were the advice manuals, children's literature, and

institutional policies and outreach that presumed that marriages meant straight marriage.

In framing interfaith marriage this way, my work moves away from most existing scholarship on Christian-Jewish interfaith families, which considers them in the context of Jewish community and life. Sylvia Barack Fishman's sociological study *Double or Nothing? Jewish Families and Mixed Marriage* (2004) explores the reasons why Jews chose to marry non-Jewish spouses as well as the rates with which and reasons why they affiliate with Jewish institutions and maintain Jewish practices, with the end goal of measuring the impact of interfaith marriage on Jewish continuity in the United States. In *Still Jewish: A History of Women and Intermarriage in America* (2009), Keren Mc-Ginity traces the history of Jewish women marrying gentile men, examining how they maintain a sense of Jewish identity in their lives and how they transmit that identity to their children. Her more recent *Marrying Out: Jewish Men, Intermarriage, and Fatherhood* (2014) asks how intermarried Jewish men take (or do not take) responsibility for transmitting Jewish identity to their children. Lila Corwin Berman uses debates about interfaith marriage as a primary data point in her exploration of how American Jews explained and presented themselves to the rest of American society in *Speaking of Jews: Rabbis, Intellectuals, and the Creation of an American Public Identity* (2009). Jennifer Thompson's *Jewish on Their Own Terms: How Intermarried Couples Are Changing American Judaism* (2014) uses ethnographic material to do exactly what the title claims: explore the ways in which interfaith couples, often living Jewish lives, are reshaping what it means to be Jewish in contemporary America. These projects are interesting and important work, but they all address interfaith marriage specifically as it relates to American Judaism.[9]

Moving outside of interfaith marriage strictly in the context of American Judaism, I situated it in terms of a number of trends in U.S. history, including religious seeking, decreasing religious affiliation, increased diversity, and the rise of multiculturalism as an ideology. In considering the impact of multiculturalism on interfaith family life, I have found Henry Goldschmidt's work on multiculturalism and religion particularly useful. Goldschmidt demonstrates that multiculturalism tends to take practices that do not operate equivalently in their social systems and make them equivalent, so that, in his work, multiculturalists view Afro-Caribbean soul food and Eastern European Jewish food as things that can be shared, missing the realities of kashrut in the lives of the Hasidic community. If Goldschmidt explores the problematic nature of this multiculturalism, my work explores the ways in which interfaith families framing practices as equivalent allows them to be combined in a blended practice. If some of the original context of the practices is lost in that combination, a new context, with new implicit logics, is reinscribed in its place.

Drawing on these networks, I interviewed fifty families and religious professionals locating themselves in Jewish, Christian, or Unitarian Universalist religious communities as well as members of a community for Christian and Jewish intentionally blended families. Most of these conversations occurred during participant observation conducted between 2007 and 2014, though sometimes individuals requested additional formal interviews, as noted in the bibliography. These families thus embody different traditions and define themselves in a variety of ways. In chapter 4, I explore the experiences of families who have chosen to formally affiliate with Judaism, demonstrating both that these families continue to include elements of Christian practice in their homes and that racially diverse families are, ironically, more free to be religiously complex while still affiliating with Judaism than are white families. In chapter 6, I analyze the experiences of four of those blended families: the Brewster-Kaplan family, who have located their moral center in an alternative "back to land" ethos; the Groff family, who have become Unitarian Universalist; the Kimball-Geller family, who are raising their daughters to be both Mormon and Jewish and who are part of both Mormon and Jewish communities; and the Miller family, who are part of a community called the Interfaith Family Project, or IFFP. I chose these families in part for access—the Miller family, for instance, happened to be preparing for their son's bar mitzvah when I got in touch, but also because they spoke unusually articulately about themes touched on by many other families: connection to religious community, wrestling with contradictory truth claims, reenvisioning narratives, and negotiating questions of religious practice.

These families break down the either/or dichotomy that so often characterizes descriptions of interfaith family life, demonstrating that while being neither or both, they can create their own vibrant moral and ritual-based lives that give them strong senses of identity, though sometimes at the price of not having a religious community. My analysis contributes a new understanding of religious studies by exploring how Americans combine multiple religious traditions in their lives. While we know that many Americans do so, scholarly studies tend to focus on individuals who, as religious seekers, take on practices that they find personally fulfilling, often from Eastern or nature-based traditions. My research both examines often taboo combinations between Christianity and Judaism and examines how those combinations are intentionally and unintentionally fused when the issue at stake is not the spiritual development of a single seeker, but rather the negotiation of the potentially competing needs of a multireligious family.

My work adds questions rooted in religious studies generally, and American religious history in particular, to examine the ways in which interfaith families are characterized in American imaginations as well as the practices maintained by and growing out of interfaith family life. In doing this, I draw from practice theory, specifically Pierre Bourdieu's understandings of *habitus* and *dispositions*, and from Michel de Certeau's concepts of strategy and tactics, considering the ways in which practices form and shape an individual's range of dispositions.[10] I also consider the ways in which individuals consciously and unconsciously use their acts of consumption—of services, of goods, but also of traditions as tactics—to shape their family identities, sometimes against the logic of the institutions in which they locate themselves.

As a scholar, I am deeply formed by American religious history and that field grounds this work. I start from an assumption that the religious lives and realities of the interfaith families themselves are as important as the official policies of their religious organizations toward such families. At the same time, I understand that while those official statements and attitudes reflect and shape interfaith family life, so do images of blended families in popular media and the narratives that families create about themselves. While I investigate the way that my sources define religion, often in terms of formal affiliation, I draw from Gary Laderman's expanded definitions of the sacred and Robert Orsi's framing of religion as a network of relationships between, among others, the living and the dead. Scholarship on interfaith families has tended to see families that live outside of Christian or Jewish institutions as being without meaningful religious lives. For such families, however, and at times for their religiously affiliated counterparts, the theologically sanctioned points of wonder and transcendent meaning do not necessarily apply. My work uses these definitions of how religiously oriented communities and networks exist to examine the ways in which a family becomes invested in practices not traditionally understood as religious, such as transmitting family recipes. Because these experiences lie outside of the boundaries often drawn for interfaith families, they provide particularly fruitful sites for combining aspects of Christian and Jewish heritages, combinations that, in certain contexts, can gesture toward greater meaning.

The consumption of goods and experiences is central to the ways in which interfaith families define their identities; indeed, the objects of consumption (or lack thereof) as well as the location of the consumption serve as important markers of identity. Work by scholars such as Leigh Eric Schmidt and Andrew Heinze mark the ways in which the market has long been tied up in expressions of religious identity, be they private family practices or public displays of piety.[11] These explorations of lived religion and consumption, however, have not studied the ways in which modes of consumption might police or trouble the lines drawn between religious distinctions and identities, as they do in interfaith families. The classic example, once again, is the celebration of Christmas. In many cases, celebrating Christmas, not necessarily with church attendance and tales of the savior's birth, but rather with a tree, stockings, presents, and viewings of *A Christmas Carol*, often marks an interfaith family as not being Jewish or not being Jewish enough. In fact, couples often had to explicitly promise to exclude a Christmas tree from their home in order to have a Jewish wedding, rather than, for instance, promise to light Shabbat candles. While, under those circumstances, the family may attend Christmas festivities in the home of a Christian relative, and participate in all of the consumption implicit in the holiday, the special distinction preserves the interfaith couple's home as Jewish.

A note on terms: there is no universally accepted term for couples from two different religions or the families that they create. Currently, the most commonly used term, by these families and organizations that most explicitly support them, is "interfaith families" and that is the term that I have tried to most consistently use throughout my text. There are moments, for instance, in my historical treatment of materials, when I sometimes use "mixed marriage," an older term that is making a comeback in some circles. I have tried to avoid using the term "intermarried," except where dictated by my sources. While certain Jewish organizations still use the term "intermarried," many members of interfaith families are offended by the term, because it has often been used derogatively. Even when it is not used derogatively, it often signals a distinctly Jewish (and less intentionally inclusive) perspective than many of my informants preferred.

That is not to say that "interfaith" is a perfect term. Some Jews object to the word "faith" as a Christian perspective on religious identity. Some interfaith couples who have chosen a third path (for instance, Unitarian Universalism) say that they have different religions or heritages, but one faith. Still others come from Christian or Jewish heritage, but are not believers and therefore object to the term "faith" because they are not people of faith. I acknowledge the validity of all of those concerns and, in the end, have chosen to use the term because it is the most commonly used and accepted by the families that I study and in the literature that I examined. I hope, by choosing the term that is best suited for Google, I have also chosen the term that will offend the fewest people.

In addition, because most literature by and about interfaith families is created by Jewish institutions, the members of the interfaith couple are often referred to as the Jews and the non-Jewish partners. The non-Jewish partner, of course, brings his or her own heritage to the table and, therefore, throughout my writing on Christian-Jewish interfaith couples, I have tended to describe the spouses as "the Christian spouse" and the "Jewish spouse," or better yet, when possible, to name the Christian's specific kind of Christianity. Because Jewish identity is often framed in ethnic or cultural terms in addition to religious terms, this choice has worked well for the Jewish members of interfaith families. It is a less perfect fit for the many people in interfaith marriages who were raised Catholic or Protestant and no longer believe in the teachings of their familial tradition, or attend its institutions, because these people no longer consider themselves Christian. I have chosen to refer to them as the Christian spouse anyway, in part to give them a more robust identity that the fact that they are not Jewish, and in part because central to my approach is that Christian identity is far more than its creeds. Like Judaism, Christianity has rich (and sometimes problematic) cultural and familial contexts.

Every now and then, despite the fact that I am committed to avoiding the term "non-Jewish," I find myself using it. I do so when I am describing material that was explicitly created from a Jewish point of view, where the identity of the Jewish spouse is important, but it does not really matter what kind of identity the partner has. Increasingly, Jewish material tries to be respectful of diversity, even among interfaith families, and so, while the non-Jewish spouses are most often Christian, sometimes they are not. When I can be specific (because there is a concrete example to which I am referring), I am. At other times, ideologically, I would like to say "Christian/Hindu/Muslim/Buddhist/Zoroastrian/Lakota," and so on. As that is not practical, I have, at times, been reduced to the term "non-Jew."

Chapters 1 and 2 analyze two competing reactions to rising rates of interfaith marriage between 1965 and 1980. During this era, marriages between Christians and Jews rose exponentially, gaining attention from both religious leadership and popular media. Chapter 1 traces the policies of the Central Conference of American Rabbis, the Catholic Church, and the attitudes of the Protestant mainline to interfaith marriage in the 1970s, as each group tried to come to terms with rapidly rising interfaith marriage rates. Chapter 2, by contrast, explores portrayals of interfaith marriage in popular media, examining one text that focuses on the child and presents potential problems with being raised in an interfaith family before turning to media representations of happy and assimilation-oriented interfaith love and unhappy, less successfully assimilationist interfaith love.

Chapter 3 addresses attempts to create Jewish families out of interfaith marriages. Focusing on the 1980s through the early 1990s, it presents both conversations around how to achieve this goal on the part of the Reform hierarchy and advice manuals that serve as outreach to interfaith couples. Chapter 4 focuses on the lived religion of Jewishly affiliated interfaith families, including substantial analysis of families that do not fit the traditional depiction of Christian-Jewish intermarriage because they are multiracial.

Chapter 5 introduces the concepts of multiculturalism and optional ethnicity as they exist in ethnic studies, and it traces their implications for a new multicultural model of interfaith family life, arising in the mid-1990s and continuing into the first decade of the twenty-first century. Chapter 6 offers four case studies, explicating a range of approaches taken by interfaith families who have, in some way, chosen to raise their children with both Christian and Jewish religious practice, or with neither practice. The chapter explores the practices that the families develop and the ways in which they contextualize those practices, exploring points of continuity and discontinuity with the model of the multicultural interfaith family in chapter 5, to demonstrate that while each family creates their own pastiche of practices, they have their own moral framework that anchors their choices.

The conclusion addresses the ultimate question posed by the debates about interfaith marriage: What about the kids? It draws from the range of religious identities with which adult children of interfaith marriage identify. Specifically, it articulates how those children of interfaith marriage understand their blended religious heritages and how their experiences do and do not likely predict the experiences of children growing up in such homes today. It also asks how the Christian-Jewish example offers insight into other forms of interfaith family life in the contemporary United States.

Ultimately, through an examination of institutional opinion, popular culture, and ethnographic studies, this book redefines interfaith families and their relation to American culture. Far from easily slipping into one religious tradition or another, these families—and the conversations around them—fall into a new category altogether that is, regardless of how and where the families locate themselves, inherently hybrid. The reality of traditions struggling for dominance, coexisting, and fusing, not in public space but instead within the

American home, is increasingly part of the new American reality. Without grappling with how society imagines interfaith families and more importantly, with the many ways that those families live out their lives and with the hybrid identities that they create, it is no longer possible to understand religion in the United States.

CHAPTER ONE

To Stem a Rising Tide

Interfaith Marriage and Religious Institutions

In 1966 the General Commission on Chaplains and Armed Forces Personnel produced a pamphlet presenting the Catholic, Jewish, and Protestant positions on interfaith marriage.[1] During the Cold War, political rhetoric construed the American family, rooted in both capitalism and religion, as one of the nation's strongest weapons in the battle against communism.[2] Similarly, religious leaders found themselves battling the threat of American secularism, and interfaith marriage, which had the potential to tear at the tightly woven religious fabric of the home, provided a threat to American organized religion. They feared anything that might draw American families away from organized religion and traditionally defined religious practice. To religious and other American leaders, marriage across religious lines therefore posed a serious threat, to their religious communities and also to national security and stability. To combat the increasing threat of marriages across religious lines, three high-ranking chaplains in the U.S. Armed Forces authored a pamphlet, entitled *What About Interfaith Marriage?* In it, these chaplains—a Catholic, a Jew, and a Protestant—all defined marriage across faith lines as inherently dangerous, not to the religious groups themselves, but to the strength of the marriage, and by extension, to the sanctity of the American family.

These pamphlets offer an entry point into how leaders in those three religions crafted their responses to interfaith marriage and their own Americanness. In an era when, according to the *New York Times*, Americans considered it "narrow-minded, intolerant, almost un-American to raise objections to marriage on the basis of creed," these chaplains suggested that there were serious problems with interfaith marriage on multiple levels.[3] Printed under the auspices of the American military, the pamphlet framed interfaith marriage as a danger to the marital bond and therefore the American home, while hinting at deeper differences. The pamphlet provides insight into how Protestant, Catholic, and Reform Jewish leaders navigated their theological and communal objections to "mixed marriage," while at the same time balancing the concern that such disagreements could be viewed, as the *New York Times* article suggests, as "un-American."

Reform Jewish, Catholic, and mainline Protestant leadership drew from their distinct theological and American social perspectives to respond to interfaith marriage. Thus, while no group strongly supported marriage across faith lines, they brought very different understandings about what was at stake for interfaith marriage. All three chaplains agreed that the home and the family were of religious importance, and both were central to how children developed religious identities. Implicit in their arguments was the centrality of the American family to the American nation-state and to rhetoric that placed the American family at the center of national security. This domestic ideology foregrounded two parents, a working father and homemaker mother, with the home as both an oasis in the midst of the threats of the outside world and a defense against them. The white middle class was most able to enact this ideal, and the middle class was largely Protestant.[4]

By the 1970s, however, other new threats seemed to put this American institution at risk. Throughout that decade and the next, the number of middle-class mothers working outside of the home climbed, as did the divorce rate. These realities were tied to a number of factors, including rising costs of living and an increase in no-fault divorce laws. The rise of second-wave feminism increased the opportunities for women to have meaningful careers and to secure economic independence, should they need to leave unhappy marriages. While much has been written on conservative religious reactions to these changes, their implications often unnerved religious liberals as well. Liberal Protestants and Jews might embrace feminist changes, but those changes also increased their concern for the stability of the family. As the baby boom generation began to come of age and marry—and to enter interfaith marriages in record numbers—their religious leadership, many of whom were members of the "greatest generation," worried that interfaith marriage would upset the stability of the family, a stability that seemed newly fragile and was, in their minds, at least implicitly tied to larger, national concerns.

Institutional discussions about "mixed marriage" or "intermarriage" evolved in the mid-twentieth-century trifecta of religion in America: Protestant, Catholic, and Jew (mainline Protestantism, non-ethnically oriented Catholicism, and Reform Judaism). The idea of tri-faith America was not descriptive language. It was *pre*scriptive language that depicted a homogeneous, "Judeo-Christian" American identity. "Extreme" religious positions, including Jewish observance, "old country" Catholicism, and evangelical separatism, undermined that nationalist project, while more moderate expressions of religion provided a language of cohesion for the nation of immigrants among those willing to downplay their differences. The overlaps and tensions inherent within the conversations of the Reform movement of American Judaism, the Catholic Church, and mainline Protestantism structured how each arm of organized religion staked a claim to its place within the American landscape, while defending the particular nature of their communities.

Friction developed between the groups as religious leaders tried to reconcile competing claims for control of the domestic sphere. The stakes of Protestants, Catholics, and Jews were overlapping yet distinct. With an emphasis on privacy and autonomy that both informed and reflected pervasive American notions of individualism and freedom, mainline Protestants felt the least tension about intermarriage. In addition, as the majority group, they were the least afraid of losing members. Broadly speaking, the primacy of the individual believer had a strong history in Protestant theology and dominated twentieth-century mainline Protestant thought. Both lay Jews and Catholics and their religious leaders, however, negotiated between the traditional claims of their own religious communities and American cultural norms of family privacy and individual rights with which those traditions sometimes conflicted.

Despite their differences, the terms with which the three groups discussed interfaith marriage were largely the same. The institutional leaders chose to focus on a particular kind of boundary, one that they defined as "religious." These leaders defined religion as a specific set of commitments and affiliations, ones that they could police and (at least attempt to) control. They were primarily concerned with conversion, religious education for eventual children, practices that a family might include or exclude, and, lastly, theological and legal questions such as "Is a covenant between a Jew and a non-Jew valid under Jewish law?" or "What does it mean to enter into a marriage that is not a sacrament according to the Catholic Church?" These institutional leaders were primarily interested in defining interfaith marriage in ways that could be solved within the institutions. Their solutions were varied, and tiered. For Jewish and Catholic leadership, the goal was to prevent interfaith marriages, either by encouraging endogamous dating or by encouraging conversion so as to create a religiously unified home. If interfaith marriage could not be prevented, religious leaders across the board, Protestant, Catholic, and Jew, argued that children should be raised with one religion. While creating single-religion families through conversion strove to resolve institutional concerns regarding affiliation, these moves did not always answer the concerns of Jewish, Catholic, and Protestant community members—neither those embarking upon interfaith family life nor those who were not.

The steady hum of disagreement surrounding the issue remained constant through the long 1970s. For Reform Jews, the concern was one that had been present since they first came to America: how to preserve a Jewish community and generational continuity in a world in which Jewishness could be easily shed—a process historically facilitated by interfaith marriage—while at the same time working within the highly universalizing language of mid-twentieth-century American Reform Judaism. Ultimately, the inclusion of "intermarried" families in synagogue life and maintaining the purity of a Jewish home crystallized as concerns of primary importance. For Catholics, the problem was slightly different: how to reconcile a strong theological view of the Church as an authoritative mediator between God and individuals—via the sacraments—with an American individualism. These concerns touched on both the sacramental nature of marriage and the necessity of bringing up the children of intermarriage in the Church. Additionally, both Jewish and Catholic hierarchies shared the problem of how to discuss their concerns with intermarriage, so often in tension with their goal of their religions being accepted as American. At the same time, institutional leaders also had to come to terms with the fact that they desired more institutional reach into the homes and family lives of American Catholics and Jews than their congregants necessarily wanted to give them.

If popular media in the 1970s largely portrayed interfaith marriage as a social good, part of the path to a shared American identity, the responses of religious institutions were, as the General Commission on Chaplains and Armed Forces Personnel pamphlet demonstrates, considerably less enthusiastic. More important than the objections raised by Jewish, Catholic, and Protestant leaders were the terms of their debate. While television shows and movies tended to portray the conflicts of interfaith marriage as humorous and largely rooted in ethnic stereotypes and class differences, focusing on practices that could easily be mapped onto food, dress, language, and mannerisms, religious leaders framed the debate according to formal religious affiliation and addressed theological concerns with interfaith marriage. These preoccupations demonstrate that if popular depictions played up "ethnic" or "cultural" qualities, religious leaders focused on aspects of Judaism and Christianity that they could define as "religious" and could control within institutional life. Nonetheless, the terms of their discussion were influenced by their attempts to redefine Judaism as an American "religion," over and above an ethnically oriented self-understanding.

Both Reform Jews and Catholics had extensive internal conversations about how to address the rising intermarriage rate. While both groups began

with strong statements against intermarriage, they also needed to accommodate congregations and parishioners who were going to intermarry, with or
without clerical support. The institutional structures of American Judaism
and American Catholicism were distinct, as were their histories and social
positions in the United States, and so were their responses. If the Reform
movement moved from debating whether rabbis should be allowed to perform interfaith marriages to debating how best to encourage interfaith
families to join and participate in Jewish communal and home life, the
post–Vatican II Catholic Church was most concerned with the sacramental
nature of Catholic marriage and policing its boundaries while maintaining
positive relationships with American Protestant society. American Protestants,
meanwhile, responded to interfaith marriage from a position of social strength.
They were concerned about maintaining the strength of the institution of
marriage and the American family, but they were less concerned about threats
either to the truth claims of their religion or to the social survival of their religious point of view. Their dominance of the American landscape allowed
them to respond comparatively tolerantly toward intermarrying couples.
In addition, Protestant dominance, and guilt about the role of Protestant
churches in delaying American involvement in World War II, allowed Protestants to respond favorably to Jewish attempts to convince intermarrying
Protestant-Jewish couples to raise their children as Jews. Inter-Christian tensions, however, prevented Protestants from supporting Catholic attempts to
persuade members of Protestant-Catholic marriages to choose Catholicism.

To Officiate or Not to Officiate: The Central Conference of American Rabbis, the Union of American Hebrew Congregations, and the Implications of Officiating at Interfaith Weddings

During the 1960s, 1970s, and early 1980s, the Reform movement's leadership
was much less interested in coping with interfaith marriage than they were in
preventing it. Samuel Sobel, the executive secretary of the Armed Forces
Chaplains Board, contributed the Jewish section of the military pamphlet on
interfaith marriage. His task was, in part, to stake out a firm stance against
mixed marriage without suggesting that his stance either indicated Jewish racial identity or detracted from Jewish "Americanness." Sobel realized that
drawing sharp boundaries around Jewish identity entailed risk: Jewish tribal-
ism had the potential to undermine their status as Americans in a country
that privileged Protestant nationalism. For much of the twentieth century,

Jews had been "torn between their commitment to Jewish racial distinctive-ness and their desire to be seen as stable members of white society."[5] In the decades after World War II, American Jews came to see themselves, and be seen by the dominant society, primarily as a religious, rather than a racial, group. As Sobel demonstrates, the "Jewish home" served as one substitute for a Jewish racial identity that had fallen into disrepute. Sobel therefore ex-plained that Jewish objections to interfaith marriage did not "arise from a sense of Jewish superiority or exclusiveness."[6] Rather, he argued, "one has not gotten to the heart of Judaism and the concept of Jewish peoplehood unless he grasps the great ethical principle of the home."[7] Sobel focused on the Juda-ism of the home, specifically arguing that "husband and wife together, united for life, bring the spirit of God, the spirit of holiness, into the household." The home, he argued, was more central to Jewish identity than any institution or organization, including the synagogue.

By pointing to the Jewish home, and the choice of a Jewish marriage part-ner, as both foundational to Jewish identity and an important unit of Ameri-can life, Sobel was also echoing decades of pointing to sociological work to defend Jewish endogamy. Beginning with research in the 1930s by Ernest Bur-gess and through the 1940s with the work of Ruby Jo Reeves Kennedy, a Jew and a Gentile, respectively, sociologists argued that religiously endogamous marriages were more successful, as marriages. Because such couples brought shared values and worldviews to the table, these scholars argued, their marriages would be happier. Furthermore, social scientists such as Julius Drachsler argued that intermarriage (be it interfaith or interethnic) resulted in assimilation. Even though assimilation was generally understood to be best for the American nation, Drachsler claimed that endogamous marriage would be best for the nation in the long run. Not only would these unified marriages create more stable homes, they would result in a gradual and there-fore more "harmonious" process of creating American unity. American rab-bis, particularly those in the Reform movement, drew on this sociological literature as much or more than they drew on Jewish law when arguing against interfaith marriage.[8] They felt they had science on their side in explaining that Jewish marriages (or Catholic or Protestant marriages) were better, both for the couple and family and for the United States, than the seemingly as-similationist interfaith marriage. When Sobel put the Jewish home at the cen-ter of Jewish, and therefore American, life he was speaking as part of an intellectual trajectory of sociologists and rabbis who had long made similar arguments.

Interfaith marriage, then, was a problem for the Jewish community and for the American nation because it undermined the potential sacrality of the home—in intermarriage, Sobel argued, the home would be "divided against itself," and its essential Jewishness seriously depleted.[9] By depleting the religious glue of the home, the interfaith marriage weakened the home, potentially endangering the bedrock of postwar American life. By using a Civil War metaphor to describe the challenges, Sobel subtly underscored the Americanness of Jews at the same time that he drew a boundary between them and their fellow citizens. Sobel was careful to explain that a "stranger" might enter Judaism through conversion, as did the biblical Ruth. Otherwise, marriage between Jews and non-Jews was discouraged because the absence of religion in the home or the presence of competing religions in the home was seen as "not conductive to the peace and harmony, love and understanding, which God has designed for marriage and which the intimate, sacred relationship of marriage must foster."[10] While Sobel presented his concerns with interfaith marriage as particularly Jewish, because he was talking about protecting the home for a place of religious development and sanctuary, there was little in his argument that could not, potentially, be extrapolated to other religious communities. By framing his argument in terms of what made for a healthy home, he deflected objections to the exclusive nature of endogamous marriage.

Sobel's comments were part of a larger trend in liberal Judaism that sought to define and preserve a Jewish tradition perceived to be under threat from various internal and external forces. At the same time, in the 1970s, while the Reform movement struggled with a dramatic increase in the interfaith marriage rate, it also attempted to form a response that would manage to strongly oppose interfaith marriage without alienating either the broader American public or the rising numbers of intermarried Jews. If their opposition to interfaith marriage implicitly criticized Protestants or Catholics, they might jeopardize their carefully constructed and hard-won status as an "American religion," possibly while invoking frightening language about Jewish racial identity. Meanwhile, since the Reform leadership was primarily concerned that interfaith marriage would cause Jewish numbers to decline, they wanted to find a way to oppose marrying non-Jews while still convincing blended families to join synagogues. While there were questions about how to incorporate families of interfaith couples into synagogue life, those questions gained more widespread attention in the 1980s and 1990s. In the 1970s, American rabbis focused simply on the phenomenon of mixed marriages: what to call them, whether rabbis should perform interfaith marriages or demand that the non-Jewish spouse convert, and what the status of the children of intermarriage would be in synagogue life.[11]

Throughout the 1960s and 1970s, the Central Conference of American Rabbis (CCAR), the rabbinical branch of the Reform movement, maintained the policy toward interfaith marriage laid out in a 1947 Responsum, which clearly opposed interfaith marriage.[12] In the 1940s, when the intermarriage rate was below 7 percent, this position did not create much comment.[13] Throughout the 1960s and 1970s, however, demand for rabbis to perform interfaith marriages rose dramatically, causing tension within the Reform movement and in the Jewish community more broadly, as rabbis and their congregants debated whether rabbis should accede to demands for mixed marriages.

By the 1960s and early 1970s, more and more Reform rabbis were allowing interfaith marriage without conversion, and debate within the Reform movement had reached a fevered pitch, as had responses from other Jewish leaders about the Reform approach. For instance, in 1973, a resolution was introduced to the New York Board of Rabbis, a committee made up of representatives from the Reform, Conservative, and Orthodox movements, which denied membership to any rabbis who performed mixed marriages.[14] Reform rabbis responded to this resolution with conflicted and even contradictory reactions. Reform rabbi Harry Essrig responded vehemently to this resolution, writing to the chairman of the Ethics Committee of the CCAR with the extreme request that ethics charges be brought against the three rabbis who had sponsored the bill. While Essrig considered interfaith marriage a violation of "the most sacred elements of the Jewish tradition," he simultaneously defended the CCAR's right to make its own decisions about the practice of its rabbis, rather than holding them accountable to other movements.[15] He pointed out the other movements were "meddling" in what was a very contentious moment for Reform Judaism. Internal Jewish debates about how to address rising rates of intermarriage, then, were closely tied to debates about the relationship between the different Jewish movements. In Essrig's view, the 1973 New York resolution violated the Jewish legitimacy of the Reform movement and its rabbis.

Likewise, at the 1971 national conference of the CCAR, the question of whether to officiate at interfaith weddings took center stage in the debates of the Reform rabbinate. Reform rabbis debated whether performing mixed marriages was a legitimate Jewish action. Roland Gittleson and David Polish proposed a resolution with extreme language, declaring that "mixed marriages are contrary to the tradition of the Jewish religion" and calling on "its members not to officiate at such mixed marriage ceremonies."[16] This was a shift in language from the earlier resolution, passed in 1909 and reaffirmed in 1947, which stipulated that mixed marriage was "contrary to the tradition of the Jewish religion, and should therefore be discouraged by the rabbinate." The change in language here is slight but significant. While the Reform movement had always disapproved of what it then called mixed marriage, prior to 1971, rabbis could use whatever methods they felt appropriate to discourage the marriages and then, if they felt that performing the marriage was the best course of action in order to keep the couple in the Jewish fold, were permitted to do so. In short, while the 1947 Responsum condemned interfaith marriage, it allowed rabbis to officiate if, for some reason, the individual rabbi thought that choice was best. The Gittleson-Polish amendment attempted to take away that bit of rabbinic autonomy. Supporters of the amendment believed that rabbis should not perform interfaith marriages. For some, the reason was strategic. They believed that to perform the marriage was to give tacit approval to interfaith marriages. Additionally, many hoped that if they could not persuade Jews to date other Jews, they could convince non-Jewish significant others to convert, using the incentive of a Jewish wedding and, in theory, guaranteeing a Jewish home. For others, the issue was rooted in understandings of the definition of Jewish marriage. Because of the covenantal nature of Jewish marriage, a religiously valid marriage could not occur between a Jew and a non-Jew. Therefore, the question of officiating at such a union became irrelevant.

The Gittleson-Polish amendment would have forbidden Reform rabbis from performing interfaith marriage outright—a distinct tightening of the regulations. These restrictions were met with swift resistance. The 1971 proposal was to be finalized at the annual conference the following year, but in April of 1972, sixteen rabbis condoned a new position, issuing a statement advocating for a return to the original resolution. They pointed out that polls from 1962 demonstrated that the CCAR supported the 1909 resolution "almost unanimously."[17] Further, they argued that "there is such a great diversity of individual opinions and practices in the Conference with regard to the professional implications of the intent of this resolution that no CCAR member may rightly claim that his opinion or his practices represent those of a clear majority of the conference membership."[18] As a result of the range of opinions within the CCAR membership, the sponsoring rabbis argued that the original statements should stand, since limiting or defining rabbinic practice would "serve no meaningful purpose and may well cause a serious breach within both the Conference and the American Reform movement."[19] Condemning mixed marriages outright, they feared, would cause irrevocable rifts within and beyond the Reform movement.

Opposition to the blanket ban of the Gittleson-Polish amendment reflected a desire for institutional and communal harmony far more than for a consistent theological stance. The majority of CCAR members believed that rabbinic autonomy was more important than an utterly constant policy toward rabbinic officiation at interfaith marriages, a position that exemplified their own internalization of American notions of individualism and their inherent similarity to mainline Protestant theological commitments. Indeed, that view ultimately prevailed, and the CCAR passed a resolution that strongly opposed rabbinic officiation at interfaith marriages but preserved the right of individual rabbis to disagree and officiate without losing their professional standing. Other rabbis opposed the Gittleson-Polish amendment because they believed that such a declaration was not in the best interests of *klal yisrael*, or the entirety of the Jewish people, as its language would alienate Jews within mixed marriages.

Rabbis opposed to the Gittleson-Polish amendment suggested that it was best for the continuity of the Jewish people for rabbis to be allowed to officiate at interfaith marriages. Specifically, they followed an argument that Hillel director and author Rabbi David Max Eichhorn made, in a 1957 article for the *CCAR Journal* that was recirculated in 1971.[20] Eichhorn was chair of the Committee on the Unaffiliated, appointed by the CCAR to explore the idea of outreach not to non-Jewish spouses in interfaith marriages but to unchurched and unbaptized Americans who might be in need of a religion. While Eichhorn was not in favor of interfaith marriage, he did not believe that refusing to marry such a couple would prevent the wedding. Someone else would simply perform it, on someone else's terms. He argued that a couple who came to a rabbi for an interfaith marriage and was turned away would likely be "bewildered, frustrated, and resentful" rather than understanding the rabbi's position.[21] They would cease to regard the rabbi as a "credible religious teacher." As a result, Eichhorn believed that turning away interfaith couples was a high-stakes choice: it would result in more alienated Jewish spouses, fewer non-Jewish spouses converting to Judaism, fewer Jewish homes, and fewer children being raised as Jews.[22] According to Eichhorn, the rabbi had two responsibilities when presented with an interfaith couple: "to move in a direction that will not weaken but will possibly strengthen the Jewish religion and also to move in a direction which will increase the chances for happiness of this couple as individuals and as the establishers of a home and family."[23] In his view, by performing the marriage, the officiating rabbi continued to have an influence in the life of the interfaith couple and became a positive, rather than an alienating, Jewish presence in their lives.

Eichhorn also tackled terminology in the name of *klal yisrael*, arguing for a switch from "mixed marriage" to "interfaith marriage." While the terms could be understood as synonymous, many people found the phrase "mixed marriage" to be offensive because of how often it was spoken of negatively and denoted people with a second-class status within Reform communities, and possibly because it hinted at racial mixing or miscegenation. Previously, in Jewish circles, the term "interfaith" marriage had been used to refer to marriages in which one partner had converted to Judaism, a problematic distinction because it underscored that, historically, converts to Judaism have been considered second-class Jews, unlike converts to Christianity, who are often understood to be every bit as sincere, if not more so, than those born in the fold. Eichhorn argues that, because of the conversion, these marriages are "in every respect, Jewish marriage[s]." Therefore, the distinction being made between mixed marriages and interfaith marriages was a false distinction, and there was no reason not to replace the offensive "mixed marriage" with what he saw as the more neutral "interfaith marriage."

While Eichhorn was an advocate for rabbinic officiation at interfaith marriages, his support was contingent upon his definition of Jewish continuity. He would advocate for interfaith marriage only under certain conditions. He did not require the non-Jewish spouse to convert, and in fact, if there was to be conversion, he insisted that it take place after the marriage so as to ensure that a future spouse was converting for love of the faith and the Jewish people rather than under coercion in order to have an officiant or out of love for the other partner. He did, however, require the couple to promise, "word of honor, that they will (1) rear their children as Jews; (2) give their children a formal Jewish religious school education; (3) make the home religious atmosphere conform to the teachings of the Jewish religious school that their children attend; (4) have no non-Jewish religious symbols or celebrations of any kind in the home."[24] With this list of requirements, Eichhorn hoped to naturally bring about the conversion of the non-Jewish spouse and to give the children a solid Jewish upbringing, securing their sense of themselves as Jewish.

In rationalizing his decision, Eichhorn explained that the real concern in interfaith marriages was not the marriage itself. While he agreed that religiously homogeneous marriages were preferable, he argued that no "reputable sociological study" proved that interfaith marriages had higher divorce rates. Though the debates about interfaith marriage had focused on prevention, and therefore on the couple, Eichhorn argued that the real potential casualties in an interfaith marriage were the children. In making this point, he was one of the first voices to shift the debate from the couple to their offspring. "There seems to be quite general agreement among psychologists that the major psychic damage which such marriages may cause does not fall on the husband and wife but upon their children. If the children of mixed marriages are not given a solid orientation in and a strong attachment to just one religion, these children are very likely to come to adulthood as insecure, unsteady, mixed-up individuals, whose lack of inner religious strength and stability will manifest itself in a thousand and one anti-social ways."[25] This was speculation and armchair psychology, demonstrating a belief that religious identity could be separated from other forms of identity and that confusion over religious identity could result in deep-seated dysfunction. Eichhorn's solutions to the dangers interfaith marriage posed to children could be solved with a singular religious education and a uniform set of religious symbols. In later chapters, as we turn to both popular depictions of interfaith families and various narratives of interfaith family life, a much more complicated and much less easily controlled depiction of interfaith family life unfolds. For Eichhorn, however, creating a monoreligious home was tantamount to and dependent on defining "religious" such that a religiously homogeneous home was possible.

Eichhorn framed his concern for what was best for the children in the general language of American social psychology, rather than by focusing on the impact to the Jewish community should these children fail to become Jewish. This concern for the children would echo through advice to interfaith families in subsequent decades and even played out in the popular young adult novel *Are You There, God? It's Me, Margaret*, by Judy Blume. In a context in which Reform leaders were deeply concerned about the impact of interfaith marriage on Jewish continuity and about the position of Jews in American society, concern for children's mental well-being provided a socially acceptable way to encourage exclusively Jewish education and home environments for children of mixed marriages. Thus, the argument of "what is best for the child" veiled an ulterior motive: the continuity and strength of the descendants of the baby boom generation, whose ties with normative Judaism were weakening rather than building off of their parents' commitment.

The most important aspect of this issue, on both sides of the debate, was the question of what was best for the Jewish community. Was it best to refuse to marry interfaith couples because such a refusal best served Judaism, sending a strong message that interfaith marriage is not acceptable, as inter-

pretations of Jewish marriage law did not allow rabbinic officiation? Some
even argued that it was better for Judaism to have fewer, but more committed,
people. Was it best to bless interfaith unions because then a rabbi could encourage the couple to become members of the community, requiring them to
promise to raise their children in Jewish homes, without elements of Christian religious tradition? Either way, the needs or wishes of the couple were
not of primary importance; the needs of the Jewish community outweighed
any particular familial desire or circumstance. Eichhorn's comment that "no
reputable sociological study" demonstrated that interfaith marriages were inclined to failure pointed to a widely held belief in 1970s America that interfaith marriages were dramatically more difficult and therefore more prone to
failure than religiously homogeneous marriages. Again, as Eichhorn and
others argued, the failure to provide children with a consistent religious message would harm them. Because interfaith marriages were believed to be difficult as well as damaging to children, the Reform leadership of the 1970s
concluded that it was best, for the couples, for their potential children, and
for the survival of Judaism, to dissuade such couples from marrying.

To that end, in 1979, Alexander Schindler, president of the Union of American Hebrew Congregations (UAHC), the congregational arm of the Reform
movement, called for the creation of a Reform agency, the Jewish Outreach
Institute, that would address the problem of intermarriage. "The tide of intermarriage is running against us," he argued. The intent of the agency was "to
turn the tide which threatens to sweep us away into directions which might
enable us to recover our numbers and, more important, to recharge our inner
strength."[26] While the agency was to be multifaceted, one of its primary functions would be outreach to intermarried couples. Schindler, whose immediate post–World War II visit to Germany informed his decision to become a
rabbi, is sometimes thought to have expanded Jewish outreach in response to
what he saw as similar crises in Jewish life—large numbers of interfaith marriages and declining Jewish affiliation. Through making Judaism more welcoming, he hoped to "stem the tide" of these demographic changes.[27]

Individual couples, however, did not experience the refusal of rabbis to
perform their weddings as being in their best interests, and some of Eichhorn's predictions about their responses proved true. Interfaith couples had
often felt unwelcome in synagogues, which failed at explaining Judaism to the
non-Jewish partner. In addition, both members of the partnership were framed
as a threat to Jewish continuity and community. This "outreach," then, was
intended to make interfaith couples feel welcome in synagogue life. While
Schindler opposed rabbinic officiation at interfaith marriages, he cautioned

that the rabbi who refused to marry a couple need not turn them away from Judaism. Rather optimistically, Schindler suggested that a rabbi explain why he could not officiate at interfaith marriages and emphasize that the couple and their future children were welcome in the synagogue. In order to keep interfaith couples within the Jewish fold, he admonished that the Reform movement "must remove the 'not wanted' signs from our hearts. We are opposed to intermarriage, but we must not oppose the intermarried."[28] In essence, Schindler encouraged Reform clergy and laity to take the "hate the sin, love the sinner approach." Rabbis and congregants were encouraged to disapprove of intermarriage and prevent it if possible. Only when that failed was the Jewish community encouraged to make intermarried couples comfortable and welcome in their communities. While the intent of this was to ward off intermarriage if possible, while welcoming those who did intermarry, this mode of outreach had mixed results, especially initially. Interviews with interfaith couples who married in the 1970s and 1980s, and with children of interfaith couples who came of age in those eras, demonstrate that while they sometimes assimilated into Jewish community life, at other times they found themselves expected to commit to a Jewish community that pathologized them and their families.

Schindler proposed three radical steps to change this scenario and welcome intermarried families into Reform congregations, addressing converts, interfaith couples, and the children of interfaith families. First, Schindler proposed a new approach to converts to Judaism. While not all converts to Reform Judaism did so because of marriage, in his role as chair of the Committee on the Unaffiliated, Eichhorn conducted a study in the early 1950s that found that a full 93.9 percent of Reform conversions were in conjunction with marriage to a Jew.[29] As Schindler believed that, since the best outcome for an interfaith couple was for the non-Jewish partner to convert, Jews needed to shift their attitude toward converts. Too often, he explained, "born Jews" assumed that "since only a madman would choose to be a Jew, the convert is either neurotic or hypocritical."[30] Not only were their motives suspect but converts to Judaism existed as second-class citizens, considered to be less Jewish than "born Jews," a situation that needed to be rectified

The Reform leadership addressed negative attitudes toward converts largely in the context of interfaith marriage, as part of an attempt to make conversion an appealing option. In hoping for the conversion of non-Jewish partners, Schindler made it clear that he was not considering "stealing" believers from other respected religions (i.e., the Catholic Church or mainline Protestantism). Rather, he was interested in the unchurched spiritual seekers, to whom, he argued, Judaism could offer universal truths. Schindler's response underscored a desire to demonstrate Judaism as a good ecumenical player—at the same time that they wanted the non-Jewish partner in interfaith marriages to convert. Reform leaders carefully did not frame that person as Christian, in part to maintain good relationships with the Protestant and Catholic leadership with whom they collaborated as part of "tri-faith America." Encouraging conversion was not poaching on Christianity's turf—rather, it was helping to create stable, religious nuclear families. Couples from similar religious backgrounds would, the leadership trusted, be less likely to get divorced. The homes would be happier, and the families have more to hold them together, in a moment when the family seemed under threat by the emerging feminist movement.

This framing of Judaism as a "universal religion," common in the Reform movement particularly in the early to mid-twentieth century, would have profound implications for the larger conversations about how to address the growing presence of interfaith families. The idea that Judaism was universal, separate from a connection to Jews as a distinct people, both set conversion up as efficacious—one could join Judaism, and it was irrelevant whether that resulted in becoming a Jew—and allowed Judaism to trump Christianity in a debate about which of the two religions a couple should choose. Leaders like Schindler used the universal nature of Judaism to argue that interfaith couples should, together, be Jewish because Christians subscribe to all of Judaism while Christian belief in Jesus was not universal and therefore not something that the Jewish half of a couple could share.

Second, Schindler charged the outreach agency with finding ways to include non-Jewish partners in Jewish communal and ritual life. He controversially argued that the "halachah permits non-Jews to be in the synagogue, to sing in the choir, to recite the blessing over the Sabbath and festival candles, and even to handle the Torah. There is no law which forbids the non-Jew to be buried in a Jewish cemetery."[31] Schindler's claims for the role of a non-Jewish spouse were shocking, flying in the face of conventionally held boundaries between Jew and non-Jew. By including non-Jewish partners as fully as possible in the rituals and life cycles controlled by the synagogue, practices that Schindler coded "religious," he hoped that they themselves would initiate processes of conversion and be comfortable raising their children to identify as Jews.

Schindler's third and final concern dealt with raising children as Jews. He argued that including children of patrilineal descent in the Jewish community was central to an outreach mission—a position that foreshadowed the movement's inclusion of children of patrilineal descent four years later. He pushed for including all children of interfaith marriage in Jewish ritual, regardless of whether or not the mother was the Jewish parent, making the child technically Jewish according to traditional Jewish law. The Reform movement had long before discarded a traditional relationship with the law, and Schindler saw no reason to use traditional definitions of "who is a Jew" if they ran counter to contemporary needs. It would be off-putting, he argued, to require that the child of a Jewish father convert in order to have a bar mitzvah, especially if the parents had raised the child exclusively as a Jew.

Schindler's position was radical, would reverse long-standing tenets of Jewish law in a mode that had ramifications beyond the Reform movement. While the Reform movement had long been the branch of Judaism with the most distance from traditional interpretations of Jewish law, a synagogue's choice to keep a kosher kitchen or support its membership driving on the Sabbath did not affect the unity of the Jewish community. Changing the rules of patrilineal descent, however, would. If the Reform movement began to count the children of Jewish men and non-Jewish women as fully Jewish, while the Conservative and Orthodox movements continued to follow Jewish law, the result would be lack of agreement between the movements as to who counted as a Jew—a reality that could result in people who had been raised Jewish and understood themselves as Jewish needing to convert (with all of that potential stigma) in order to be accepted into many Jewish communities.

The concern, for the upper echelons of the CCAR and the UAHC, ultimately centered on how the children of interfaith marriages would fare, in both their psychological health and their commitment to the Jewish people. Other than the decisions to grant all the children of non-Jewish mothers full participation in synagogue life, there was little conversation about how to interact with children from interfaith homes themselves. While ultimately, as chapter 4 will explore, the Reform movement focused its conversations on how to encourage interfaith families to create Jewish homes, for most of the 1970s, conversations within the CCAR and the UAHC focused on the prevention of interfaith marriages rather than on the needs of such families. Similarly, they discussed the need to include these blended families, but paid little attention to how to implement such plans.

By framing their objections to interfaith marriage in terms of the psychological health of the children, Jewish leaders were able to speak out against interfaith marriage without seeming to be un-American or biased against Protestants and Catholics. The shared national concern that social changes were undermining strong families, with unified marriages and psychologically healthy children, meant that conversations about how to buttress the family were more acceptable to the American public—even if the answers (endogamous marriage) seemed to run against the American message of assimilation. The question of how to create an "authentic identity, a solid core of personality that would allow the individual to withstand the pressures toward mindless conformity," defined the middle of the twentieth century, for Jews and Protestants alike.[32] As a result, the Reform hierarchy framed their public statements around the question of how best to care for and raise healthy children with a firm sense of identity, even as their internal correspondence was preoccupied with the best outcome for Jewish continuity.

Rabbis and other Jewish leaders, then, were able to argue that science, in the form of both sociology and psychology, supported the position that a singular religious identity was best for children. They encouraged couples to find a home in Judaism when one person had a Jewish identity and the other person was a largely secular American, adrift from other religious communities or perhaps seeking a religious identity. Judaism was not threatening to Christianity, they argued, though it might well be a rational choice for those who had already left Christian communities. This understanding required using a reconfigured understanding of Judaism as a universal religion rather than an ethnic identity, both making the synagogue more accessible to the intermarried spouse and unintentionally undercutting some of the traditional arguments against intermarriage.

The Catholic Church and the Sacrament of Marriage

If Jews were concerned about marriages between Jews and Christians, Catholics were predominantly concerned about marriages to Protestants, a position that was largely shaped by an anti-Protestant, pre–Vatican II sensibility. At the same time, that attitude needed to be articulated in a manner that was palatable to an American public that had only recently recognized Catholicism as a viable American religion, provided it played by certain rules.[33] Specifically, as had been shown in the presidential campaign of John F. Kennedy, American Catholics needed to demonstrate to the rest of the American public that their primary allegiance was to the United States, rather than to Rome. In the military pamphlet on interfaith marriage (mentioned at the beginning of this chapter), the spokesman for Catholicism, Monsignor Joseph Marbach, Chancellor of the Military Ordinariate, expressed a concern about interfaith marriage formed by Catholic theology in a language that was palatable to the

American public. Like his Jewish colleague, he contended that "mixed marriage" should be avoided because it would lead to marital unhappiness. If, however, a couple insisted on such a marriage, he suggested a negotiation of their differing backgrounds that was based on the shared worship space of a military setting, presumed a Protestant-Catholic marriage, and applied a logic that ultimately favored Catholic practice.

Like the Jewish leadership, Monsignor Marbach used the language of psychology rather than that of theology when he wrote that the Catholic Church did not favor mixed marriages, because the different religious backgrounds would add stress to the marriage. "To paraphrase a well-known columnist," he quipped, "marriage is a war enough without making it a holy war."[34] In this sentiment, he echoed the concern (and war metaphors) of his Jewish coauthor to extend the idea that marriage is of importance beyond the couple. He moved on, however, to suggest that while successful interfaith marriages are possible, they are likely to succeed only when couples can agree on certain ground rules, which he describes through the metaphor of shared worship space. He argued that a couple could compromise on their family's religious practices just as interfaith religious spaces could compromise on decorations for worship space. Just as Catholics might agree not to display a picture of the Blessed Mother, as long as Protestants allowed a depiction of the Holy Family, similar compromises, he argued, must be made in a marriage and must be made in a way that at least considers the views of the party that wants "more." After all, he pointed out, if Protestants have two or three sacraments and Catholics seven, a child raised as a Catholic will believe in all of the sacraments held dear by a Protestant parent. This position, then, presents Catholicism as the logical choice for the Protestant-Catholic interfaith couple.

Marbach's comments reflected a Catholic Church of the 1960s and 1970s that was actively renegotiating its stance on mixed marriage under the watchful eyes of Protestants eager to spot attitudes toward intermarriage that seemed to threaten the ecumenical spirit of the age. At the same time, like their Jewish counterparts, interfaith marriage presented some very serious practical and theological problems for the Catholic hierarchy. In the 1960s, the American Catholic Church's guidelines for mixed marriages shifted slightly as a result of the Second Vatican Council (Vatican II).

While a thorough study of the formal theology of marriage and concerns of the Catholic hierarchy toward mixed marriage in the decades immediately preceding Vatican II fall beyond the purview of this book, they grounded the Catholic Church's theological concerns around mixed marriage.[35] The Catholic Church regarded itself as the sole authority over all Christian marriages, to the extent "that it makes marriage more a contractual pledge binding the two persons to the Catholic Church than a free, mutual, and inviolable contract between each other."[36] Given that legalistic understanding, in which each party in the marriage entered into a contract with the Church, it prohibited marriages between Catholics and non-Catholics, whether the non-Catholics were baptized Christians or not.[37]

The Church had particular theological concerns with marriage between Catholics and Protestants. Catholic theology considers marriage a Sacrament of the Life, which means that it can only be undertaken when one is free from sin. Additionally, the Sacrament of Marriage is only a sacrament if both of the people being married are in a state of grace. If one or both of the people is in a sinful state, then the marriage is a lifelong contract, but not a sacrament. While it would be theoretically possible for a baptized non-Catholic to be in a sin-free state, as an article by Abbot Richard Felix pointed out, "the well informed Catholic will ask himself the question 'Is the Sacrament received worthily?'"[38] While a Catholic prepared for marriage by going to confession, the non-Catholic could not and therefore was more likely to be married in a state of "moral or grievous sin," rendering the marriage legally valid but "sinful and sacrilegious."[39] Again, Church literature, such as the *Our Sunday Visitor* column "Why" on the subject of "Mixed Marriage," was careful to point out that it was perfectly possible for a Catholic to marry in a sinful state, but the fact remained that Catholics, unlike Protestants or Jews, had a way to cleanse themselves of sin.[40] Those who married outside of the Catholic faith sacrificed the sacramental nature of their marriage, then, which lessened the odds that Christ would dwell in their marriage. The marriage would not only have the strains that clergy feared would weaken a marriage, but because a mixed marriage was not a sacrament, theologically, both the marriage itself and the role of the Church in the life of the believer would be diminished.

In fact, before Vatican II, Catholic literature drew on traditional Church history to oppose marriage to Protestants, referring to them as heretics or schismatics.[41] In 1932, American bishops instituted a policy that before a priest performed a mixed marriage, the Catholic partner had to meet with the priest alone. The bishops believed, in the words of John Francis Noll, Bishop of Fort Wayne, Indiana, that "most mixed marriages could be prevented if the priest had a friendly chat with the Catholic party before he or she promised too much, or at least the dangers which we fear from every mixed marriage could, in large part, be overcome."[42] This view, deliberately naïve or not, suggested that a Catholic believer's attachment to his or her Church would be, once he or she was reminded of it, greater than his or her attachment to a beloved. Once again, Catholic and Jewish understandings of the role of the clergy in these marriages intersected; their first priority was prevention. If prevention failed, however, the question was how to minimize the damage, both to the couple and to the religious community.

In the event that the priest could not convince the Catholic to break the engagement, the couple and their priest were required to seek a dispensation from Rome for the marriage, as mixed marriage violated Church laws.[43] Dispensations could only be granted under specific reasons, the majority of which centered on securing Catholics for the Church. The Church would grant dispensations under the following conditions: the priest truly believed that the Catholic in the couple would, if not granted a dispensation, commit apostasy by being married in either a civil or a Protestant ceremony; the priest had a "well-founded hope" that the Protestant partner would be converted to Catholicism through the marriage along with his or her family, including any children from a prior marriage; the Catholic lived in a place in which there were few other Catholics and to deny marriage to a Protestant might prevent the Catholic from marrying; or the marriage would prevent a scandal, such as an illegitimate pregnancy or cohabitation.[44]

Here, then, the concern shifts from questions of personal faith to those of communal continuity. In order to be eligible for a dispensation, the couple had to make a specific set of promises, and the Catholic party had to make an additional pledge. Together, the couple had to promise that they would not divorce; that all children born to the marriage would be educated and baptized exclusively as Catholics; that the non-Catholic would not interfere with raising the children as Catholics; that if the Catholic partner died, the survivor would continue to raise the children as Catholics; that the Archbishop or his representatives had the right to enforce the contract; and, lastly, that all of the above conditions be transferable to their heirs. Additionally, the Catholic party promised to work faithfully for the conversion of his or her spouse, to refrain from practicing birth control, and to have only one marriage, before a priest.[45]

The requirements for a dispensation and the agreements required from the couple are noteworthy for a number of reasons. First, they demonstrate a concern with the creation of new Catholics, through both the potential conversion of the Protestant and his or her premarital family and through the guarantee that all future children would be raised as Catholics. Second, the language of the ante-nuptial agreement was legal language, referring to the marrying couples as "parties" and using the nomenclature of contract law. In the 1940s, the American Catholic Church was particularly interested in whether these contracts could be upheld in the American civil courts.[46] Without the support of the civil courts, the Church could only enforce the contracts as long as the family remained a part of the Church. If the family left the Church, the Church had no way to retaliate. If the contracts could have been upheld in a civil court, then the Church would have been able to declare marriages null if the couple did not fulfill their agreements and potentially take custody of the children, in order to guarantee their Catholic upbringing. In this moment, the Catholic Church, which had historically been a religion of outsiders, was contemplating turning to the legal system for protection, indicating their own sense that they had "made it" as an American religion. The American legal system might protect Catholic religious contracts.

Not everyone agreed that these prenuptial contracts deserved protection from the U.S. legal system. After these concerns were raised in *American Catholic Magazine*, the *Yale Law Journal* took up the question of "whether these completely un-American pre-marital contracts as drawn up by the Catholic Church on instructions from Rome could be upheld and enforced by the civil courts in the United States, and, if so would it be advisable to do so."[47] Specifically, the authors argued that it was un-American to argue that a couple could not change their religion or the religious orientation of their family. Ultimately, the *Yale Law Journal* decided that the contract was legally binding and therefore could, theoretically, be upheld in a U.S. civil court. According to the 1941 pamphlet "Mixed Marriage and the Catholic Church," however, "in the opinion of the article in the *Yale Law Journal*: to force an issue that concerns a difference of religious opinion in to a decision of the civil courts is not in keeping with our vital democratic principle of separation of church and state."[48] The American Catholic hierarchy chose, therefore, not to pursue support from civil courts for maintaining the Catholic nature of interfaith homes, at least in part because of the implication that to do so was un-American. For a Catholic Church that sought to affirm its mainstream acceptance, such legal challenges posed too many risks to be useful. While the Church might win in the court of law, it risked losing in the court of public opinion, sacrificing hard-earned acceptance as an American religion.

Given that the Catholic objections to mixed marriage applied to all non-Catholics, it is worth examining why their objections focused on Protestants rather than on Jews. On the surface, one might think that a Catholic-Protestant marriage would be the best kind of interfaith marriage (if religiously mixed marriages were going to occur), far better than one between a Catholic and a Jew, as Catholics and Protestants were both Christians. Nevertheless, the Catholic Church was not overly concerned with Catholic-Jewish intermarriage.

Primarily, the Catholic concern with Protestants was simply a numbers game. Statistically, the Church's hierarchy believed that one in four American Catholics married a non-Catholic, and the majority of those marriages were to Protestants. Protestants, then, who represented the mainstream in American culture, posed a particular threat to the Church. Second, Protestant clergy were often more willing to perform interfaith marriages than were Jewish clergy, and so the Catholic hierarchy felt united with Jewish leadership on an issue that remained contentious with Protestant leaders. In this way, Catholics and Jews shared a minority status that lent urgency to their opposition to both marriages to Protestants and the adoption of Protestant practices, but also rendered that opposition somewhat politically risky.

Lastly, the ecumenical movement gave Catholics considerable reason for concern. As Catholics and Protestants found increased common ground in social justice arenas and carried on more conversations together as American Christians, the Catholic laity became increasingly less concerned with divisions between the Catholic Church and Protestant denominations, particularly High Church denominations like Lutherans and Episcopalians. As a result, the Church tried to couch its objections to mixed marriage in acceptable language, claiming, "It cannot be stressed too emphatically that the Church in her legislation on mixed marriages intends no offence whatsoever to anyone. On the contrary, she is vitally concerned about the happiness of both parties to a marriage, and seeks through her laws to safeguard conjugal happiness for all."[49] The objections and requirements, nevertheless, did not sit well with mainline Protestant denominations. As ecumenism took root, liberal Protestants became more and more interested in creating ties across Christianity and therefore came to object less to marriage with Catholics. In part because of this disapproval, Protestant clergy were often willing to perform mixed marriages. As a result, Protestants posed a threat to the Catholic hierarchy that the Jews did not. Perhaps the Catholic hierarchy did not need to express deep concern about marriages between Catholics and Jews because the Catholic bishops could rest assured that if priests refused to marry Catholic-Jewish couples, rabbis would do so as well (or at least the governing bodies of the Jewish movements strongly encouraged rabbis to do so). Since they shared similar fears of assimilation and decreased relevance, their positions on interfaith marriage reflected those concerns. Institutionally, Catholics and Jews thus presented a united, more conservative front on the subject of mixed marriage.

Vatican II shifted many arenas of the Church, including opening up questions on mixed marriage. While discussion on mixed marriage was raised in

1963, the Council decided in 1964 to put the question before the Pope for his consideration. In 1966, Pope Paul VI issued an Apostolic Letter, "*Motu Proprio* Determining Norms for Mixed Marriages."[50] The papal letter signified a distinct shift in attitudes toward mixed marriage at the same time that it condemned the practice. In the letter, the Pope observed that the contemporary world, in which Catholics were living in closer proximity to Protestants and other non-Catholics, made the question of mixed marriage more pressing than it had been in the past. The apostolic letter rebutted the somewhat popular idea that mixed marriage might bring about greater Christian unity through the conversion of Protestants. Rather, Pope Paul VI feared that disagreements within and about mixed marriage would increase tension between Protestants and Catholics.[51] Additionally, he was concerned about the implications of mixed marriage for Catholic worship, for the education of children, and on the family structure, which he referred to as the "living cell of the Church."[52] As a result, the Church, "conscious of her duty, discourages the contracting of mixed marriages, for she is most desirous that Catholics be able in matrimony to attain to perfect union of mind and full communion of life."[53] With its focus on the home and its outright condemnation of the practice, the Catholic Church officially entered the era of rising rates of interfaith marriage with the same position as all of institutional Judaism: against contracting marriages across religious boundaries.

Nonetheless, the apostolic letter flagged two major changes in tone, if not in substance, in the Church's response. Paul VI noted that "although in the case of baptized persons of different religious confessions, there is less risk of religious indifferentism, it can be more easily avoided if both husband and wife have a sound knowledge of the Christian nature of marital partnership, and if they are properly helped by their respective Church authorities."[54] This wording is a notable shift in language here from earlier sources, where Protestants were "heretics" or "schismatics." Now they were fellow Christians, in communion, however imperfect, with Christ. The acceptance of Protestants as potential, if not ideal, marriage partners, however, underscored that Jews, who did not accept Christ, were much less appropriate spouses for Catholics and ranked below Protestants. The Pope was not willing to condemn even those marriages, however, arguing that "even difficulties arising in marriage between a Catholic and an unbaptized person can be overcome through pastoral watchfulness and skill."[55] While the Church certainly opposed interfaith marriages, the Pope was willing to acknowledge that though more difficult, and less than ideal, success was possible with appropriate guidance from a religious authority. In this, there were similarities between the formal position of the Reform movement and the Catholic Church (with the exception of the issue of rabbinic autonomy).

In "Determining Norms for Mixed Marriages," however, the Pope did not endorse mixed marriage, defined primarily as marriage between Catholics and Protestants. He staked out the Church's disapproval and its concern for its children. He continued to require dispensations granted on the conditions that all Catholics remain "steadfast in their faith" and raise any children as Catholics, but he did not rearticulate the requirement that the Catholic work for the conversion of his or her spouse. Again, as in Reform Judaism, the continuity of faith and community—as manifested through the children—took center stage.

While the Catholic hierarchy created monolithic policies, some clergy offered noncanonical perspectives on interfaith marriage. For instance, as *The Christian Century* noted, Father Hans Kueng, the Swiss-born dean of the University of Tübingen and a priest, argued throughout the 1960s for a much more liberal stance on mixed marriages. Specifically, he opposed viewing children of marriages between a Catholic and a non-Catholic outside of the Church as illegitimate and opposed the requirement that the Catholic partner work for the conversion of his or her spouse. Assuming mixed marriages were between Christians, Kueng suggested that it was necessary for spouses to respect each other's Christian faith. Additionally, he opposed the Church's requiring the children to be reared as Catholics, arguing that questions of baptism and education were "better left to the conscience of the parents."[56] Kueng voiced these opinions prior to debates on mixed marriage during Vatican II and again in 1967 during a Synod of Catholic Bishops that led, ultimately, to the positions proposed in the Papal *Matrimonia Mixa*.

Complicating the debate within the Catholic hierarchy, lay Catholics (like Jews) did not always agree with the positions of the Church. In 1980, for instance, *U.S. Catholic* published an article by a Dominican nun, Daphne Mould, arguing that in fact the Church should encourage mixed marriages. She believed that mixed marriages were "ecumenism in action." Once again assuming that both members of the marriage are Christian, mixed marriage "is pioneering the loving unity of two different Christian traditions." This, she noted, required people of mature and courageous faith, but the potential, she argued, was immense. In order for the couple to approach this loving unity, she argued, the Catholic Church could not demand that the couple make "its old mixed marriage promises" in which the couple had to raise the children as Catholics and that the Catholic spouse had to work for the other's conversion. These requirements, she pointed out, "gave the other church involved the legitimate grievance that it was 'being bred out; in a sort of matrimonial genocide.'" Rather, she argued, the "happy marriage begins with boy meeting girl, and pastors and churches must realize that helping these people is the vital thing." In staking out this position, Mould took the stance that marriage was a matter of romantic love between individuals, who were to be helped in their path together, rather than an affair of the churches for any other goal.

While Mould did not minimize the potential troubles facing Christians from different traditions, she argued that, with the goal of Christian unity, the churches involved would best help the couple by minimizing those differences rather than accentuating them. Specifically, she suggested interchurch baptismal services that would welcome children into both of their parents' faiths and would "give them the run of their parents' churches." With such strong grounding, the children could then select Catholicism or a Protestant denomination when they reached adulthood. She called for dual officiation of marriages and, whenever possible, full participation in each other's churches. Churches should reach out and welcome spouses from other Christian traditions into community life. As was *U.S. Catholic*'s practice with articles in its "Sounding Board" section, Mould's article was precirculated to a number of subscribers for their feedback along with a survey. *U.S. Catholic* then printed survey results and a representative sample of responses to the article. Notably, while 79 percent of the respondents wrote that they would prefer that their child not marry outside of their faith, 41 percent agreed with the statement "I would rather see a Catholic marry a Protestant or a Jew of strong faith than a baptized Catholic of weak faith"; only 46 percent disagreed.

That almost half of the Catholic readers polled expressed preference for a person of strong, but different, faith over a weak Catholic demonstrated a fundamental difference between Catholic and Jewish populations. While Jews, regardless of differences in observance, tended to regard each other as Jews and therefore part of the same community, *klal yisrael*, across degrees of faith, Catholics were primarily interested in a community of the faithful. For some lay Catholics then, it was easier to imagine being in community with the differently faithful than with the nonfaithful. The Catholic laity had, by the 1980s, come to accept the concept of a tri-faith America, laid out by Herberg a generation before: they accepted that Protestants and Jews were their compatriots in American religion and that within tri-faith America, strong faith mattered more than its form.

Almost two-thirds of the readers polled believed that marriage between Catholics and Protestants would improve Christian unity. That did not, however, mean that a similar majority agreed with Mould that marriage to Protestants should be encouraged. Rather, for the bulk of the respondents, Christian unity was a positive outcome of an unfortunate marital choice. Readers, however, considered marriage to Protestants regrettable not because they were theologically suspect, but because they believed that mixed marriages added unnecessary burdens to the challenges of married life. Despite the variety of opinions on mixed marriages, one thing was clear: in 1980, 80 percent of the survey respondents said that if their child announced a mixed marriage, they would "tell them of the difficulties involved but express their acceptance." The tide had shifted in the Catholic world—mixed marriage was worrisome because it was potentially harder, not because it was sinful.

Within this lay Catholic conversation, members of interfaith marriages (largely to Protestants) brought very different experiences to the discussion that spoke to the everyday realities of negotiating practice, family, and community. In addition to survey results, *U.S. Catholic* included some readers' comments, representing a range of viewpoints.[57] Among those responses were opposing views from intermarried couples. As Cynthia Rutter of Oklahoma wrote, "As a Catholic married to a Protestant, I assure you that being of different faiths does make a big difference. You not only have to explain and defend every facet of your Catholicism to your partner, but also to your partner's family. It is especially trying when a joyous occasion, such as a baptism, is ruined when it must be done 'over the dead body' of a parent-in-law. Being a Catholic is a way of life—not just a 45-minute attendance at Mass on Sunday."[58] If Rutter experienced deep pain at the familial resistance that she felt from her spouse and his family, Patrick Hanley of Alaska wrote in to say that while he had experienced some difficulties in his marriage to a Mormon, he had been happily married for seven years and that those difficulties were "certainly not enough to destroy the marriage." Others presented dissenting opinions about the idea of raising children in two churches. D. E. Halpin of Florida worried that a dual religious upbringing put the children in the position of "serving two masters—perhaps neither one very well," whereas an anonymous respondent from North Dakota wrote that her children were Catholic, but had "no problem accepting anyone's faith." Their attitude, she explained, was "Dad's a great guy, so his faith must be, too!" The respondents did not offer a consensus of agreement or disagreement on the question of interfaith marriage, good or bad, though they tended to agree that while the Church should accept it, they should not advocate for it. Concerns did not focus on the sacramental concerns outlined in some of the debates over whether a Protestant could be free from sin at the moment of marriage. Rather, *U.S. Catholic*'s respondents centered their dialogue on issues of family life: the presence or absence of familial tension, and the clarity or confusion of the children's religious identities.[59]

Defense of Marriage, Defense of the Individual: The Protestant Mainline Responds to Interfaith Marriage

Protestant responses to interfaith marriage were much less overtly articulated than those of Jews and Catholics. These more muted reactions were influenced by the status and assumption of Protestant Christianity as the baseline for mainstream American culture. As both Jewish and Catholic literature noted, particularly when arguing for rabbis and priests to officiate at intermarriages, Protestant clergy could be counted on to officiate at interfaith marriages, largely because of Protestant belief in the moral agency of the individual subject. This idea that marriage and sexual activity within marriage are the concerns not of the family or the community but of the individual is central to and rooted in early Protestant understandings of what it meant to be free from church control.[60]

In his section of the Armed Forces pamphlet *What about Interfaith Marriage?* Fredrick W. Brink, the Force Chaplain for the Cruise Deployer Force of the U.S. Atlantic Fleet, outlined some of the key concerns of Protestant reflections on interfaith marriage, and while his comments revealed concerns about the implications of interfaith marriage for the American family, they were also deeply rooted in the understanding of the individual's ability to make autonomous religious and marital choices. This assumption of individualism not only lay at the heart of Protestant understandings, but also was braided into mainstream American ideas about citizenship.

Brink's first undertaking was to point out that there were many internal differences between Protestant churches' ideas on marriage: for instance, whether marriage was considered to be a sacrament. Nonetheless, he viewed his task as only speaking to the commonalities in Protestant views of marriage. He argued that Protestants view marriage as a relationship "instituted by God, for the welfare and happiness of mankind. . . . It is a blending of the lives of the man and the woman in a manner acceptable to God, for their mutual growth, benefit, and happiness." Across the various Protestant sects, Brink maintained that Christian marriage was understood as originating in God and including God. While each individual denomination (and in some cases each congregation) had the right to "circumscribe marriage with rules that apply to that church's own adherents . . . Protestants insist[ed] that no one church [had] the right to force its own rules upon persons who are identified with another church." In short, the individual believer had the right to choose her own Christian community according to the dictates of her own conscience, though once in that community, she was supposed to abide by the dictates of that denomination. If she then married a member of another religious group, she could freely choose to follow the dictates of that religious community. If she did not do so, she could not be compelled to by their moral and theological dictates.

Brink outlines key Protestant tenets of marriage, in a clear attempt to diffuse Catholic critiques of Protestant positions on both divorce and birth control. Protestants, he claimed, view the marriage relationship as permanent. Though divorce is permitted, there is no assumption that marriage is to be entered into or exited lightly. Second, Protestants believed that the "to-be-desired completion of a marriage is the presence and training of children." In other words, the couple's relationship had to be considered, not only in terms of whether it was good for them, but whether it would make them good parents. If the Jewish and Catholic chaplains explained away the differences between their views of marriage and other groups, the Protestant leader underscored similarities between the three religions and their understanding of marriage, a position that demonstrated the power of being the largest, dominant religious group in the nation.

Given these two points as a base, Brink then turned his consideration to marriages between differing faiths. Protestants, according to Brink, believed that a marriage is an individual's own marriage before God and therefore do not believe that the clergy of any church can have "exclusive authority" over the marriage. The clergy only had authority over the partner who is their adherent, not the other spouse. Second, marriage is a process rather than an event. He argued that love was built over time and that elements of disruption, such as differing religious backgrounds, should not exist from the beginning of the relationship. Third, he claimed that marriages are strongest when the spouses have similar cultural backgrounds and Protestants, Catholics, and Jews have strong differences, not only in religious practice and obedience but also in their understandings of those elements. Fourth, and in direct contradiction to the Jewish and Catholic views on interfaith parenting, Brink maintained that children should be nurtured by both of their parents, and it is damaging to the integrity of the parent-child bond to require one parent to remain silent about matters religious. In the end, however, he presents Protestants as agreeing with their co-religionists in so much as he depicted interfaith (or "mixed") marriage as difficult and therefore unwise. "It is far wiser, for the lasting success of the marriage, for the training and development of the children, for the permanent harmony of the home, to forgo a marriage involving conflicts of faith than to establish a marriage where almost certain friction and violation of integrity can be expected." Interfaith marriage was problematic not because the other religious groups were somehow inherently lesser but because the tension that existed between these groups would undermine the marriage and the home. The claims of the differing religious communities rather than inherent differences in belief could undermine the peace and strength of the private family at a time when the social changes of the late 1960s and 1970s, ranging from youth revolts and feminism to rising divorce rates and urban riots, seemed to be undermining the very stability that the family both needed and represented.

Brink's concerns encapsulated many of the Protestant mainline's concerns around interfaith marriage and generalized American concerns about the divorce rate. While other Protestant public voices shared his concerns about individualism, they did not agree that interfaith marriage might weaken the marital bond. As a result, mainline Protestants were supportive of couples hoping to intermarry, as evidenced by the fact that when *The Christian Century*, the publication that served as the primary collective voice of the Protestant mainline, discussed mixed or interfaith marriage in the 1960s and 1970s, it largely framed those discussions as criticisms of the Catholic position.

The Christian Century approached intermarriage from a position of confidence in the continued social relevance of marriage and of support for individual rights that led to support, if not for intermarriage, than for the right of individuals to enter into such marriages. The Protestant debate on interfaith marriage was one that focused on the individual rights of the marrying couple, a conversation that was in marked contrast to the conversations among both the Catholic and the Jewish hierarchies, though it would later be picked up in popular culture and by individual intermarrying Catholics and Jews. As a result, interfaith marriage discussions in *The Christian Century* tended to focus on Protestant frustrations with the Catholic position, rather than on critiques of interfaith marriage itself.

The magazine was dismissive of the concern that intermarriages were more likely to cause divorce. For instance, in 1963 one author, Clark Elizey, endorsed that idea, writing, "It seems clear that interfaith marriages are much more likely to break down than marriages between a man and woman of the same faith. Moreover, on the whole, couples concerned about religious values tend to remain married."[61] He then asked whether staying married was actually the greater good. He pointed out that none of the survey data addressed the question of why religiously endogamous couples were more likely to stay married and suggested that it was possible that some of these couples stayed married for fear of community censure rather than for psychologically healthy reasons. If, he implied, divorce was the psychologically healthiest option, then it was better to divorce than to stay married. As a result, Elizey undercut one of the primary objections to interfaith marriage—the argument that it created unstable families—by suggesting that divorce was not, in and of itself, a bad choice in a marriage and by undermining the claim that, just because a religiously similar couple stayed married, their family life was notably better than that of an interfaith couple who did not.

Underscoring their confidence in the institution of marriage itself, a 1967 article by Earl Brill entitled "Is Marriage Dying, Too?" came to the conclusion that not only would marriage likely remain relevant, but also social changes would likely strengthen the institution. He argued, "You may be sure that even with the pressure off, most young people will probably decide to get married just the same. If we can ever reach the point where they can do it as an act of real freedom, then we will have made marriage more meaningful, both for those who decide for it and those who decide against it."[62] Rather than saying that marriage would remain safe, the argument in this *Christian Century* piece suggested that marriage becoming an optional social practice would, in time, actually strengthen the institution of marriage, because those who entered it would do so with intention and the all-important American quality of freedom. Marriage, therefore, was safe from irrelevance and, in this framing, would be compatible with both the increased options available to women and the emphasis on personal freedom articulated by the youth revolts. While the article did not go so far as to say that intermarriage was part of this larger choice, the aspect of choice placed intermarriage firmly within the range of acceptable options. This emphasis on choice, while central to Protestantism (and therefore to American legal understandings of marriage), was not shared by the Jewish and Catholic leadership, who hoped that appeals to communal and theological concerns would be stronger than the individualist message of either Protestantism or secular America.

Protestant attitudes toward mixed marriage are clearest in their attacks on Catholic resistance to it. Repeated print space was given to the idea that Catholic laws on mixed marriage were among the strongest impediments to the ecumenical movement.[63] *The Christian Century* published pieces by and about Catholic leaders who disagreed with the Vatican's policy on mixed marriages, both to undermine the logic of those policies and to point to the hope of a more accommodating Church.[64] An editorial in *The Christian Century* outlined the Catholic position as unacceptable for five primary reasons: the Protestant is asked to cede all religious influence in the lives of his or her children; the Catholic laws put two basic human drives, those of love and religion, in opposition to each other; the Catholic laws weaken the marriages of interfaith couples; rather than creating strong Catholics or Protestants, the Catholic position drives couples away from religious institutions; and, lastly, the Catholic Church's policies on mixed marriage were, in the view of the editors of *The Christian Century,* in direct opposition to the Church's own Declaration on Religious Liberty. Two of these points, that the Church's position on interfaith marriage weakened marriages and drove families from organized religion, are fairly straightforward: to demand that the Protestant (or the Catholic) "betray" his or her religion created "handicaps" in the marriage, which were "often crushing."[65] Similarly, rather than interfaith marriages creating more Catholics, as the Church had long hoped, the editorial suggested that both Roman Catholics and Protestants were learning that mixed marriages resulted in a "wide exit from the church."[66] The Protestant argument, articulated in this editorial, was that the Catholic Church and Protestant denominations would both be better served by trying to keep interfaith couples engaged in church life broadly, rather than giving them strict and potentially painful requirements in order to stay involved.

The other three arguments are revealing largely because of the language that the editorial employed. First, while the Catholic instructions on mixed marriage were offered in the spirit of reconciliation with Protestants, *The Christian Century* argued that it did "elementary injustices" to human beings, particularly Protestant ones. According to this Protestant viewpoint, the Catholic Church required the non-Catholic to "relinquish orally, though not in writing, all influence over the spiritual destiny of his unborn children and, moreover, to confer upon an institution in which he does not believe tyrannical power over his children's religious education."[67] The issue at stake, in this example of the Protestant imagination, is the "tyrannical power" over the individual conscience. In the end, the individual has greater right to the spiritual care of his child than does a religious institution, as they hoped the properly thinking Protestant would agree.

Because the Catholic Church would still not consider Protestant marriages to be valid, the Protestant who wanted to honor the religion of his or her intended was essentially over a religious barrel. "If he has in him a grain of the Protestant principle that such an absolutizing of the future is evil, that such tyranny over him and over his children violates the conscience's sacredness, he must bury it under a Catholic altar as he speaks his marriage vows."[68] The language here is striking and indicative of violence—this Protestant periodical is accusing the Catholic Church of doing violence to the sacredness of the individual conscience in the very set of laws that the Church saw as a way to reach out to Protestants. The language also made clear the importance of the rights of the individual in Protestant thought.

The rights of the individual are echoed throughout the other critiques of Catholic policy toward interfaith marriage. The National Council of Churches objected specifically to the Catholic restrictions on Protestants entering into mixed marriages with Catholics, stating that

> religion is a basic interest in human life, and differences of religion, if these are fundamental, may strain a marriage to the point of breaking, especially when they are aggravated by ecclesial interference. No religious body which confesses itself Christian can tolerate the imposition upon one of its own members of the requirements of another religious body by which the religious scruples of that member are aroused, or action repugnant to reason and conscience is forced upon him by an authority which he does not acknowledge. . . . If either partner enters upon the union as a propagandist, determined through the intimacies of marriage to subvert the religious faith of the other, disaster is immanent.[69]

The National Council of Churches articulated the concern that ecclesial disapproval increased the odds that the interfaith marriage would fail and that if the Catholic partner followed the Church's dictate to attempt the conversion of a spouse, he or she would put an impossible strain on the marriage. More importantly, the council argued that the Catholic hierarchy's attempt to control the behavior of the Protestant member of a Catholic-Protestant marriage was an affront to the couple's shared Christianity.

The Christian Century followed a similar theme. Because it is "demonstrably true" that an interfaith couple that remains interfaith can have a happy marriage, the Catholic mixed marriage laws dealt "unjustly with the sacred rights of men and women by playing against each other two of the most elementary and powerful human drives: romantic-sexual love and religious devotion."[70] The violation of these rights is strongest for the Protestant partner because he is the partner who must betray "one or the other of these drives—his love or his religion. He must promise the Catholic Church what his own church has taught he has no right to promise" or must walk away from love.[71] In perhaps the most striking critique of Catholic marriage law, this Protestant editorial suggests that, in fact, the Catholic Church shares the value of individual rights: "[Vatican Council II's Declaration on Religious Liberty] senses profoundly and expresses unequivocally the sacred and inviolable rights of the individual conscience, rights which many of us believe are infringed by the mixed marriage laws."[72] In the Protestant view, the Catholic stance on interfaith marriage failed to live up to the promises of Vatican II, making its position on interfaith marriage hypocritical in the extreme.

If the Protestant media was deeply unsympathetic and even adversarial toward the Catholic position, however, they had much more patience for the Jewish perspective. Indeed, in discussing intermarriage, *The Christian Century* rarely spoke of Jews. Rather, Jewish concerns about intermarriage came up in defense of American Jewish "stridency" in defense of Zionism. On May 11, 1961, for instance, a group of rabbis prepared a statement in opposition to anti-Zionist remarks made by the historian and anti-Zionist intellectual Arnold J. Toynbee. Though the *Christian Century* editors found the Jewish response to be somewhat extreme, they conceded that its tone was the result of an understandable "insecurity." Though patronizing in their response, the editors were sympathetic to Jewish fears of extinction, particularly in this immediate post-Holocaust world, where Jewish survival was understood to be extremely fragile. The editors pointed out that American Judaism faced the threats of "intermarriage, adaptation, and assimilation," more even "than the rabbis might believe exists or hope for."[73] Though the editors argued that the rabbis overstated the full force of these threats, they wrote, "But in spite of their illusions, we would give this round to the rabbis on points: if there are values in Jewish religion and race, they are best uttered out of a nurturing tradition, out of the Arcanum of Jewish thought. Quite obviously, intermarriage would score against the Jewish future. That Judaism has the right to legislate in relation to those who choose to be identified with it is obvious; that such legislation is wise or effective is another question. But it is always ungracious for the "outsider" to wish non-being on a group having a valid religious heritage."[74] While the editorial staff of *The Christian Century* was not certain that the Jewish response to interfaith marriage (which was, in the 1960s, to simply refuse to perform interfaith marriages and to sustain a strong community conversation against it) was the best one, they acknowledged fully that intermarriage posed a strong threat to the Jewish future. Jewish leaders were given the understood right to legislate the terms of Jewish marriage, because to allow an outsider, such as Toynbee or the editors themselves, seemed to also be legislating the potential nonexistence of the Jewish people. While the editors may not have fully agreed with the Jewish approach, that skepticism takes a very different tone than their deep frustration with the Catholic position. Interestingly, even as the interfaith marriage rate rose throughout the 1970s and 1980s, mainline Protestants did not raise objections to inter-faith couples choosing to create Jewish homes. Rather, many of the memoirs and advice manuals advocating for raising the children of interfaith marriage as Jews were written by Christian partners and spouses. In addition, as the interfaith marriage rate rose, mentions of interfaith marriage (whether between Protestants and Catholics or Protestants and Jews) in the *Christian Century* declined. Endogamous marriage was simply not a hot-button issue for the Protestant mainline, who came from a position of cultural strength and who lost far more people to secularism than to interfaith marriage.

Why, then, the different Protestant responses to Catholic and Jewish reactions to interfaith marriage? First, Catholic objections to interfaith marriage between Catholics and Protestants had quite a bit to do with the lesser status of Protestants. If after Vatican II Protestants were seen as being in less perfect communion with Christ, as little as a decade before, official Catholic writings had referred to Protestants as heretics. While it did not needle Protestants to have Jewish leaders prefer that Jews marry Jews, implicit in the Catholic opposition to Catholic-Protestant marriage was the argument that Protestants were at best lesser Christians and at worst not Christian at all. Second, Jews were a tiny proportion of the American population, and awareness of the devastation of the Holocaust was growing in the American consciousness in the 1960s. While individual ministers were indeed happy to marry Christian-Jewish couples who were denied marriage by their rabbis, it would have been a very different matter for a leading Protestant publication to criticize attempts to stem the tide of Jewish intermarriage.

Conclusion

In examining the conversations being held among Jewish, Catholic, and Protestant leadership circles about interfaith marriage, the issues are much more complicated than a simple split in opinion between Christians and Jews. Both because of the ideological and practical changes brought on by the feminist movement, including an increase in middle-class women working outside the home and the rising divorce rate in the 1970s, Jews, Catholics, and Protestants all addressed the implications for interfaith marriage on the health of the couple and their home, though they came to distinctly different conclusions. Additionally, each group brought a distinct set of concerns to the table. The Central Conference of American Rabbis was deeply concerned about the impact of interfaith marriage on a dwindling Jewish population. Their response to interfaith marriage was torn between marking the boundaries of the group (by attempting to halt the tide of intermarriage) and by their belief in the universal qualities of Judaism, which suggested that an unaffiliated spouse could find meaning in the "Jewish faith" at the same time that it made it hard to present a clear reason why one should not intermarry.

For the Catholic hierarchy, in the United States and internationally, communal standards around the importance of the sacraments and the authority of the Church were changing in ways that had a direct impact on marriage. On the one hand, the Church held tightly to a sacramental theology of marriage that made marriage outside of its followers deeply problematic. On the other, Vatican II decreased the practices that made Catholics' and Protestants' lived realities markedly different, and as the Church moved into ecumenical relationships with Protestants, it tended to emphasize (though not enough for Protestant tastes) its commonalities with other Christians. The Catholic laity shared some of the views of their leadership, but demonstrated a very different set of concerns than did the leadership—they were interested not in questions of marital theology, but in the negotiations of daily life.

Mainline Protestants, meanwhile, had the most fluid understandings of community and largely put the communal interest second to the needs and rights of the individual. As they were the group with the broadest cultural influence, they were also the group most in step with general American understandings of marriage in the time period. These community needs and standards, however, were not fixed points. How to respond to interfaith marriage and families was not a question with a monolithic answer, but instead, the beginnings of an ongoing conversation that continued to change and grow as each community did the same.

A discussion of an interfaith family's religious practice(s) or of the quotidian details of interfaith marriage was remarkably absent from the conversations in the 1970s (or, in the case of the Catholic Church, of the policies that remained relevant in the 1970s). Rather, across the board in the 1970s, religious groups were concerned with the question of how to prevent interfaith marriage; whether to prevent it; and for Catholics and Jews, if they could not prevent it, how to ensure that the family became part of their religious community. This conversation largely disappeared after the 1980s. Marriage between Catholics and Protestants ceased to be a central focus of debate for either group, sacrificed in the name of ecumenical unity on other issues. While Catholic policies remained in place, individual priests and couples implemented them as they saw fit, and receiving a dispensation became a matter of course.

In Reform Jewish circles, however, the topic of interfaith marriage remained immediate and pressing, both for the leadership and for the laity. The focus, then, became the Christian-Jewish marriage. While this chapter details the real divisions between Catholics and Protestants, those conversations lost salience in a public debate about interfaith marriage that became about whether or not a couple could or should have a Christmas tree, whether traditions could or should be combined, and what it meant for Christian women to raise Jewish children. By the end of the 1970s, the Reform leadership had largely realized that they could not prevent interfaith marriage, and the conversation shifted to how best to address the reality that perhaps as many as 50 percent of Jews would marry non-Jews. The development of that conversation is explored in chapter 4.

As noted above, the Protestant understanding of the individual as the autonomous moral unit has deeply influenced American culture. That reality is also traced out in the following chapters, as each depiction or negotiation of interfaith family life has to address the reality that young American couples see themselves as having the right to marry and consider their primary obligation to be to themselves and each other, over and above religious institutions, ideologies, or communities. While the Protestant mainline expressed the least interest in persuading interfaith couples to join their congregations, in many ways, they already had their hearts and minds.

Lastly, while the religious groups were most interested in the patrollable boundaries of communal life and in theological distinctions, television, film, advice manuals, and ethnographic experience point to a number of other factors in understandings of interfaith marriage: class, gender, and practice were also central to conversations about interfaith marriage. Thus, these initial institutional conversations establish a baseline for the vocabulary—and disagreements—that will follow.

CHAPTER TWO

Blended or Transcended

Interfaith Families in Popular Culture, 1970–1980

The opening montage of the 1972–1973 CBS sitcom *Bridget Loves Bernie* depicts a young couple falling in love. A swarthy taxi driver sees a beautiful blonde unsuccessfully trying to hail a cab. Despite being off duty, he picks her up and drives her to work. At the end of the school day, when the lovely teacher emerges surrounded by her young students, there he is waiting for her. The sequence continues with an idyllic day of courting in iconic New York City settings, racing through Central Park and making out in the cab by the LOVE sculpture. After their afternoon together, Bridget pulls back from a kiss to reflect, "You know, this is crazy. I do not even know your full name."

"Bernie," he replies, gazing fondly into her eyes. "Steinberg. What's yours?"

"Bridget," she answers. "Bridget Theresa Mary Colleen Fitzgerald."

"I think we, uh," Bernie begins, before the couple finishes in unison, "I think we have a problem."

This opening montage establishes key tropes of Christian-Jewish interfaith marriage, as it appears on the large and small screens. As they fall in love, Bridget and Bernie do not experience conflict because of their different backgrounds. In fact, the opening montage focuses on what they have in common, being young in New York City, only introducing the differing backgrounds when they share their names in the final moments (and only spoken words) of the montage: Bernie's name simply, but distinctively, Jewish, Bridget's comically, Catholically long.

Bridget Loves Bernie encapsulates the mainstream media's response toward interfaith marriage in the 1970s, a position largely at odds with religious leaders of the era. While postwar Catholic and Jewish religious leaders worked toward acceptance as "mainstream" American religions, they also prized distinctive elements of Catholic and Jewish life and community, fearing that acceptance would lead toward assimilation and secularism. As the interfaith marriage rate rose through the 1970s, leaders in these communities, particularly in Jewish communities, largely condemned it, but television and movie writers often celebrated it as a key step in the path to assimilation. Religious leaders feared that the assimilation championed in the imagined world of American popular culture would result, not in Americanized Catholics and

t in Americans who were no longer Catholic or Jewish. Indeed, on
e and small screens, interfaith marriage provided Catholics and Jews a
to the American secular, a way of existing in the American society that
was theoretically neutral but is, in fact, based in a Protestant-inflected secularism.

In these media representations of interfaith marriage, Jews could marry
Protestants and shed their Jewishness. Similarly, Catholics and Jews could
marry each other and, together, shed the excess ethnicity of their families and
communities to enter into a way of being American that was a form of secular
Protestant whiteness perceived as neutral, not ethnically marked. These intermarrying characters are rarely portrayed as having excess ethnicity to shed
themselves of—they are candidates for interfaith marriage in the first place
because they are portrayed as already forward-thinking Americans, rather than
mired in the provincialism of their backgrounds.[1] Rather, their parents—
members of an older generation—are depicted as clinging to older, outmoded,
and fundamentally un-American mind-sets and forms of embodiment that
prevent them from becoming "appropriately" modern and assimilated. In the
logic of Hollywood, then, romantic love and marriage provide young Americans
the motivation to detach from their families or communities, who are depicted
as somehow too much: too materialistic, too loud, too physical. While these
depictions were largely (though not exclusively) of marriage rather than of
childrearing, the viewer can envision the kinds of homes these marriages
would create: the children would grow up with one less ethnic layer to strip
away and therefore be already closer to the ideal of assimilation to a white,
American "norm."

These television and film renditions generally depicted interfaith marriage
as favorable, leading to happiness for the couple, provided the marriage aided
in their assimilation to an American mainstream. In television programs such
as *Bridget Loves Bernie* and *Little House on the Prairie*, and in movies like *The
Comeback Kid*, scriptwriters posited the challenges of interfaith marriage as
easy to overcome, functionally through a falling away of difference. The conflicts they depicted were located in the parental generation, whose differences
were rooted in ethnic identities that their assimilated children rejected and
which therefore did not cause disruption to the new marriage. Implicit in this
narrative is the screenwriter's understanding of the married couple, their life
choices, and their resulting nuclear family as the concern of the individual
couples and not of their religious organizations, which were notably absent
from the dramas and only somewhat the concern of the previous generations.
While this process was largely, in these examples, presented as becoming

freed from religious tradition, it was also a deeply Protestant way of framing family, in keeping with mainline positions outlined in the next chapter. In some sense, then, while interfaith families were presented as becoming American, marriage was also a means of assimilating into a Protestant identity. Ironically, because the 1970s saw an increase in Jewish outreach attempts for interfaith families, this was also the decade in which interfaith couples began to reverse the trend of interfaith marriage resulting in Protestant or secular homes.

Cinematographic interfaith relationships did not always, however, result in happy, successful marriages. In the moments when they failed, notably in *Annie Hall* and *The Way We Were*, the failure of the relationship was tied to a failure of assimilation. Neither Alfie nor Katie grow more like their WASPY significant others over the course of their respective films, with the differences between the members of each couple (positive and negative) largely rooted in stereotypical depictions of Jew versus Gentile.[2] These relationships failed both as romances and as attempts at assimilation, underscoring the belief that interfaith couples were successful only if the couple blended into mainstream America.

These early representations of interfaith marriage did not explicitly engage in debates about religion versus culture, as later advice manuals sometimes would. Instead, these representations drew from various stereotypes of Jews, and to a lesser extent Catholics, to depict these identities as ones that could be overcome to enter into an equally stereotypical American secular (or Protestant) identity. The elements of these stereotypes were drawn from across a spectrum of religious practices but were largely located in excess. Jews (and, to a lesser extent, Catholics) were too much. They were too noisy; too lower class; too rooted in bodily experiences of illness, food, comfort, or sexuality; too particular in their religiosity.

As many scholars have argued, nations have a shared imagination, or communal ideology, and in the United States, the dominant imagination appears to be a shared, secular vision of a couple with 2.5 children and a white picket fence, an ideal that is deeply rooted in a Protestant history.[3] In the American context, the perfect "secular" citizen was formed through a Protestant lens, a lens so self-evident and normative as to ultimately become invisible. As a result, an American public arose that tolerated any religion that existed exclusively in private (namely in the home) and that saw its public space as free from religious life and values. That public space, however, had what Robert Orsi refers to as an "embedded moral schema" that owed its very categories, as well as its moral claims, to an inherited Protestant tradition.[4] The result, then, was an American public that saw itself as separate from, yet tolerant of, religion, but was in fact dramatically more tolerant of particular kinds of Protestant religious expression, privileging "rational, word-centered, non-ritualistic, middle class, unemotional" forms of Protestantism that were most closely allied with the power brokers of American society.[5] This system could and did adapt to include Catholics and Jews, insofar as they were able to embody this particular kind of secular identity derived from white Protestant liberalism.

Marriage, as an institution, was, in fact, particularly important to this kind of secular state, and interfaith marriage had long provided a path to assimilation for Catholics and Jews who wanted to enter the Protestant mainstream. Before the Protestant Reformation, while most premodern Christians had lived out their lives within marriages, Christian teaching idealized the celibate, communal lives of monks and nuns. Protestant Reformers such as Calvin and Luther, however, considered marriage the ideal form of Christian life. Ideal Christian marriage was defined by individuals, exerting their own morality by freely choosing both the restrictions of marriage and the spouse with whom they would enter into those restrictions. As Janet Jakobsen asserts, "The switch to marriage as both norm and ideal, then, is part of the production of the modern individual, and of that individual as free."[6] The very notion of modern marriage, then, allowed, even required, a couple to separate from the church and from family and to create a space for them to exert their own moral agency. By the late twentieth century, popular understandings of marriage included ideas of companionship, romantic love, and sexual desire, but at the core, they were embedded in inherently liberal and theologically Protestant ideals of individuals as autonomous moral agents.[7] When Catholic and Jewish men married Protestant women, they were often able to join their fathers-in-law in business and, through the family connections provided by their wives, to become "secular" American citizens. Similarly, Jewish and Catholic women who married Protestant men could maintain Jewish and Catholic homes, without posing any problem as long as their sons followed their Protestant husbands into "secular" American citizenship, marked by business and civic engagement. While not all marriages between Jews or Catholics and Protestants resulted in the minority groups disappearing into the Protestant mainstream, from colonial times through the mid-twentieth century, many had found marriage provided an opportunity to join the more powerful majority, and to do so as individuals.[8]

Assimilation and Interfaith Marriage on the Large and Small Screens

In the 1970s, interfaith marriage as depicted on television and in the movies echoed the historical experience and was both shaped by and a shaper of an American imagination that framed marriage as the union of individuals who were free moral agents, more beholden to their own goals as secular citizens than to the communities that shaped them. The differences that television and film chose to highlight also provide us with insight into what differences animated the American imagination. In their representations of interfaith marriage, Jews and Christians were not different because of belief in Jesus, or necessarily because of religious observances. Rather, interfaith couples were presented as navigating (or failing to navigate) gulfs caused by social class, mannerisms, politics, and food, as much if not more than those of belief or affiliation. Popular representations of interfaith marriages in the 1970s, then, portrayed them as a social good as long as they resulted in the transcendence of ethnicity and difference such that the young Catholic-Jewish couple, or the Jew marrying a Protestant, became more completely American.

The theme of intermarriage as a component of assimilation was not new in the 1970s. *Abie's Irish Rose*, a play by Anne Nichols, ran on Broadway from 1922 to 1927. It was, at the time, the longest-running Broadway show and the longest-running touring play in the United States. The play tells the story of Jewish Abie and Irish Catholic Rose, who were secretly married by a Protestant minister as they knew that neither of their widowed fathers would support the marriage. The play provided a prototype for the modern, Americanized young couple, juxtaposed against the Old World, older generation. Abie's and Rose's fathers provided the humor in the play, largely by airing any number of stereotypical and bigoted opinions.

Abie's Irish Rose, which was made into films in both 1928 and 1946 and prompted a NBC radio spin-off that ran from 1942 until 1944, demonstrated a hope for the assimilationist nature of interfaith marriage. The fathers were funny precisely because they were stuck in their Old World Irish and Jewish ways. In fact, in their dedication to a strict Catholicism and an Orthodox Judaism, they were more rigid than the priest and rabbi who performed second and third weddings for the couple. In the original script, Nichols underscores the Americanness not only of the young couple, but also, in an artistic foreshadowing of Will Herberg's *Protestant, Catholic, Jew*, of the supportive clergy (minister, rabbi, and priest), by making them all veterans of World War I, where Abie had been a wounded soldier and Rose, his nurse.[9]

Coming on the heels of huge waves of immigration and during a time of anxiety that brought about the quotas of the Immigration Act of 1924, *Abie's Irish Rose* and its spin-offs were born out of anxiety more about immigration than about intermarriage, as intermarriage rates between Christians and Jews were quite low in the first half of the twentieth century. The themes of these programs, however, were reprised almost 50 years later, reflecting not so much fears of immigration, but the postwar ideal of an American melting pot in which Catholics and Jews could join Protestants as members of an American secular. Timed for a moment when rates of marriage between Christians and Jews were skyrocketing, these plays depicted what was, for some, the promise of America, but it was predicated on a washing out of ethnic identity, which was, for others, one of the primary perils of life in the United States.

The Ghetto Girl and the Shiksa Goddess: Gendered Stereotypes and *The Heartbreak Kid*

The idea that interfaith marriage provided a seamless entry into American life is aptly demonstrated by the 1972 film *The Heartbreak Kid*, directed by Elaine May and written by Neil Simon. The movie, which is more of a romance than a romantic comedy, represents interfaith marriage as socially acceptable, understandable, and even desirable by using a long-standing and highly gendered trope of assimilation: the ghetto girl and the shiksa goddess.[10] Like in *Abie's Irish Rose*, the trope of the ghetto girl harkened to the era of Jewish immigration to America and represented anxiety about how Jewish women adapted to the new American landscape. American prosperity freed the archetypal ghetto girl from the restrictions of poverty and tradition that shaped Eastern European Jewish life, and the ghetto girl used her newfound freedom to become grasping and crass, interested in material, gustatory, and sexual acquisition. She demonstrated neither the virtue of her Old World counterparts nor the refinement of the native-born American. *The Heartbreak Kid* juxtaposes the two marriages of Lenny Cantrow, played by Charles Grodin: the first to Lila Kolodny, played by Jeannie Berlin, and the second to Kelly Cochran, played by Cybill Shepherd. The contrasts between the brides, who represent Jewish imaginings of archetypal Jewish and Gentile women, clearly privilege the refined Kelly over the crass Lila. The women are contrasted throughout the film: Lenny and Lila arrive for their honeymoon at a fancy resort, where Lila comments loudly on how nice everything is. Kelly, however, is clearly in her natural environment—she is comfortable in her surroundings and does not call attention to herself by calling attention to them. If the original ghetto girl was overcome by the wonders of America, Lila is excited by how the better half lives, but the awe that she expresses at the opulence of their surroundings and her loud enthusiasm demonstrate that she, and therefore they as a couple, cannot assimilate into the upper-class, "nice" American society.

The starkest contrast between the two women comes in the film's depictions of Lenny's sexual encounters with them (or theirs with him). The film opens with the New York Jewish wedding of Lenny and Lila. After a wedding and lunch, shot through a soft filter and yellow light that serve to make the wedding seem both drab and unreal, the couple departs for their Florida honeymoon. The couple's wedding night takes place in a motel room lit by the headlights of passing cars, where, undeterred by the lack of ambiance, Lila climbs onto Lenny to have loud and vigorous sex while he stares at the ceiling. After she finishes, she dismounts, announcing her need to "tinkle." In contrast, Kelly and Lenny first make premarital love by firelight in the privacy of a secluded winter lodge. Or at least the view infers that they do—while Lila and Lenny have sex on camera, Kelly and Lenny are shown beginning a mutual seduction before the scene fades away. The scene is romantic, shot with a soft focus, and staged to be appealing, rather than comic and mildly repulsive. Even in this most embodied of moments, the cinematography, with is soft focus and lighting, constructs their relationship in terms of romance, implying their emotional intimacy, rather than the physicality of their sexual encounter.

Lila's bodily excesses tie her, and therefore Lenny, to their lower-class, Jewish social location. Insatiable in both her carnal and gastronomic appetites, she is a ghetto girl for the modern era—someone who is grasping, overbearing, greedy, and abrasive. In this way, the ghetto girl resembles another trope of Jewish womanhood, the Jewish mother—she is too ethnically marked to be included in a modern story of assimilation and she cannot be trusted to raise suitably assimilated children. For that, the Jewish man of the screen needs a Gentile bride.[11] In *The Heartbreak Kid*, Kelly represents the quintessential American girl, the shiksa goddess. Lenny first spots the blonde and delicately lovely Kelly frolicking in the waves while they are both alone on the beach. The viewer gets very little sense of Kelly as a person, with interests or a personality; she exists largely as a reflection of Lenny's desires. By the time Lenny tells Lila that he wants a divorce and sets out to woo and marry Kelly, the narrative arc of the film has established Lenny as a sensitive man who has accidently yoked himself to a parody of "lower-class" habits. In leaving Lila, then, he is not a husband deserting his wife, but a man freeing himself from a marriage that traps him and keeps him from the life that he *could* lead. Kelly and her family offer Lenny what interfaith marriage had always been portrayed as offering the young Jewish man (and what it often had histori- cally offered him): access to a higher social standing and an "All-American" life.

The Cochran family is from Minnesota, a place that represents an Ameri- can ideal of wholesome "niceness" in the media world of the 1970s.[12] A mon- tage of Kelly on a college campus, in a blue winter hat that sets off her blonde hair, in the company of other coeds and surrounded by football players in letterman jackets, underscores her All-American, Midwestern charm. As the viewer watches Lenny watch Kelly, she represents a world, more than a love interest—Lenny and Kelly are never shown conversing. He desires her because of the world that she represents.

Kelly's wholesome, "American" beauty is coupled with her family's ability to elevate Lenny into a new social milieu. The closing scenes of the movie are of the couple's wedding reception, surrounded by Kelly's family and their circle. No one from Lenny's earlier wedding is in evidence. Lenny has left them behind as he has assimilated into this new environment, and if he seems a bit stiff in his new world, the implication is that his children will fit in, com- fortable with the privileges that they, like their mother, will take for granted. In *The Heartbreak Kid*, the characters do not discuss the differences between Lenny's and Kelly's backgrounds, either in terms of class or religion. We know that Kelly is Christian only from the shots of their wedding, a montage set in church with a minister in vestments, and from the implicit reality that American audiences recognize the markers of WASP culture—the letterman sweaters, the pastoral campus, the Minnesota nice.

In showing intermarriage as a path to assimilation, *Heartbreak Kid* repre- sents a long-standing link between intermarriage and assimilation into a domi- nant Protestant, American norm. White, European Jews could become American through proper acculturation.[13] As Lenny became part of the Cochran family's world, there was no sense that he was losing anything in giving up his city, his family, his traditions, or beliefs. The picture is of an appealing social ascent in which Lenny transcends his Jewishness, rather than incorporating his Jewish past into his new life.

While the extreme example of the Jewish wife, divorced for a Gentile bride, did not frequently recur in film, most of the interfaith couples on the screen did portray Jewish men married to Christian women. Similarly, even though *The Heartbreak Kid* was extreme in its depiction of assimilation as desirable and inevitable, the assumption that "American" is preferable to "ethnic," and that "American" is associated with the Christian family, floated beneath the surface of other media depictions of interfaith marriage, occasionally bubbling up as a topic of particular concern. The lack of conversation about this process is remarkable: Lenny simply became "American" and to be American is, in part, to be able to thrive in Protestant society. Lenny's example exemplified the pattern of interfaith marriage before its dramatic increases in the 1970s, when marriage to a non-Jew had provided many Jewish men, or their children, with entrée into mainstream, upper-class society.[14] Because historically this model dominated interfaith marriage, it represented precisely why Jewish leadership opposed interfaith marriage throughout the 1970s and why, late in the decade, the Reform movement transitioned into formal outreach to interfaith couples. *The Heartbreak Kid*, however, demonstrated the popular embrace of such an act of assimilation.

Bridget Loves Bernie and the Conflict between Religious Leaders and Media Images

If the interfaith relationship in *Heartbreak Kid* barely acknowledges potential tensions caused by a romance between members of different religions, the one-season CBS hit *Bridget Loves Bernie,* presented a considerably more fraught relationship in its depiction of a young interfaith couple and their parents. As the opening vignette demonstrates, *Bridget Loves Bernie* features a Catholic woman married to a Jewish man, a relationship that encompassed not just religious differences but a wide class divide.

Bridget came from a wealthy family while Bernie's family lived over their deli. *Bridget Loves Bernie,* its popularity, and the anxiety that it triggered all provide insight into how popular culture and formal religious communities were not always in agreement about this contentious issue. Indeed, like *Bridget Loves Bernie* (henceforth referred to as *BLB*), popular depictions of interfaith marriage in the 1970s demonstrated different concerns than those of religious leaders, based in many cases on different understandings of what was important about Jewish and Christian identity: social class, food habits, rituals, and religious identity of the children, with much of the humor based in differences in attitude between the intermarrying couple and their parents' generation. As subsequent chapters will demonstrate, these differences, between the territory of the synagogue and the markers of Jewish home life, would echo through the lives of many real-life interfaith families, as they tried to fit into Jewish communities whose written rules were often quite different from the unspoken social codes that governed them.

FIGURE 1 Meredith Baxter and David Birney in *Bridget Loves Bernie* (1972).
Used with permission from mptv images.

The sitcom appeared during the early stages of a skyrocketing American intermarriage rate. It captured some of the heightened anxiety around interfaith marriage that these rapidly shifting demographics caused for religious communities and for intermarried families. Like *Abie's Irish Rose*, BLB depicts a young, modern couple differentiating themselves from their immigrant parents and assimilating into American society. This representation was not new; indeed, the show was a fairly overt remake of *Abie's Irish Rose*. Though the sitcom had some structural differences in the makeup and geographies of the families, it echoed specific scenes, for instance, parents insisting on Jewish and Catholic wedding officiants. If in *Abie's Irish Rose* the couple had three weddings performed by a Protestant, Catholic, and Jew, respectively, in *BLB*, the couple chose a secular wedding before a justice of the peace before marrying again at the behest of their parents in a co-officiated ceremony with a rabbi and a priest, a scenario that would not have been likely in the real-life 1970s.

While one episode of *BLB* addressed observance of Jewish holidays and prayer to Catholic saints, most often the plotlines stressed differences of language, food, class, and appearance, along with the occasional question about religious practice to depict the pitfalls of interfaith life. Following the formula set by previous generations' depictions of interfaith family life, these concerns are presented as those of the older generation, in this case the parents of baby boomers. Demonstrating that these are generational problems, the young couple's strongest ally remains Bridget's brother, Father Mike. Since Mike is a Catholic priest, the audience might expect him to respond with concern to the young couple's announcement of their desire to marry. Mike's character, however, is not representative of the voluminous, and largely disapproving, literature on intermarriage produced by the Catholic Church. He far more closely approximates the views of the Protestant clergy of the 1970s. He is depicted as tolerant of interfaith marriage, seeing the couple and their love as more important than their competing religious upbringings. In the pilot episode, when the not-yet married Bridget and Bernie come to Mike for advice, rather than objecting to their relationship, he takes them out to breakfast. Surprised and almost indignant, Bernie demands to know why Mike is not listing traditional objections to interfaith marriages, asking "What kind of priest are you?" Mike responds, "An understanding one, I hope." Even a member of the baby boom generation dedicated enough to become a priest is, in the logic of the sitcom, able to move beyond the "parochialism" of demanding endogamous marriage into supporting the loving and assimilationist marriage of two individuals. When pressed for concerns, his answer underscores the generational nature of the conflict: "I was saving my two big arguments for after we had our scrambled eggs, but you pushed me . . . our mother and father." While Bridget's brother has no concerns with her marriage, despite being so dedicated to the Church as to have become a priest, he reminds Bridget of what her facial expression tells the audience she already knows: their parents will not understand or approve of her decision to marry a non-Catholic.

In the sitcom, food represents religious and ethnic tensions between the Steinbergs and the Fitzgeralds, and it demonstrates the generational nature of those conflicts. In the pilot episode, food customs allow writers to depict the differences between the Steinberg and Fitzgerald parents, to show the parents actively using their different backgrounds to discourage the new relationship, and to indicate that these differences exist for the older generation far more than for the young, American couple. In the pilot, then, food, and the different foods of each family, plays a starring role: the courting couple has a meal with each family. In this instance, food customs demonstrate a way to depict the families as drawing their religious and ethnic boundary lines, and to make it very clear to the young couple (and to the viewer) exactly who the outsider is.

After deciding to marry, Bernie takes Bridget home to meet his parents and his Uncle Moe over a dinner filled with traditional Ashkenazi fare, including gefilte fish and horseradish, most of it prepared by Bernie's mother, Sophie. The meal is a hazing ritual of hospitality: the table is groaning with food, while Sophie ladles matzoh balls onto soup plates and cuts blocks of kugel. Bridget is pressured to eat gefilte fish and horseradish. The conversation is similarly abundant—the Steinbergs speak over each other, mixing Yiddish with English, but explaining through laughter that the jokes do not "translate so funny." Bernie, however, is frustrated by his family's superabundance of ethnicity: "I've lived with you people all my life! Now why, all of a sudden, is everyone being so Jewish?" Sophie, who has been drawing attention to Bridget's Catholicism, and their own Judaism throughout the meal, looks up and says, meaningfully, "Already, it starts." The script does not make it clear whether family is emphasizing ethnic clannishness to remind Bridget that she is an outsider, or whether they are as they have always been, and Bernie only minds because of Bridget's presence. Either way, the scene underscores that Bernie does not share, or does not choose to share, his family's ethnic markers—with Bridget, he can, and does, step beyond them.

Specifically, Bernie must move beyond Sophie. If, in *Heartbreak Kid*, Lenny's first wife represents the ghetto girl, a kind of woman whom the assimilation-inclined Jewish man must escape, Sophie represents the trope of the Jewish mother. In the 1970s, when *BLB* aired, the Jewish mother was a figure of power and authority, controlling her children through her love—the ethnic version of "momism."[15] The Jewish mother trope was stock footage in the comedy routines of the Jewish resorts in the Catskills, though in less comic forms, she also appeared in literature, for instance as Sophie Portnoy.[16] Infinitely loving, the Jewish mother was also smothering, controlling her children through worry about them and their futures and through her desire for emotional connection. In depictions of the Jewish mother, meals served as one of her primary tools: she expressed her love through copious amounts of food, and she extracted guilt through reminders of how she had labored to produce it.[17] Though her desires are different, like the ghetto girl, the Jewish mother is a figure of excess: she loves too much, and needs too much love; she worries too much; she demands an obedience that smothers her children. Ironically, the very strength of her desire to protect her children has the potential to hobble them such that, narratively, they must escape her in order to assimilate into the American mainstream.

The fundamental tension between Jewish mother and Gentile bride is highlighted in episode nine, "How to Be a Jewish Mother," an episode that revolved around food. The central tension of the episode arises when Sophie stops by as Bridget is cleaning up breakfast and discovers that Bernie has not finished his breakfast. She explains to Bridget that the menu is at fault. "Eggs with ham? I am not surprised." Bridget, puzzled and a bit defensive, responds, "Well, I make it for him every morning. It is practically his favorite breakfast." Sophie argues that although Bernie may *say* that he likes ham, and that he may even *believe* that he likes ham, "deep down, he is Jewish" and that living with "Catholic cooking" will eventually harm him. While Sophie argues that Bridget's cooking is Catholic, there is nothing distinctly Catholic about her breakfast choice (nor is it associated with a known Catholic ethnic group, like Italian pancetta or Irish corned beef). Rather, Sophie is asserting her authority by objecting to the fact that Bridget is not maintaining Jewish dietary laws for Bernie and is therefore moving their household toward mainstream American (non-Jewish) foodways.

Sophie successfully undermines Bridget's confidence such that Bridget cooks a kosher dinner of matzoh ball soup and boiled chicken. Bridget offers the *hamotzi*, the blessing over bread, in Hebrew before the meal, and when Bernie's uncle offers a toast, everyone says "*L'Chaim*," except for Bernie, who says "Cheers." Throughout the rest of the episode, Bridget takes on the role of Jewish mother, encouraging Bernie to take on any number of practices, until he complains that the house has become a Jewish folk festival. He retaliates by co-opting elements of Catholicism—for instance, saying a prayer to St. Jude to ask that he sell a play. His exaggerated Catholicism helps Bridget realize that, just as she does not want a Catholic husband, Bernie does not want her to be Jewish. Essentially, this episode does not depict Bernie as becoming less Jewish because of pressure from his Catholic wife. Bernie assimilated away from Sophie's Old World manners and concerns, and Bridget appeals to him precisely because of her differences from Sophie. Sophie, rather than Bernie, suggests that Bridget should be more Jewish and when she acts on the idea, Bernie essentially points out that he does not want to be married to a "Jewish mother." Despite Sophie's meddling, together the couple creates a neutral and American space to inhabit, marked by neither Jewish nor Catholic elements, not because that neutrality is a compromise, but because it is presented as their most authentic space.

If Bernie's family is depicted as overwhelmingly Jewish and exorbitantly ethnic, Bridget's family is presented as a uniquely mid-twentieth-century kind of Catholic. While the Catholic father in *Abie's Irish Rose* was a whiskey-swilling Irish laborer, Bridget's parents represent a very different, yet unmistakable, moment in Catholic assimilation. The Fitzgeralds are post-Camelot Catholics, and "Kennedy and his family demonstrated that loyalty to Catholicism could effortlessly accompany intelligent patriotism, urbane sophistication, and coolly detached Cosmopolitanism."[18] Bridget's maiden name even echoes the Kennedy family—the F in JFK stands, after all, for Fitzgerald. Bridget's parents, then, could hobnob with delegates to the UN (Amy Fitzgerald asks Bernie if he knows Golda Meir, a "lovely woman"), serve on the board of the Metropolitan Museum of Art, and drink martinis like other members of New York City's elite, all the while remaining dedicated to the Church.

While the Fitzgeralds do not demonstrate excess in the same way that the Steinbergs do, their Catholicism still shows on their bodies—even the extremely hip Father Mike is usually in clericals and a Roman collar, and in one episode, an aunt visits in a full habit. When Bridget's mother finds out that Bernie is Jewish, rather than black, she crosses herself in relief, adding a layer of complication to which we will return. No matter how worrisome interfaith marriage was, many saw it as preferable to interracial marriage. Bodies then, stand in the way of full assimilation—the Fitzgeralds mark their bodies with their Catholicism, and they fear the idea of racially marked bodies that would prevent their daughter from maintaining their social position in space that was increasingly free from religious boundaries, but still functionally, if not legally, racially segregated. Despite their success as upper-class Americans, the Fitzgeralds do not aspire to full assimilation. As Walter Fitzgerald tells Bernie, wanting to underscore that their objections to the marriage are not rooted in anti-Semitism, "We would feel the same way about you if you were Protestant."

The generational tensions of Jewish interfaith marriage were particularly relevant in the 1970s. The younger generation of Jews was intermarrying at a higher rate than ever before, with varying estimates averaging at about 30 percent for the early 1970s. In part, this was because they were raised in an implicitly white, middle-class, postwar, suburban world that accepted "Judeo-

Christian" religious difference, but was much less tolerant of a range of other differences, including those of language and race, but also mannerism and decorum. In that worldview, if the religions of Protestants, Catholics, and Jews were now acceptable American religions, marriage could happen across those lines and be part of the national good, especially as it aided in assimilation.[19] (Contemporary ethnic studies scholars nuance this perception of sameness, pointing out that the very act of trying to be the same could make Jews and Catholics "hyperconscious of... difference.")[20] Additionally, these couples were products of the 1960s, a time that valued individualism and spiritual seeking and was skeptical of institutional loyalty, whereas their parents had been formed by both the Great Depression and World War II.[21]

If generational conflict was part and parcel of 1970s pop culture, there were also historical factors that made it particularly applicable in representations of the interfaith family. As young adults in 1973, Bridget's and Bernie's characters were part of the first generation to be raised in a post–World War II, Protestant-Catholic-Jewish world, where religious identity was not supposed to conflict with American identity. As long as Catholics and Jews erased the boundaries between themselves and the American Protestant secular, they could, in theory, be fully included in American society and have access to the newly realizable American dream.[22] As characters like Bridget and Bernie modeled, however, inclusion in that American life required that Catholics and Jews move away from some of the markers of identity that were as much or more located in foodways or speech patterns as in observance of fast days, prayers in Hebrew, or prayers to saints.

Their parents, however, were in a very different place. The parental generation had been shaped by a pre–Vatican II Catholicism, when the Latin mass and habited clergy marked Catholicism as an Old World religion, separate from the American democratic impulse. The changes of Vatican II erased many practices that separated Catholics from their Protestant neighbors, easing obligations of fast days and encouraging lay participation in local church governance, modernizing reforms that also brought the experience of the Church more in step with the American mainstream.[23] While some members of the Greatest Generation were excited by the potential to be urbane and sophisticated Americans while remaining deeply Catholic, their Catholicism had still been formed before Vatican II, whereas baby boomers experienced a Catholicism that was both in flux and marked by an embrace of modernity. Elements of the parental commitment to Catholic life can be seen in *BLB* when, for instance, Bridget's father suspects that she may convert to Judaism and laments the thirteen years of Catholic school that he had provided for her.

At the same time that Catholic parents had different cultural attachments to the Catholic Church than did their children, the cultural shifts that made intermarriage possible also put a kind of long-denied cultural status within the grasp of Catholic parents. The social acceptability represented by Bridget's Upper East Side parents, with their desire to know the correct people and serve on the board of the Metropolitan Museum of Art, was not something that Catholic parents necessarily wanted to see their children surrender through an alliance with Jews, who, for all of their assimilation, remained more on the edge of mainstream American culture than Catholics who, in the end, shared Christianity, if in a different form, with the Protestant majority. There was, after all, no Jewish Camelot. Outside the Fitzgerald social climbing, questions of Catholic assimilation are absent from the light sitcom world of *BLB*. They do, however, lurk behind the generational conflicts that shape the show, suggesting that questions about assimilation were also deeply resonant with its historical moment.

While conflict around interfaith marriage was portrayed as generational, *Bridget Loves Bernie* also suggested that the interfaith couple could serve as a model for their parents, bringing them out of their ethnic enclaves into a more American space. In the penultimate episode of the sitcom, titled "The Information Gap," the show addresses what for many religious leaders and interfaith couples was the central question of interfaith marriage, "What about the children?" In "The Information Gap," Sophie Steinberg hears Bridget and Bernie discussing their "new arrival." While the couple is making plans to adopt a dog, all four parents come to the conclusion that they plan to adopt a child and begin arguing about whether the child will be Catholic or Jewish. Otis, Bernie's African-American best friend, agrees to drive Bridget and Bernie to pick up their puppy, as long as Father Mike can babysit his niece while he does so. As a result, when the would-be grandparents arrive, in a pitched battle about the baby's potential religion, they find Mike at home with a black infant. Not realizing that the child is Otis's niece, all four "grandparents" are initially horrified at the thought of a black grandchild. Mike plays along with their mistake, specifically to convince both the Fitzgeralds and the Steinbergs that they can move beyond race and religion to simply love each other as human beings and accept the baby into the family. In this message about the humanity beyond religious and racial identity, *BLB* places itself firmly in the camp of the younger generation and an idealized America, segregated by neither race nor religion.

Bridget Loves Bernie addresses social, cultural, and class differences and sets up the difference between Bernie's working-class roots and Bridget's wealthy parents as equally—if not more—important than their religious differences. To a certain extent, this means that the sitcom conflates the concepts of Judaism and working-class status and Catholicism and upper-class status. The show therefore sidesteps religious faith, which makes the harmony of this couple relatively easy. The audience sympathizes with Bridget and Bernie as they struggle to avoid the meddling of their parents, as Bridget's parents try to include them in their high-society life and Bernie's try to increase the expression of Judaism in their home. Since American society is deeply interested in both "princess and pauper" stories and the myth of a classless society, the transgression of class lines seems natural and appropriate. Similarly, as religion in the 1970s became less about community and more about the individual,[24] it was possible for Bridget and Bernie, in contrast to the older generation, to see religion as one of the differences between them that serves to make them more attractive to each other, but that does not need to be shared or taken to "extremes." Indeed, at no point in the show does either member of the couple demonstrate any attachment to practices or beliefs that are depicted as Jewish or Catholic. This contrasts sharply with the form of home that is intelligible to their parents, in which traditions are maintained through the shared goals of the family, and the need to accommodate other American lifestyles ends when one walks through the front door.

Although *BLB* was immensely popular, CBS pulled the sitcom after receiving letters of complaint and public criticism from Jewish groups and individuals about the title characters' interfaith marriage. Prominent Jewish groups, including the Synagogue Council of America, quickly denounced the network's new show, which went into reruns after twenty-two episodes and stopped airing at the end of the 1972–73 season. Thomas Swafford, the vice president in charge of program practices, explained that CBS understood the "long-run consequences" of what bowing to censorship would do to television generally.[25] Officially, therefore, CBS claimed that it canceled the show because of a ratings dip in the Saturday-night lineup, between the popular shows *All in the Family* and *The Mary Tyler Moore Show*, and not because of Jewish objections.[26] For most of its first (and only) year on the air, however, *Bridget Loves Bernie* ranked in the top five of the Nielsen ratings, making it, as of this writing, the most highly ranked show to be canceled in the history of television.[27]

Whether the protests were the reason that CBS canceled the show or whether CBS really was concerned about a slight ratings dip in its lineup, complaints were certainly vociferous, at least in the Jewish press and in some Jewish communities. Not only did the Synagogue Council of America arrange to meet with Swafford, but individual rabbis and laypersons from locations around the country wrote letters to CBS and used their pulpits to object to the sitcom's content.[28] The Rabbinical Council of Greater Washington called for "sincere-minded members of every religious denomination to show their disapproval of 'Bridget Loves Bernie' by refusing to watch the show, by boycotting the products of the program's sponsor, and by writing letters of protest to WTOP-TV and to the CBS network in New York."[29] They were not alone in calling for boycotts—numerous congregational rabbis publicly listed sponsors of the show and called for Jews and others to write to sponsors, local networks, and CBS.[30]

Viewers had specific concerns about the show. Articles in the Jewish press expressed concerns that *BLB* downplayed the problems faced by interfaith couples, making such relationships more appealing than they actually would be in real life. Letters to the editor in the *New York Times* echoed these concerns, suggesting that the sitcom would make Jewish young people think that it was "romantic and chic" to marry a Gentile and would therefore encourage intermarriage by offering such an attractive example.[31] Others, writing out of the belief that intermarriage was the greatest threat to Jewish continuity in the late twentieth century, suggested that the show was in massively poor taste, with one letter to the *New York Times* comparing *BLB* to "a series about the merry adventures of a Jewish family on their way to the gas chambers."[32] This perspective articulates the deepest Jewish fear of interfaith marriage: that it posed a serious threat to Jewish continuity. If the children of interfaith marriage did not grow up to identify as Jews and raise Jewish children themselves, American acceptance of Jews (as exemplified by interfaith marriage) ran the risk of "completing Hitler's work for him."[33] For all of these writers, Jewish-Christian intermarriage was simply unacceptable, and television had a social responsibility not to make light of, or seem to support, such a lifestyle. The response from Jewish leadership, across movements and from some Jewish lay voices, demonstrates significant tension between the popular American response to interfaith marriage and the fears of those who worried about the impact of intermarriage on communal Jewish life and even Jewish survival. This tension stemmed from the suggestion that the young couple could transcend his Judaism and her Catholicism in order to be young American individuals in love.

Though Houston's Rabbi Jack Segal noted an article in the *Catholic Visitor* disapproving of its portrayals of Catholic-Jewish intermarriage, lay Catholics and leaders in the Catholic Church were largely absent from the protests against *BLB*. In her work on controversial prime-time television, historian Kathryn Montgomery points out that Catholics spent the 1973–74 television season protesting CBS for another reason: they were largely occupied with protests against the contemporaneous CBS sitcom *Maude*, in which the title character has an abortion.[34] Additionally, while Jews were deeply concerned about interfaith marriage to Christians, Catholics were primarily concerned with marriage between Catholics and Protestants, not between Catholics and Jews. While the Catholic Church did not approve of Catholic-Jewish marriage, it was simply not an issue that raised the same amount of concern in Catholic circles.

In Jewish and Catholic lay and official responses to *BLB*, we see that the two communities had radically different responses based on the perceived threat of the show to their community's future. Catholics, who objected strenuously to Maude's abortion, protested because they believed themselves to be a large-enough share of the American television market to be able to dictate what versions of morality appeared on prime-time television. Whether or not they appreciated the depiction of interfaith marriage in *BLB*, they did not feel the need to object strongly. If Catholics responded from a position of strength, Jewish responses underscored their sense of numeric instability in the United States. To glorify interfaith marriage struck leaders and laity across a range of Jewish communities as nothing so much as a strike against the Jewish community, at the same time that the message clearly struck a chord with the many viewers who bumped it to the top five in the Nielsen ratings.

Little House on the Prairie: The Close of a Decade

Little House on the Prairie ran on NBC from 1974 to 1984. A series created to highlight Michael Landon in the role of Charles Ingalls, or "Pa," it was only loosely based on the young adult books by Laura Ingalls Wilder, telling the stories of her pioneer girlhood in the late nineteenth century. It was an immensely popular show, with high ratings throughout its time on the air. Rather than confine itself to themes rooted in the nineteenth century, *Little House* occasionally addressed hot-button issues of the 1970s, such as women's rights or disability rights. It was in this vein that they chose to address the question of interfaith families. Whereas seven years before, *BLB* had been removed from the air because of pressure from Jewish groups about the portrayal of interfaith marriage, in 1980, during the show's sixth season, the writers of the popular *Little House* series were able to choose interfaith marriage as one of the social issues worth addressing in the show's plotlines without causing social comment. This shift in response suggests that interfaith marriage had become a more acceptable topic for mainstream television.

Little House on the Prairie reprises many of the themes that had reoccurred throughout the decade, with an important twist. For the first time, in *Little House*, Protestant culture is portrayed as having a material culture and set of practices that its adherents might value, rather than simply being the social neutral into which overly Jewish or Catholic individuals might assimilate. In other cases, such as *Heartbreak Kid*, Christianity is presented as having a distinct social location based in economic and social class, but largely absent from these depictions of Christianity are religious belief and practice, material culture, and familial traditions. Instead, to be Protestant is to be a member of the dominant and largely secular American culture—even to be free from an excess of religion. Even in *BLB*, where the Christian family's Catholicism allows for the sight gags of a family that includes a priest and a nun, the concerns of the Catholic family are largely rooted in class-consciousness rather than in religious identity. *Little House*, however, addresses both material culture, in this case artifacts such as a christening gown, and religious practices of Christianity as well as of Judaism, giving a more complete picture of two lived religious cultures combining in family life.[35]

In season six of the series, one of the supporting characters, Nellie Olsen, finds herself struggling to run the hotel and restaurant that her mother has given her. Enter Percival Dalton, a short and scholarly young man from out of town who is hired as a consultant. The couple falls in love and decides to marry, at which point Percival announces that he cannot be married in the church. "I'm Jewish," he explains, introducing a new plotline and comedic element into the show. Percival, as it turns out, was born Isaac Cohen and has assimilated to avoid discrimination as he travels through the American West. Nellie and Percival's interfaith household did not mirror the deeply contentious interfaith home in which producer/director Landon was raised, but the extended family offered a chance to explore interfaith family life in a show that Landon had consciously structured around wholesome "family values."[36]

While the interfaith marriage factors into Nellie and Percival's wedding during season six, it is most prominent in season seven when Nellie's character becomes pregnant. Though interfaith conflicts are part of the running gag of the Olsen family, the primary conflict around the interfaith family reaches its apex in an episode entitled "Let Us Reason Together." The episode focuses on the four grandparents awaiting the birth of their grandchild and the implicit assumption on the part of the writers that, if they "reason together," a solution to their cultural differences will emerge. As in other depictions of interfaith marriage, the older generation portrays a cultural rigidity that the younger generation must move beyond. It offers, however, two notably new elements. First, Mrs. Olsen, a Protestant parent, is every bit as problematic as Mr. Cohen. Second, for the first time, the show treats the older generation with some sympathy, suggesting that whether or not their approach is ideal, something is lost in the process of assimilation.

As in *BLB*, food provides a flashpoint for establishing the family traditions. Both Mr. Cohen and Mrs. Olsen find the other family's foodways unacceptable. Mr. Cohen expresses disapproval of the fact that the Olsen son, Willie, drinks milk with his meal, observing that milk and meat are not to be served together. The script element serves to highlight the differences between the families, rather than to accurately depict a misunderstanding, because Jews are well aware that non-Jews do not keep kosher. Mrs. Olsen is offended when Mr. Cohen refuses to eat the roast beef because it is not kosher, though she later bonds with Mrs. Cohen over chocolate cake. ("Is chocolate cake acceptable or is it sinful?" Mrs. Olsen asks. "Only sinful for the waistline," Mrs. Cohen quips. "God does not mind a sweet tooth.") Mrs. Olsen has her own chance to disapprove when the Cohens, Daltons, and Olsens gather for Shabbat dinner at Nellie and Percival's restaurant—walking in, she gripes that she does not want to eat Jewish food. Similarly, in an earlier episode, she mistook Nellie's morning sickness as a reaction to sharing Jewish food like matzoh and kreplach with her husband. Similarly, when Mr. Cohen comments that the grandchild will have many family Shabbat dinners, Mrs. Olsen counters with the idea that they will gather often for Sunday dinner.

The episode "Let Us Reason Together," however, suggests that something other than a hidebound and backward-looking tendency connects Mrs. Olsen and Mr. Cohen to their heritages. In an attempt to bond with Mrs. Cohen, Mrs. Olsen brings out Nellie's christening dress, which she had saved since Nellie herself was a baby. For Mrs. Olsen, the christening dress represents continuity—the thought of Nellie in her christening dress and of seeing Nellie's own baby in the same dress moves her to tears. Similarly, when Mr. Cohen argues that the grandson must be Jewish, he says, "Who will say kaddish at your grave if your son does not learn Torah?" Rather than focusing solely on the comedic conflicts between and stereotypes of Jews and Christians, *Little House on the Prairie* underscored the deep-seated familial longing to share traditions with their grandchildren that is motivating both Mr. Cohen and Mrs. Olsen.

Significantly, Mr. Cohen asks what assimilation means for a relationship to Judaism and is clearly pained and troubled by his son's decisions. In more than one extended scene between the father and son, Mr. Cohen makes his disappointment at Percival's assimilationist decisions known. To Mr. Cohen, the fact that Percival prays on Sunday, in church with Nellie, makes him a Gentile. Percival responds, "It's just a building, Papa. How can the roof over my head change what I am?" To Mr. Cohen, however, Percival's words are not reassuring—Percival's Christian practices may or may not change what he is, but they suggest, at best a lack of filial respect and, at worst, open rejection. Furthermore, he worries that Sunday dinners with the Olsens and attendance at church will confuse his longed-for grandson—that the child will not be Jewish and will, in fact, not know what it is to be a Jew. The character's concerns are significant because, while in the end, Percival is more sympathetically drawn, and he does not value the kinds of Jewish observance that his father desires, Mr. Cohen's prime-time character is the first to give voice to the fears that assimilation through intermarriage might damage Jewish survival or, at least, disconnect the children of intermarriage from a valuable heritage. In the end, however, despite some sympathy for Mr. Cohen's and Mrs. Olsen's positions, the script ultimately places these concerns, for religious belief and tradition, with the grandparents, not with the parents, and therefore relegates them to the past. Nellie and Percival are both upset by the families arguing, but they are not presented as being divided by these issues themselves. Percival is untroubled about going to church with Nellie; and when he asks Nellie if she is upset that he hid his original name, she observes, "I married you, not your name!"

The evening of the grandparents' decision, that a granddaughter will be Christian and a grandson Jewish, Nellie and Percival lie in bed laughing about the proposed solution and how silly they found the entire conversation—there was no sense that either parent had any stake in the religious upbringing of their children. One could argue that the young couple were depicted going to church together and would probably have raised Christian children, but even then the script suggests that they would have done so by default, rather than because of clear conviction. (The fact that the town doctor, rather than the minister, performed their wedding suggests that they would have trended toward the secular rather than the Protestant.) Together, they care about family peace, a peace that might occur at the expense of religion. As Percival observes after a particularly loud clash between Mrs. Olsen and Mr. Cohen, "Is this what religion is all about? Anger? Fighting? Hatred? Because if it is, Nellie and I do not want any part of it." Nellie, Percival, and their parents, then, echo the generational difference reflected throughout the decade: the intermarried couple, whether or not they have children, is portrayed as unconcerned about the difference between Jews and Christians. The concerns and investments in Christian and Jewish formation, whether they stem from bigotry, sentiment, or commitment to continuity, are the territory of the previous generation.

In the end, with classic television closure and echoing the solution in the original *Abie's Irish Rose*, the babies are born, and they are just that—babies, a boy *and* a girl, a Jewish grandson for Mr. Cohen and a Christian grand-daughter for Mrs. Olsen. The solution is presented as a happy one: each grandparent gets what he or she wanted. Fundamentally, though, while their Solomonic solution of twins prevents one grandparent from "winning," in no way does it resolve the tensions surrounding identity. Mr. Cohen has, all along, expressed concern that Percival has fallen away from Judaism—whatever prayers he says, he says on Sunday mornings during a Protestant worship service. He eats non-kosher meat and does not keep the Sabbath. He has not promised a shift in his life and in the life of his family because they have had a boy. Similarly, Mr. Cohen feared that Sunday dinner, after church, would confuse a Jewish grandchild. Presumably, according to the terms of the compromise, the daughter will be raised Christian. Not only does that mean that the family will continue to have Sunday dinner, but it suggests that church and Christmas will continue to be part of the Dalton family life.

While the compromise results in a joyous family celebration, it does not offer a clear plan for going forward—will the Jewish son be raised Jewish in the way that Percival has chosen to live or will the couple take on the practices that matter to Mr. Cohen? Will both children participate in family rituals? Subsequently Nellie and Percival continue as they had begun. In this way, though *Little House* was responding to a social issue of the late twentieth century, Percival, like Lenny in *The Heartbreak Kid*, replicated what was, in fact, the nineteenth-century pattern of assimilation: he married a Protestant woman and became part of her Midwestern family's life, leaving behind his Jewish New York background.[37] While the script acknowledges some ambiva-lence around assimilation, and while officially one of the grandchildren will be Jewish, in the end, the answer is an assimilation to a secular mainstream—the identity that both parents have embraced, having rejected religion as divisive.

Unsuccessful Assimilation, Failed Relationships

Not all on-screen interfaith couples managed successful relationships. Two iconic, romantic films of the 1970s, Sydney Pollack's *The Way We Were* (1973) and Woody Allen's *Annie Hall* (1977), both link the couples' failures to their differences—not in theology or religious practice, but in worldview and mannerisms. In the story arc of both movies, this gulf, rooted in social and cultural differences between WASP and Jew, proved insurmountable for the couples, largely because the Jewish partner was unable to contain her or his emotions or neuroses.

The Way We Were offered a counterexample to the depictions of successful and happy interfaith families. In the 1973 film, blond, All-American Robert Redford plays Hubbell Gardiner, and quintessentially Jewish Barbra Streisand was nominated for an Oscar for her performance as Katie Morosky, in a romance set between the late 1930s and early 1950s and drawing its dramatic tension from the couple's differences. While in *The Heartbreak Kid* Lenny's Jewishness and Kelly's Christianity are left largely unstated, Streisand's character threads references to her Judaism through the film, gleefully exclaiming "Happy Rosh Hashanah" as Hubbell opens a gift or making reference to the early summer holiday of Shavous while Hubbell's All-American WASPiness is unstated but evident in his letterman sweaters and in the suave, moneyed sophistication of his friends. The differences in their backgrounds are underscored when, for instance, Katie first tells Hubbell that she is pregnant. Spinning a third-person anecdote, she nervously notes, "loud-mouthed Jewish girl from New York City tells her gorgeous goyische guy" that she is pregnant. Not only does Streisand's character narrate their differences, she does so with Yiddish, the very language that underscores her ethnicity. Notes of Katie's Jewishness (and of Jewish women as less desirable than their Gentile counterparts) echo through the film, with, for instance, the recurrent motif of Katie ironing her hair, one of the many beauty regimes in which Jewish women have participated in order to look less ethnic.

While Katie is willing to iron her hair, however, she is unwilling (or unable) to tamp down her political passions, a part of her personality that Hubbell partially admires but ultimately cannot share. In the end, Katie's political passions, not her references to Jewish holidays, end the relationship. Hubbell cannot live with Katie's uncompromising insistence on calling people on a failure to engage with, or a tendency to make light of, political happenings. In the structure of the film, the couple is not depicted as growing apart. Rather, these differences in approach had always existed. During their college days, she was a Marxist student radical, and he was a fraternity boy with a varsity letter. As a couple, those differences spark tensions when he tries to bring her into his lighthearted, implicitly WASP world. Katie cannot tolerate a social world in which people joke about politics, when the issues at stake are, to her, desperately important. Katie's inability to fit into Hubbell's world is strikingly demonstrated in a scene set immediately following FDR's death. The couple is at a cocktail party and Hubbell's friends, all more conservative than the late president, are making cynical jokes about FDR, his politics, Eleanor's looks, and her public involvement. Katie, who had wished that FDR had taken the New Deal further, exploded with anger, not only about their dismissal of FDR's politics but also about their fundamental disrespect for the dead. That difference, light and detached humor versus passionate engagement, is the core difficulty in Katie and Hubbell's relationship, one that comes to a head while they are in Hollywood, when Hubbell "chickens out" at a House Un-American Committee meeting.[38]

The first time they consider breaking up, Katie identifies the problem. "I don't have the right style for you, do I?" Hubbell agrees that the problem is her style. "You push too hard, every damn minute. There's no time to ever relax and enjoy living. Everything's too serious to be so serious." While in that moment, the couple reconciles, the fundamental difference of Katie's seriousness and intensity is, in the end, what drives them apart. Years later, they encounter each other on the street. Hubbell has not become a gifted writer; rather, he is one of the anonymous writers for a sitcom. Katie is outside protesting. They have remained true to themselves, but cannot be together.

A couple of points are worth noting here: the most basic is that Katie's way of being is, in point of fact, Jewish. The issue here is not the religious differences (for a commonsense definition of religion—i.e., matters of belief, observance, or holidays), but rather worldviews that are coded, inherently, as WASP and Jewish, carefree and intense, polite and political. Katie and Hubbell cannot be together, not because they cannot agree on whether to baptize a child but because the very traits that initially made Katie intriguing, her intensity and engagement, are the self-same things that drove them apart. And those things are tied to differences of WASP and Jewish identities. At the same time, while Katie's Jewishness makes her an unacceptable mate, the film is not anti-Semitic. Katie offers to change and Hubbell tells her not to do so—he recognizes the value in her approach to the world. In the final scene of the movie, in their final encounter, Hubbell acknowledges what Katie knows: he was his best self when she was with him. Katie cannot exist within Hubbell's world, but the film does not disparage her in suggesting that her failure to assimilate ends the relationship.

The theme of the impossible relationship between Jew and Gentile was equally pronounced in Woody Allen's Academy Award–winning movie *Annie Hall*, with the interfaith romance even sparking two of the movie's possible titles, *Me and My Goy* and *It Had to Be Jew*.[39] In *Annie Hall*, Allen's character, the neurotic Jewish comedian Alvy Singer, becomes romantically involved with the enthusiastic, but somewhat ditzy and unintellectual Annie Hall, late of Chippewa Falls, Wisconsin, played by Diane Keaton. In one of their first conversations, their different backgrounds as New York Jew and Midwestern Gentile become clear. Standing on her balcony, Annie observes, "You are what my Grammy Hall would call a real Jew." Alvy, unsure how to respond, settles on "Thank you," to which Annie replies, "Oh, she hates Jews." From their earliest conversations, the film establishes that Alvy fulfills not just the stereotypes of Jewishness, but specifically negative stereotypes, and that Annie sees him, in part, in light of those tropes.

When with Annie, however, Alvy sees himself as the archetypal Jew as well. Much later in the movie, when Alvy takes his standup routine to a Wisconsin college campus, he and Annie have Easter dinner with her family. The scene cuts from the outside of the Halls' perfectly groomed colonial home to the dinner table, where everyone politely compliments the ham. When Alvy says that the ham is "dynamite," Grammy Hall makes a silent expression of distaste. The camera focuses on her face as she watches Alvy, and then cuts to her perspective on him: a Hasid, with a full beard and *payos*. The conversation continues with a restrained discussion of swap meets and country club meetings, when Alvy breaks the scene in order to address the camera. As a self-conscious narrator, Alvy tells the audience that Grammy Hall is a "classic Jew hater" and reflects that Annie's family looks American and healthy, "like they never get sick." "They are nothing like my family," he explains. "The two couldn't be more different. Like oil and water." The scene cuts from the sedate dinner in the spacious Hall family dining room, where pauses stretch between comments, to a table in a crowded apartment, where the people lean across each other to reach for food and loudly interrupt each other to discuss the medical conditions of shared acquaintances. While Allen's depiction of the Hall family dinner is a parody of the Minnesota nice that defines Kelly's family in *The Heartbreak Kid* and not necessarily a warm or appealing family scene, Alvy's comments frame them as the American norm. Alvy, in this depiction, is neurotic because he is a New York Jew, a member of a tribe that lacks physical and emotional boundaries. In the end, when he and Annie fall apart because of their incompatible neuroses, those neuroses are clearly the result of their very different backgrounds. Like Hubbell and Katie, Annie and Alvy cannot be together because they cannot break free of where they came from.

Conclusion

During the 1970s, interfaith couples were strikingly visible in popular culture, with a presence both on television and in the movies. Although religious leadership was concerned about the rising rate of interfaith marriage, popular culture embraced interfaith marriage, on the condition that the couple's relationship moved them away from religion and into a shared secular and American space. Often this did not require the couple themselves to change—they were portrayed as essentially different from their families, less extreme in their embodiment, less committed to religious expression. Rather, the successful relationship requires that the Jewish partner, always portrayed as male in these successful relationships, separate himself from his family and their excessive ways. The onus to move beyond parents does not, however, rest solely on the Jewish man. In both *Bridget Loves Bernie* and *Little House on the Prairie*, the Christian women are depicted as being free from the class prejudices and anti-Semitism of their parents. While the Jewish men are acceptable because they are without the extremes of their families—the food, the mannerisms, the loud voices—the Christian women are without the exclusionary attitudes of their parents. Neither excessive ethnicity nor overt bigotry were acceptable attitudes in the American secular. The fact that they were not acceptable is demonstrated by the extent to which differences rooted in stereotypes of WASPS and Jews undermine the romantic relationships of two of the most famous movies in the 1970s. Interfaith marriage, then, was to be celebrated in media representations, as long as it encouraged a drift toward an American secular that remained largely defined by the norms of white Protestantism. When an interfaith marriage or relationship failed to bring the more ethnic partner in line with the specifications of "Minnesota nice," however, the relationship was not successful—even as *The Way We Were* and *Annie Hall* did not glorify the WASP mannerisms or necessarily denigrate Jewish ones, they still suggested that the differences between the couple were too vast to be bridged.

CHAPTER THREE

One Roof, One Religion

The Campaign for a Jewish (Interfaith) Family

In its 2003–4 season, HBO's hit series *Sex in the City*, which featured the lives and loves of four single women in New York, presented conversion to Judaism as a solution to the dilemma posed by interfaith love. For the first five seasons of the show, WASPy Episcopalian Charlotte York had been the series' most traditional leading woman. A Smith graduate of the sweater-set variety and former sorority girl, Charlotte believed in the ideals of romantic love and Emily Post etiquette. Her faith that true love and marriage would carry the day caused Carrie Bradshaw, the show's narrator, to call her the "Park Avenue Pollyanna" in voice-overs. Charlotte's dedication to an idealized version of upper-class WASP standards of behavior and aesthetics makes it particularly surprising when, in season six, she meets and falls in love with her divorce lawyer, the sensitive but homely Harry Greenblatt. A relationship with Harry promises fulfillment that her previous marriage had lacked, so when he explains that he cannot marry a non-Jew, Charlotte pursues conversion.

As Samuel Freedman commented in a review for *USA Today*, "no television show had ever presented a conversion with such visual and theological detail. Even more important is what the approving portrayal represents: a reversal of the entertainment industry's tradition of viewing Jewish identity as something to be shed in the quest to become American."[1] Following traditional Jewish conversionary practices, the rabbi rebuffs Charlotte the first two times she approaches him. She undergoes a study process with the rabbi and his wife, learning Jewish religious laws and customs, and she ultimately converts at a *mikveh*, or ritual bath. When she realizes that becoming Jewish means giving up Christmas, Charlotte holds Christmas in July, setting up her tree and her ornaments and celebrating one last time, clearly mourning a loss.

Charlotte exerts a great deal of effort in her conversion to Judaism. Her pride in her accomplishment is evident when she first cooks a Shabbat dinner for Harry. Not only does she prepare traditional Eastern European dishes, but her beatific expression as she lights the Shabbat candles and recites the blessing in Hebrew suggests piety. The scene implies that while the conversion had been undertaken for Harry, Charlotte ultimately finds meaning in Judaism's rituals. As part of her conversion process, Charlotte's rabbi requires that she give up (and mourn the loss of) Christmas. She does so, before exchanging her Christian practices for those of Judaism. By her religious conversion, Charlotte creates a single-faith marriage and home for herself and Harry.

While the overt message of the storyline suggested the efficacy of conversion, the narrative also suggests fundamental tensions in what it means to create single-religion homes out of interfaith marriages, as well as an inherent gender imbalance regarding expectations of conversion. Harry has different plans for the Friday night on which Charlotte cooks her first Shabbat dinner. He arrives home and immediately turns on the Mets game, muting it and watching it behind Charlotte's back as she recites the blessing over the candles. Charlotte is hurt and outraged when she discovers that he is watching a ballgame on Shabbat—less because of the sacredness of the day and more because it undermines her efforts. "I gave up Christ for you," she exclaims. "Can't you give up the Mets for me?" Harry responds that it was going to be a long life together if she continues to hold her conversion over his head. "Take out the garbage, I gave up Christ for you," he yells.

This plotline in the popular television show demonstrates how a number of early twenty-first-century assumptions around interfaith marriage grew out of a series of conversations in much earlier decades, largely within Reform Judaism. Having realized they were unlikely to stem the tide of interfaith marriage, in the 1970s and early 1980s, the Reform leadership set out to convince interfaith couples to create Jewish homes. In the early 1980s, leaders in the Reform movement defined Judaism as a religion, based in belief, education, and formal participation in communal life. Such a definition made it more possible both to count children of non-Jewish mothers as Jews and to argue that conversion to Judaism was a fully efficacious solution to the problem of intermarriage. While this understanding of Judaism appealed to the Reform leadership, because it could be easily defined, controlled, and transmitted, some in the Reform community did not support these changes because they did not think that religious conversion alone was sufficient to make someone Jewish, as often converts lacked many qualities that made them "feel Jewish" to their co-religionists. As a result, they sometimes rebuffed "New Jews" and interfaith families as insufficiently Jewish. Women with Christian backgrounds, whether or not they were actively engaged in Christian life, often took on the work of creating Jewish homes when they married Jewish men. Like Charlotte, they sometimes found that their understandings of what it meant to create such homes differed from the understandings and, at times, the desires of their communities and even their husbands.

In *Sex and the City*, Charlotte approaches conversion to Judaism as a religious experience, as the only route possible for a convert. Yet she discovers that while Harry wants her to "be Jewish," he does not necessarily want her to "do Jewish"—he wants her to inhabit the identity without needing to perform it. Harry believes that the act of conversion is enough to make their household Jewish, but Charlotte wants to enact the practices that she learned about while studying for conversion. They are working with different models of a single-faith household. For Harry, being Jewish is not tied to living an observant Jewish lifestyle. Charlotte's response emphasizes that she relates to Judaism as a belief system: she notes her sacrifice of Christ, even though the series emphasizes her sacrifice of the Christmas tree. Similarly, the plotline presents Charlotte giving up her traditions and beliefs to adapt to Harry's requirements. While Charlotte is expected to jettison her own tradition for Harry, he initially does not expect to allow her a voice in how they were Jewish—he was unwilling to moderate his ethnic Judaism with religious observance. The show, then, underscores the tension for the characters in what it meant to be Jewish—a religious identity available through conversion and observance in contrast to something more nebulous, perhaps, cooking brisket and shopping at Zabar's, the elements of the Shabbat dinner that Harry appreciates, largely because they are traditions relating to his family of origin. In doing so, it also highlights the tension inherent in the gendered perceptions of interfaith marriage: that non-Jewish women would be willing to take on Judaism for the good of their families and relationships and find personal fulfillment in doing so. In order to find that personal fulfillment, these women might have to make their husbands "more Jewish" than they were before marriage—and with a different definition of what it meant to be Jewish.

These competing understandings of Judaism are evident in the Reform leadership's attempts to convince interfaith families of the inherent value and fairness of choosing Judaism as a family religion. In outreach campaigns, they tackled complexities of interfaith home life, particularly how the relationship between practice and identity is tied to understandings of religion, culture, and ethnicity. Specifically, they revealed assumptions about Judaism and Christianity as "religions" and "cultures." Both terms suggested that Jewish identity rested in belief and culture, while Christian identity was rooted exclusively in personal belief, a distinction that they used to argue that interfaith families should choose Jewish lives. As a result, the solutions that the Reform leadership proposed for interfaith marriage often failed to account for the realities of individual lives, experiences, and understandings of identity. While outreach efforts, in the form of advice manuals for parents and picture books for children, tried to bring interfaith families into the Jewish fold and did not frame gender roles as a central concern, they reflected the expectation that Christian women would understand that the various imbalances between Judaism and Christianity meant that they should not share their belief systems with their children. These women, the manuals suggested, should sacrifice their own presumably inessential traditions to raise Jewish children. The Reform movement's campaign to prove the value that a Christian woman could find in Jewish life and in the reasonableness of her sacrifice of her natal religion for family unity was successful enough that it began to appear in popular culture depictions of intermarriage by the turn of the twenty-first century, as it did in *Sex and the City*.[2]

At the same time that the Reform movement's outreach campaign placed belief-oriented Christianity in opposition to the traditions of Judaism, their depictions of peoples' lives repeatedly troubled this distinction by exploring noncreedal aspects of Christianity. Even as the Reform movement's division between religion and culture was of central importance to the creation of Jewish homes out of interfaith marriages, depictions of interfaith family life demonstrated a strong fear of cultural Christianity. Outreach leaders such as authors Paul Cowan and Andrea King worried that children would develop "a *way of being*, a *habitual state* (especially of the body) and, in particular, a *predisposition, tendency, propensity,* or *inclination*" toward or drawn from Christianity.[3] By participating in Christian practice (either the formal practice of religious services or the family practices of Christmas trees and holiday cooking), the authors feared children of interfaith families would develop Christian, rather than Jewish, dispositions. In short, they would feel like Christians, whether or not they believed like Christians. This fear underscored a tension between the desire to define Christianity as an exclusively creedal religion and the experience of Jews as a minority in a Christian culture, a designation that implicitly suggested a range of noncreedal Christian experiences.

Defining Jewishness: Reform Jewish Leadership and Solutions to the Interfaith Family

Over the course of the twentieth century, American Judaism largely shifted from a racial and ethnic self-understanding to a religious one. This shift was essential in the process of American assimilation, one that allowed sociologist Will Herberg, writing in the 1950s, to claim Judaism as an "American religion" along with Protestantism and Catholicism.[4] In making that move, Jewish religious leaders attempted to secure Judaism's place as an American religion by framing it in creedal terms, as opposed to language that centered on race, ethnicity, or civilization.[5] If Judaism was a religion, defined by creed, Jews could be both fully American and fully Jewish. In addition, interfaith marriage could be solved by conversion; accepting Judaism could create a Jew.

The resistance in Reform congregations to including "new Jews" who were religiously but not ethnically assimilated into the community underscored some of the tensions in considering Judaism as an institutional religion alone. In part, the tendency to focus on overtly religious practice hindered the ability of American Jews to articulate their fears about intermarriage. If Judaism existed solely in religious terms and Protestants, Catholics, and Jews shared the same fundamental American values, or if a family had abandoned its religious beliefs and practice, intermarriage ceased to be a problem. Similarly, if the Gentile girlfriend could, through conversion or marriage contract, be turned into a Jewish wife and mother (legally or functionally), there was no longer a cost to interfaith marriage from the standpoint of Jewish survival as long as she raised children who attended and received education from Jewish communal institutions. These definitions of Judaism restricted Jewish identity to aspects that were, at least theoretically, under rabbinic control. They also failed to account for the full spectrum of lived religion affected by rising interfaith marriage rates.

In determining how to define Jewish identity, the Reform movement's leadership was motivated in part by a desire to incorporate interfaith families into Jewish communities. The policy debates of the Reform movement tied Jewish identity to participation in Jewish institutional life. This deliberate shift away from Jewish legal and cultural definitions of Judaism derived from an attempt to address intermarriage but also contributed to a shift from "cultural" or "ethnic" Jewish identity to a "religious" or affiliation-based understanding of Jewish life in the Reform movement. That shift suggested that attendance at services and religious school could make up for the lack of an ethnic identity in the home, one that might be determined by observance of various *mitzvoth* (commandments), but also by Eastern European cuisine, Yiddish-based speech patterns, and an affinity for the Lower East Side.[6] Additionally, the Reform movement eliminated reliance upon matrilineal descent alone, allowing Reform Judaism to be passed from either parent to a child, provided that child received a Jewish education. These definitions of Jewishness from the leadership of the Reform movement were not always ac-

FIGURE 2 Unitarian-Jewish chuppah, embroidered by the groom's mother. Visible in the chuppah are symbols of the couple's two religions, a Star of David and a flaming chalice. Image courtesy of the wedding couple, Ben and Emily.

cepted within the membership of those Reform Jewish communities, who found that the inclusion of recent converts and interfaith families shifted the tenor of the community.

Divorce cases provide particularly clear evidence of the challenges that faced the Reform leadership as they tried to ensure that the children of Christian women and Jewish men were raised as Jews. The question of interfaith marriage was inherently gendered for the Reform leadership for reasons related to Jewish law, American family law, and sociology. According to halakha (Jewish law), only Jewish women could give birth to Jewish children. Religious leaders understood mothers were more likely to be deeply involved in raising children and shaping their religious dispositions. Divorce compounded these concerns as mothers were more likely to retain custody of children when a marriage dissolved.

Reform leaders, including Alexander Schindler, president of the Union of American Hebrew Congregations (UAHC), the congregational arm of the Reform movement; Joseph Glaser, attorney and executive vice president of the Central Conference of American Rabbis (CCAR), the rabbinic arm of the Reform movement; and Sanford Seltzer, director of the Commission on Reform Jewish Outreach and director of planning and research for the UAHC, were particularly interested in ensuring the Jewish identity of children when their interfaith parents divorced.[7] Their early 1980s investigation of interfaith divorce underscores two key themes. First, the exploration itself exposes some of the assumptions of the Reform leadership about what constituted Jewish identity and about whose authority mattered in the raising of children—that of parents or that of religious institutions. The court cases also demonstrate differences between how the rabbis and U.S. courts approached that authority. Although Judaism saw itself as an American religion, tensions existed between the CCAR's sense of Jewish communal needs and the courts' commitment to individual religious freedom.

Second, the court cases themselves highlight the tension between policy and practice in the lives of interfaith families. They reveal what agreements interfaith couples made about their family lives and how those arrangements changed when the marriage collapsed. The practices of interfaith families demonstrate some of the ways in which CCAR policies and rabbinic hopes were incommensurate with the lived religion of interfaith families or the reality of the high divorce rates in the 1970s and 1980s. It's important to note that only some of these marriages were interfaith. In others, the marriages had not been interfaith, as the women had converted for the marriages. After the divorce, however, the families became interfaith when the wives returned to their original religions.

Although couples generally had to agree to raise their children as Jews in order to be married by a rabbi, after the wedding, rabbis had no way to enforce that promise either in the marriage or in divorce. Schindler, Glaser, and Seltzer were particularly interested in investigating whether, when a couple divorced, the U.S. courts could hold Christian women to their premarital promises to raise Jewish children. The Reform movement cited studies demonstrating that two to four times as many Jewish men married Christian women as vice versa and that 50 percent of interfaith marriages ended in divorce.[8] Since mothers received custody in 90 percent of divorce cases, children who were Jewish would be raised primarily in the homes of their

Christian (or previously Christian) mothers.[9] The Reform leadership feared that, post-divorce, such women would renege on their commitment to raise children as Jews. Despite Reform movement concerns that these children represented a significant numerical loss to American Judaism, Seltzer discovered that the U.S. courts would not support the Reform agenda.

The family courts were not quite certain how to navigate interfaith marriages. In two cases, from 1956 and 1962, lower courts ordered a Protestant mother to raise her children as Catholics and a Catholic woman to raise her children as Jews, respectively.[10] In each case, the lower courts' decisions were predicated on the agreement that the couple had made during their marriage for the religious upbringing of the children. The lower courts maintained the women were obligated to raise the children in the religion that the couple had, together, selected for their family. In both cases, however, the decisions were overturned upon appeal, allowing the mother, as the custodial parent, to determine the children's religious upbringing.

In the first case, the court ruled that not only should the judicial system generally not legislate the children's religious upbringing and instead leave that decision to the custodial parent, but also that "the courts have generally refused to enforce agreements between the father and the mother concerning the religious training of children but have held that the parent having custody is not bound by previous contract."[11] In the second case, the court went even further. To force a Catholic woman to bring her children to Jewish religious schools and services on a weekly basis, the court decided, "violates section 58 of the Virginia Constitution which guaranteed that no man shall be compelled to frequent or support any religious worship, place, or ministry."[12] The American legal system privileged the religious freedom of the individual over previous commitments to spouses or religious officials—a custodial parent could not be forced to raise her children in a given religion, even if she had previously agreed to do so. Thus, UAHC and the CCAR could not count on the court system to enforce premarital commitments to raise children as Jews should the marriage dissolve.

Seltzer and other members of the UAHC leadership understood that the courts would not support them in requiring Christian custodial parents to raise their children as Jews, but they were hopeful the legal system would require mothers to raise their children as Jews if they had converted to Judaism as a condition of the marriage. In an essay written for the UAHC, Seltzer argued that "such cases are of profound importance, not merely in terms of the well-being of children subsequent to the dissolution of a marriage and the maintenance of some family stability, but in terms of the legal status of Jewish conversions in the civil courts of the United States."[13] In other words, Seltzer hoped that the civil courts would see conversion to Judaism as a legally binding commitment. In the 1981 case of *Green v. Green*, Mrs. Green had converted to Judaism upon marriage. Post-divorce, she decided to return to her natal Roman Catholicism, in which she wanted to raise her children. Mr. Green argued that both her conversion certificate and their marriage contract, including the agreement that the children be raised as Jews, should be considered legally binding contracts.[14]

While the Green case was ongoing at the time of Seltzer's investigation into the legal ramifications of divorce after conversion, another case thwarted the Reform leadership's hope that the legal system would support their prenuptial contracts. Mrs. Schwarzman had been Roman Catholic before her marriage and agreed to convert to Judaism as a condition of the marriage. Both the conversion and the wedding were Reform. Their four children were named in the synagogue. When Mrs. Schwarzman sought a divorce, however, she renounced Judaism, married a Catholic man, and intended to move forward raising the children as Catholics. Mr. Schwarzman went to court to try to guarantee that his children be raised as Jews as they had been since birth. He cited the couple's oral agreement and their mother's conversion—making the children born of a Jewish mother—and their ritual naming in a synagogue. While he did not seek custody of the children or question his ex-wife's capability to mother them, he sought to ensure that she continue to bring them up as Jews. Mrs. Schwarzman, in turn, responded that she had converted under duress. The court ruled in her favor, in part because of the testimony of an Orthodox rabbi, who declared her conversion invalid and therefore the children not Jewish, because of the lack of a *mikveh* in her conversion.[15]

In this case, despite being the largest of the American Jewish movements, the Reform movement faced questions of legitimacy, not only from Jews in other denominations but also from the American legal system, because of its approach to Jewish law. The court essentially decided that Mrs. Schwarzman's conversion had not been valid and was therefore not binding. When they made this decision, the court delegitimized the Reform process of conversion because it did not meet Orthodox interpretations of Jewish law. The decision that the conversion was not valid because it did not hew to Orthodox standards was more damaging to the Reform movement's legitimacy than stating that she had the right to change her mind about her religious identity, or that if her conversion had been undertaken as a condition of marriage, she might choose to reverse her decision upon divorce.

The fact that the Reform leadership studied these divorce cases in an attempt to use the American legal system to force Christian mothers to raise Jewish children demonstrates how concerned they were about Jewish continuity in the face of interfaith marriage. When the Reform leadership sought to solve the interfaith marriage problem by requiring couples to maintain Jewish homes or by requiring the Christian partner to convert to Judaism, they officially claimed that they were reaching out to the religiously unaffiliated. The women in these court cases were not unchurched—they had sacrificed their own traditions for what they perceived to be the good of their marriage (or to access a Jewish wedding), but when the marriage ended, they were no longer interested in maintaining their own Jewish religiosity or in passing Jewish identity on to their children. By making a Jewish home a condition of marriage, the Reform leadership created a population whose commitment to Judaism was funneled through their husbands and did not necessarily outlive the relationships.

Though they struggled with these issues, the Reform movement ultimately discarded the idea of trying to legally compel non-Jewish parents to raise children as Jews. As Donald Gluckman of the CCAR's Committee on Family Life pointed out, "all such legal means of coercion would be counterproductive" and would lead to "exceedingly complex and acrimonious family circumstances," with Jewish life aggravating, rather than lessening, the strife of divorce.[16] To Gluckman, such involvement by a national arm of the Reform movement or by his committee would be "highly inappropriate"[17] because of the stress it would insert into the already difficult process of divorce and the strain it could add to the home. While the UAHC leadership was largely concerned with ensuring Jewish continuity, as the head of the Committee on Family Life, Gluckman was also concerned that the policies that they were considering would damage family life, and that if Jewish policies caused acrimonious homes, it might result in the children resenting, rather than identifying with, Judaism.

As the Reform leaders debated whether Christian mothers could be held to their commitment to raise Jewish children, they had to define what constituted a "Jewish child." The Reform leaders concluded that the children would be raised as Jews if they attended Jewish religious school and services on a regular basis. It is unlikely that anyone thought that a mother who was forced by court order to raise her children as Jews (or, for that matter, in any given religion) would create a warm and vibrant Jewish home culture. This responsibility would be left to the noncustodial parent and his extended family, who by definition would have less opportunity to influence the children's worldview. The discussion of interfaith divorce at the highest levels of Reform leadership did not address practices in the home as central to the formation of Jewish self-understanding, or as the center of Jewish life. Rather, they located Jewish identity in Jewish education and synagogue participation, goals that were theoretically possible for the non-Jewish mother raising her Jewish children and that represented a broader shift in the Reform movement.[18] With this shift to formal education as the primary marker of Jewish identity, the UAHC and CCAR leadership failed to address key questions of what made a home, or a person, feel Jewish in ways that had been immediately accessible only a generation before. While they did not explicitly draw distinctions between Judaism as a "religion" and other understandings of Judaism, they drew definitions that privileged expressions of Jewishness that fell within the purview of the synagogue and religious authority.

Patrilineal Descent: The Reform Movement Adapts to Interfaith Marriage

In 1983, shortly after the debate about custody and interfaith divorce, the Reform movement made another modification to its policies, largely in response to intermarriage. It redefined Jewishness in Reform interpretation of Jewish law. According to traditional Jewish law, Judaism was passed from mother to child.[19] The child of a Jewish father and a non-Jewish mother was not considered Jewish unless that child converted. Similarly, adopted children whose birth mother was not Jewish had to convert to be recognized as Jews. While the Reform movement had not always strictly observed this aspect of Jewish law, they formally accepted patrilineal descent in 1983. While this shift in policy was intended to more easily integrate interfaith families into Jewish life, it also put the Reform movement out of step with other definitions of "who is a Jew." Patrilineally descended Jews often found themselves shocked and dismayed when they moved outside of Reform communities and discovered that other Jewish communities and the nation state of Israel did not consider them to be Jewish. While Reform policy aimed to be more inclusive, their policy sometimes made the experience of interfaith family members more confusing and, at times, more painful. The Reform movement had made alterations to that law at other moments in their history, deciding in 1947 that infants or school-aged children would be considered Jews if they were raised as Jews, a decision that was aimed at children adopted into Jewish families. The same policy noted that once a child was old enough to give consent to his or her religious identity, he or she still needed to convert.[20] These decisions, however, were about adoption, not about patrilineal descent. Reform leaders were willing to dispense with matrilineal descent if a child was adopted into a Jewish home with two Jewish parents. While the policy set a precedent that opened the possibility of considering children with a Jewish father and a non-Jewish mother to be Jewish, it did not actually do so.

By 1961, the CCAR had changed its focus from adoption to the biological children of Jewish men and non-Jewish women.[21] That year, the Rabbi's Manual noted that while Jewish law allowed children of mixed marriages to join a synagogue or marry a Jew without conversion only if their mothers were Jewish, "Reform Judaism . . . accepts such a child as Jewish without a formal conversion, if he attends a Jewish school and follows a course of studies leading to Confirmation. Such a procedure is regarded as sufficient evidence that the parents and the child himself intend that he shall live as a Jew."[22] The Rabbi's Manual was not a formal statement of policy, however, and did not provide a definitive statement on the status of the child of a Jewish father and a non-Jewish mother. It does, however, demonstrate that the Reform practice during the era when interfaith marriage first began to increase sharply was to quietly accept patrilineal descent when combined with participation in Jewish education.

On March 15, 1983, the CCAR at its ninety-fourth annual convention formally adopted the "Report of the Committee on Patrilineal Descent on the Status of Children of Mixed Marriages." Doing so allowed the movement to be more immediately accepting of the children of interfaith marriage, but it radically changed understandings of Jewish descent in the Reform movement (or at least in the governing bodies of the Reform movement) and meant that the Reform movement would have different definitions of Jewish identity than the other American Jewish movements. Henceforth, the Reform movement would consider ás Jewish any child with one Jewish biological parent, mother or father. "This presumption of the Jewish status of the offspring of any mixed marriage is to be established through appropriate and timely public and formal acts of identification with the Jewish faith and people," the report stipulated, before going on to note, "the performance of these mitzvot [commandments] serves to commit those who participate in them, both parent and child, to Jewish life. Depending on circumstances, mitzvot leading toward a positive and exclusive Jewish identity will include entry into the covenant, acquisition of a Hebrew name, Torah study, bar/bat mitzvah and Kabbalat Torah (Confirmation). For those beyond childhood claiming Jewish identity, other public acts or declarations may be added or substituted after consultation with their rabbi."[23] Essentially, the Committee on Patrilineal Descent decided that in order to be considered Jewish, a child had to be raised in a Jewish way, outlining a set of religious practices that counted as raising the child as a Jew. Without that upbringing, a child with one Jewish parent would not be counted as a Jew, even if the Jewish parent was the mother. With the proper upbringing, the child of a Jewish father would be considered Jewish. With this move, the Reform movement privileged education over Jewish law, but also argued that the education that occurred in religious institutions held more weight than the forms of Jewish practice that might exist in a home. No provision was made for children of interfaith marriage raised in homes that saw themselves as Jewish, but existed outside of institutional structures.

This move was a distinct shift from previous Reform policy not only because it added patrilineal descent but also because it argued that matrilineal descent, the traditional benchmark of Jewishness, was not sufficient to make a child Jewish—education was needed as well. This shift moved away from an ethnic to an educational model of Jewish identity. While it did not eradicate the ethnic component entirely—a Jewish parent remained necessary—for the first time in modern Jewish history, a Jewish mother was not sufficient to claim Jewish identity. The shift to an educational model also solidified an institutional focus on Jewishness because, for the Reform movement, Jewish education became necessary to claiming Jewish status along with affiliation with a formal community. This model, however, came into play at a time in American religious history when religious affiliation was declining and claims to white ethnic identity were rising.[24] As a result, a large number of interfaith households, whose lived experiences may have included elements of Jewish tradition, ritual, stories, and food, were excluded from "counting" as Jews. Similarly, this model, which privileged religious affiliation and education as defining Jewish identity, overlooked similar elements of Christian traditions that might have existed in those officially Jewish households.

The leadership had a number of justifications for this change, but their primary motivation was to address the rising rates of intermarriage.[25] "There are tens of thousands of mixed marriages," the report points out: "In a vast majority of these cases the non-Jewish extended family is a functioning part of the child's world, and may be decisive in shaping the life of the child. It can no longer be assumed a priori, therefore, that the child of a Jewish mother will be Jewish any more than that the child of a non-Jewish mother will not be."[26] In other words, the non-Jewish members of the child's family have the potential to culturally shape the child. In order to ensure that the child has an "exclusively" Jewish identity, the child needs to participate (exclusively) in institutionally sanctioned Jewish rituals. It is unclear how these rituals would mitigate the influence of the non-Jewish extended family, but they do provide clear markers of an identity. This focus on life-cycle rituals functions as a way of looking at Jewishness as participating in formal practices and education that could be regulated by the institution. Putting primacy on those practices and affiliations allowed the cultural milieu of family and home to recede in (formal) importance.

These policies meant that children of interfaith marriage raised in the Reform movement often considered themselves Jewish and were then surprised when they discovered that other Jews did not necessarily see them as Jewish. In my interviews with members of interfaith families, rabbis, and ministers, conducted between 2005 and 2013, people told stories of the pain caused by differing definitions of "who is a Jew." One conservative rabbi noted that it is often difficult and painful when an interfaith family moves from a Reform congregation to his and learns that, because the father is the Jewish parent, the children have to convert before they can have their b'nai mitzvah (coming of age ceremonies). While he reflected that they try to make trips to the *mikveh* for conversion feel like an organic part of the b'nai mitzvah process, adolescents are often taken aback to learn that they "are not really Jewish."[27]

Not only did the Reform move to accept patrilineal descent create potential fault lines in American Judaism, but it also resulted in children of interfaith marriage having complicated feelings for Israel. In my interviews, numerous adult children of interfaith marriage spoke of their fraught relationship with Israel. Unhappy with her second-class status as a patrilineal Jew, one woman, Alyssa, formally converted through the Conservative moment, though that does not make either her or her children Jewish according to Israeli law. She works as a director of education in a Reconstructionist community that accepts patrilineal descent, has a large number of interfaith families, and maintains commitments to Israel.[28] As a result, Alyssa often worries about the ramifications of teaching students to think of themselves as Jews and to feel connected to Israel, even as the Israeli state does not recognize them as Jews.[29] As she put it, "Israel does not care about me. I have right of return, and my children do. But that is not because they care about me. They care about my father. All because my Jewish parent is my father." Israeli law allows anyone with at least one Jewish grandparent to emigrate to Israel, but only those with matrilineal descent are considered Jews by the country's Orthodox rabbinate. As a result, even though Alyssa is raising her children to think of themselves as Jews, they cannot pass right of return to Israel on to their children and, should they move to Israel, they would be unable to access marriage or burial. While the Reform and Reconstructionist leaderships' decision to accept patrilineal descent was intended to welcome interfaith families into synagogues, and has been in many ways successful, it also created problems that the policies could not smooth away. While many Reform Jews whose identity depended on patrilineal descent were perfectly comfortable with the fact that not everyone considered them Jewish, others were not. In numerous conversations, people whose Jewish identity depended on patrilineal descent described being either hurt or angered by the fact that not everyone accepted them as Jews.

New Jews and Jewish Ethnicity

The policy decision to include interfaith families in Reform communities created problems for those of patrilineal descent and, furthermore, created tension within the communities themselves. As more and more non-Jews entered Jewish communal life as members of Jewish families, they changed the ethnic identity–based character of those communal organizations. Members complained to Alexander Schindler, UAHC president and the initiator of the outreach programs to interfaith couples, that their synagogues and community centers, formerly places to relax from life in a Gentile world, no longer provided ethnic enclaves. This concern extended to "New Jews," as converts were sometimes called.

In an attempt to mitigate such reactions, different Jewish communal organizations provided various programs. For instance, in 1981, Chicago's Spertus College hosted workshops on interfaith marriage, which included spaces for participants to "develop a personal response" to "intermarriage and New Jews." These workshops were intended both to help people air their feelings about people who were part of the Jewish community by marriage or conversion but who were not born Jewish and to explore ways to include them in communal life. Ironically, the presence of large numbers of converts created a new problem in Jewish communal life. People who had been born Jewish sometimes complained that these converts made synagogues feel less Jewish.[30] Thus, the Reform leadership's definition of a Jew as one who follows a set of beliefs and practices established by a religious institution conflicted with the lived reality of Jews who defined Jewishness as a hereditary identity shaped by tradition within the context of the family household.

These concerns pointed to an ongoing debate within the Jewish world. If formal Reform rhetoric, largely under the oversight of Alexander Schindler, understood conversion as an answer to the problem of intermarriage, members of congregations and families were less convinced by a purely institutionally religious understanding of what made someone Jewish. The religious answer had a certain utility, offering a potential solution to problems of intermarriage (via conversion) and divorce (via the hallmarks of institutional upbringing), but ongoing and new forms of communal discomfort underscored more culturally inflected understandings of identity.

The fact that Jewish communities pushed back against both "New Jews" and interfaith families indicated that the understanding of Judaism as a religion, accessible through belief and practice, did not sit well with everyone in Reform Jewish communities. The new members, some argued, changed the "feel" of Jewish communal life. Barbara Friedlander of Ohio wrote to Schindler in 1992, "I cannot find a Temple that feels 'Jewish.' . . . In a world where Jews are a minority, it was always comfortable to go to Temple and be with one's own. . . . It is comforting and familiar to be with people who share your heritage and religious beliefs, and who know what it is to be a Jew in a Christian world; a world which seems to have extended right into our Synagogues."[31] Jewish spaces began to feel less Jewish and ceased to operate as minority enclaves, protected from the dominant culture. Previously, synagogues, Jewish community centers, and other communal organizations offered spaces that served as ethnic enclaves. One could sprinkle Yiddish into conversation or make critical comments about "the goyim" and their dominant Christian culture. Once synagogues contained community members who had been raised in that dominant culture, they could no longer serve such a function, in part because their leadership tried to get them to downplay ethnic elements (such as the use of Yiddish, particularly to denigrate Christians) in order to be more welcome to interfaith families and New Jews and in part because Christian spouses meant that synagogues were no longer Gentile-free spaces. Interestingly, this discomfort existed despite the fact that conversion and often intermarriage required significant study. As a result, converts were often very knowledgeable about certain kinds of Jewish ritual life—at times more so than those born as Jews. Yet this knowledge was not sufficient to make the converts "feel Jewish" to many of their fellow congregants. Advice manuals did not address these experiences, and while the Reform movement tried to address them, their policy focused on concerns rooted in ritual, not on the question of what, precisely, made people Jewish. While the Reform leadership tried to define Jewish identity in terms of characteristics under institutional control, like educational and ritual requirements, those definitions often resulted in people who did not "feel Jewish" to their fellow congregants.

Ironically, some converts had both more Jewish knowledge and more robust (intentional) practice than many who were born Jews. Thus, the "interfaith" family with a convert (who was technically no longer interfaith, but still
often regarded as such) was more "Jewish" by the official standards of Reform
Judaism than born Jews who do nothing ritually. At the same time, they were
still, to a certain degree, outsiders and as a result retained a certain "interfaith"
status despite official protests that once a conversion occurred the families
were no longer interfaith. While those families were formally religiously
homogeneous, the converted spouse (or the Christian spouse in a Jewish
household) did not necessarily share the cultural capital of born Jews and
brought their own backgrounds to their new, Jewish lives. Those differences
sometimes changed the communities that they joined and were not always
well received by existing community members.

Religious Manuals: Defining Jews, Complicating Families

While the Reform movement's formal policies focused on institutionally
shaped aspects of Jewish identity, by the late 1980s and early 1990s, advice
manuals began to delineate potential relationships between "religious" and
"cultural" practice, where cultural practice was broadly defined to include
recipes and speech patterns, but also emotional responses, modes of buying
groceries, and parenting styles. That did not prevent people from trying to
draw boundaries, either in institutional settings or in private lives. While rabbis debated the role of the Reform movement in connecting interfaith families
to Judaism, couples themselves turned to advice manuals on how to navigate
interfaith family life.

Two manuals—Paul Cowan's *Mixed Blessings: Overcoming the Stumbling
Blocks to Interfaith Marriage* (1987) and Andrea King's *If I'm Jewish and You're
Christian, What Are the Kids? A Parenting Guide for Interfaith Families* (here-
after *What Are the Kids?*) (1996)—were written to encourage couples to
choose to maintain Jewish homes and families. Both books were widely
read: 80 percent of the couples that I interviewed in my ethnographic study
of forty interfaith families ad read one or both of the books as had all of the
religious leaders. Both texts are commonly found in the collections of public
libraries and have continued to be cited in work on interfaith marriage in the
decades since their publication. Paul Cowan was a Jew whose marriage to a
Unitarian-raised New Englander had been interfaith until his wife converted
to Judaism after fifteen years of marriage. Andrea King was an Episcopalian
married to a Jew and raising their son in a Jewish home.

By the time that Cowan wrote *Mixed Blessings,* he and his wife, Rachel, were prominent spokespeople for intermarriage within non-Orthodox Jewish communities. They staunchly supported intermarriage, while advocating for couples to maintain Jewish homes. In that capacity, they had led workshops on college campuses and at Jewish cultural centers such as the 92nd Street YMHA. The American Jewish Committee sponsored the Cowans' speaking tour of six cities, and they became sought-after speakers on intermarriage throughout the decade, talking at synagogues, Jewish community centers, and Jewish campus centers. King wrote *What Are the Kids?* at the request of Lydia Kukoff, who headed outreach to interfaith couples for the UAHC. Both of these manuals, then, were written by insiders from interfaith families who were writing with the authority of relationships with formal institutional affiliations and connections.

Both advice manuals argued that children would be confused and religiously troubled if they were raised with both Christianity and Judaism. While neither manual overtly claimed Judaism as the superior religion, they both advocated for Jewish families. Additionally, both addressed some of the conflicts that could arise in an interfaith family as a result of the differing backgrounds of the couple and offered coping strategies for them. The authors' understandings of religion and culture were central to their defense of a singularly Jewish interfaith home. As much as they tried to draw neat lines between religion and culture, between acceptable and unacceptable practices for interfaith families, and between Christianity and Judaism, however, their depictions of interfaith family life and social realities often undermined their own distinctions.

The Need for a Single-Religion Household

Both manuals established a need for a single-religion household. In doing this, they identified both Christianity and Judaism as "religions," a term that they do not define, but which is revealed to be tied to holiday celebrations, specific practices, community, and morality. While King and the Cowans suggest that Jewish education is important, they do not put participation in Jewish institutional life in the foreground. These are manuals for why and how to create a Jewish *home* after an interfaith marriage. Each author uses a combination of personal experiences and his or her work with other interfaith families in order to establish this as a necessity.

Cowan uses moments in the lives of his children to argue that the failure to choose a religion for his children confused them. At a Purim celebration, the Cowans' young son ran to Rachel, threw himself into her arms, and, fearful of the story's antagonist, exclaimed, "Hamon will not come for me, will he? I am only half-Jewish."[32] For the Cowan parents, this was a red flag.[33] In the fall of 2007, when Rachel spoke at a workshop for interfaith couples at a synagogue in Atlanta, Georgia, she described her thoughts at the time: "Hmm. You can't be half a religion."[34] Her comment clearly identified Judaism as a religion, a set of beliefs or factors fundamentally different from an ethnic or cultural identity, which could exist in fractional portions as the result of blended parentage.

The Cowans were similarly troubled when their daughter asked, "Mom, would it hurt your feelings if I said that I was Jewish?" The Cowans were concerned that their daughter felt that articulating her own religious identity implied choosing one parent and therefore potentially hurting or rejecting the other. In the book, Cowan suggests that while some families do not see incidents like these as problematic, he and his wife both felt in the moment that they were worrisome and had come to believe that eliding children's questions about religion with platitudes creates a "time bomb" that would blow up later, leaving older children confused about their identities. To him, any response that might have mitigated the children's confusion in the moment would only delay the problems of a fragmented identity. They would resurface later, he contends, potentially around major life events, like the death of a parent or grandparent, a wedding, or the birth of a child, and that when the problems emerged, they would be severe. For Cowan, no degree of religious blending was acceptable. The child needed to be raised in one religious tradition or another.

Rather than define what it meant to choose a single religion, Cowan demonstrates what such a choice could look like by tracing his own family's path. When Cowan used his own family life to suggest that one must (and can) choose one religion for an interfaith family, he honed in on aspects of Jewish identity that connected to specific practices that one could adopt. For Rachel, it became an identity, marked by those practices and education, to which one could convert. They provided their children with Jewish education, holidays, and ritual practice. He describes how Hanukkah and Passover slowly started to feel like "their holidays" and the family's Shabbat practice became "sanctified time."[35] The Cowan parents, both people who had grown up without strong connections to ritual practice, committed to a life marked with Jewish observance and, by this account, found deep meaning in it. Ultimately, Rachel Cowan decided that she had come to approach God from a decidedly Jewish place. With that realization, which her husband described with the explicitly Christian (and belief-oriented) term "an epiphany," Rachel

Cowan converted to Judaism. While her conversion was sanctioned by a religious institution, it grew out of the changes that she had made in her home and in her practice.

While Cowan depicts Rachel's conversion to Judaism as religiously efficacious, such that she was in rabbinical school while he was writing the manual, he also locates many of their ongoing differences in their separate heritages. He bases his explanation on ethno-therapy, a model of family therapy that the American Jewish Committee advocated as a form of family therapy. Ethno-therapy centered on helping people understand their interpersonal conflicts as rooted in culturally conditioned emotional responses. In advocating for ethno-therapy, experts, including psychotherapists, the American Jewish Committee, and Cowan himself, frame Jewish and Christian identity in cultural terms. As Cowan put it, "When people from different cultural backgrounds fall in love, rejoice together and grieve together, raise children together, they aren't doing so as undifferentiated white bread Americans, but as men and women whose responses to issues as major as life and death, as minor as food or the best way to spend leisure time, have been influenced by their cultural heritages."[36] He notes that couples who came to their workshops often thought that they had incompatible styles for human interaction when in fact they were experiencing cultural differences in their marriages. He draws many examples from his own marriage, saying that while political differences about Zionism or overt questions of faith life came up rarely, "Our tensions over household details recurred so often that we sometimes wondered whether our marriage could survive them."[37] These tensions, Cowan argued, were rooted in the fact that though both he and his wife were American, because of their backgrounds as a Jew and a WASP, they were not only religiously different but also from very different cultural backgrounds.

Cowan acknowledges that the late sixties and early seventies were times of a great deal of change in the structure of marriage. Having allowed for tensions caused by changing gender norms, he articulates some of the specifics that he believes to have been based in their Jewish and Unitarian upbringings. Cowan located many domestic differences in their different backgrounds, with the most striking difference in their styles of negotiating and arguing. Cowan came from a "very talkative Jewish family," his wife from a "reserved Protestant one."[38] He describes arguments thus: "I argue melodramatically, exaggerating to make my point, trying to drag Rachel's feelings out of her. But what I see as a natural, heated conversation threatens her with obliteration. I think I am expressing my emotions—she thinks I am bullying her. When she withdraws or begins to cry, I feel terrible because I've been raised to think that reserved people are calmer and wiser than I am.... So I try to heal the wound I've inflicted, hovering over Rachel, asking her how she is. I punish her with words. She punishes me with silences."[39] Eventually, the Cowans found a way to make their marriage work across their differences. Even when Rachel Cowan converted to Judaism and ultimately decided to become a rabbi, however, her style of argument did not change. Cowan notes that, now, in the middle of a fight, they can "pause ... and laugh at these familiar differences."[40]

The differences that Cowan pointed out were redolent with the kinds of stereotypes that define popular depictions—understandings of Jews as loud and emotional, WASPS as emotionally distant and painfully reserved. Cowan did not explore how these typologies might intersect with individual personalities; rather, he presents ethno-therapy as a way of seeing marital differences as rooted in culture rather than in personality. The emphasis on those differences complicates Cowan's assertion that a family can choose to exist in an exclusively Jewish modality. In this telling, Cowan suggests that because Rachel's conversion was religious in nature, it was also efficacious.

Like Cowan, Andrea King argues in *What Are the Kids?* that it is best for children to have one religious identity. She bases her opinion on her observations as an early childhood educator and explained that, after working with children for years and paying particular attention to children of interfaith marriages, she realized that a sense of identity was hugely important to young children. She also determined that "children who had a clear religious identity often demonstrated a level of self-esteem that seemed to be absent in children who had an ambiguous or mixed religious identity."[41] These children, she writes, felt a strong connection to their religious communities, to religious holidays, and to life-cycle events. In *What Are the Kids?*, King formulates religious identity as a matter of making it clear to the children that they are either Christian or Jewish, a distinction that she places largely in terms of clearly definable rituals and community.

King structures the manual around two composite families, the Graysons and the Cohens. As "composites," each family theoretically combined elements of the many interfaith families that King encountered as an educator, as well as through "personal observation, formal interviews, informal conversations, and discussion groups."[42] She maintains that the "statements, explanations, feelings, reactions and events presented in this book are true and were revealed to me over a ten-year period by scores of interfaith families."[43] She explains that, for the sake of simplicity, she has combined their accounts.

That act of redaction was, of course, an act of interpretation and therefore the families are as indicative of King's attitude and approach to interfaith families as they are of the families' experiences. The Grayson family, made up of a Jewish mother, a Christian father, and three children (spanning across elementary, middle, and high school), served as King's example of a family that chose to be both Christian and Jewish. Her depiction of them underscored her valuing of formal and institutional markers of religious identity. The Graysons decided to raise their children in both traditions because it seemed unfair to ask one parent to give up holiday traditions and also because they viewed the core messages of both traditions as fundamentally the same. The Graysons attended both church and synagogue on occasion, so that the children would be familiar with both services—"when to stand up and sit down," as their father put it, in King's words.[44]

King suggests that while the Graysons believed that they were raising their children in both religions, in fact, they were raising their children in neither, to the detriment of their children. She depicts their oldest child, Hannah, explaining, "I am not both, I am nothing. It is not like having a Japanese mother and an Eskimo father, so you are half Japanese and half Eskimo."[45] Through Hannah, King underscores the difference she sees between religious identities and ethnic or cultural identities. Combining religious identities made you neither, rather than the plurality possible when combining cultural identities. In short, multiculturalism was possible for King, and, when racialized, inevitable, but multireligiosity was not.

King did not specify why she saw religious identity as separate from ethnic identity, but some possibilities are evident in her description of their practice. Hannah continued: "You know, my parents are really proud that they raised us in both religions. . . . But I don't buy it. We have extra holidays but nothing else. It seems to me that a religion should help you deal with difficult situations, but I never got any consistent Jewish or Christian information on morality or anything like that. . . . I wish I had a religion that I grew up with. I'd like to have a religion that is like a hometown—something that you can think about and know that it is yours."[46] Hannah's example points to a difference between a collection of traditions that a family might maintain and membership in a community with a shared history and set of beliefs, values, and truth claims. Implicit in this example are two assumptions: the first assumption is that Jewish and Christian identities have those shared communal elements, in a way that Japanese or Eskimo identities might not. Second, King implies that for the Graysons religion was holidays and nothing more because they were participating in two religions. She does not explore the possibility that a single-tradition family could be similarly disengaged or a dual-tradition family might choose a robust engagement with multiple traditions and values.

King's critique of the Grayson method reveals her view of Christian and Jewish identity as rooted in religious education and traditional observance within a community context. Importantly, she draws a sharp line between religious differences and cultural differences. Both Cowan and King stress the importance of having one religion for a family, arguing that religion, unlike culture or ethnicity, cannot be blended. While neither delves deeply into questions of contradictory truth claims, it seems reasonable to assume that those concerns are a piece of why they assert that religions cannot be combined.

Why Choose Judaism?

Cowan and King both argue that Judaism is the religion that an interfaith couple should choose. They avoid arguments about Jewish continuity in favor of personal sets of reasons for the couple to choose a Jewish family life. King and Cowan understand the argument that choosing to follow both traditions is the fair path, as it does not privilege one spouse's heritage over the other. They suggest, however, that such a framing presupposes that Christianity and Judaism are equivalent and fails to take key differences into account. Cowan frames these differences in terms of what he calls cultural asymmetry and King in a dichotomy between Christianity, which she presents in terms of private belief, and Judaism, which she labels a religion and a culture. Cultural asymmetry allows Cowan to suggest that, in fact, a Jewish home is the more fair and healthy option, because it allows both partners to have a religious life that they would find enhancing and enjoyable. In order to make such an argument, however, he has to downplay cultural aspects of Christian identity, so as to minimize the potential loss for the Christian spouse.

Cowan argues that interfaith couples should choose to maintain Jewish homes because "Judaism and Christianity live and interact asymmetrically" on theological, cultural, and psychological levels.[47] Theologically, according to Cowan, because Christians believe in the Old Testament: "When Christians worship with Jews, there is almost nothing they cannot affirm. . . . They [may feel that Jesus is missing] but they can participate fully without reservation in the liturgical life of the synagogue, Holy Day rituals, even family rituals."[48] In this reading, Cowan actively perpetuates an understanding of Judaism as being, in essence, Christianity without Christ, a reading that requires downplaying huge aspects of both Christian and Jewish experience. He avoids the many differences between their worship experiences, home rituals, and holidays in order to argue that Christians can fit seamlessly into Jewish life. Cowan argues that this is not the experience of Jews worshipping with Christians, who find that "almost nothing is accessible, almost everything is problematic."[49] Not only are New Testament readings problematic for Jews, so are the reinterpretations of the Hebrew Scriptures in light of the teachings of the New Testament. Cowan does not address whether the *failure* to read Hebrew Scriptures in light of the New Testament would make those shared texts inaccessible to Christians—rather, he focuses on the fact that the texts themselves are shared.

Cultural asymmetry existed between Christians and Jews, according to Cowan, because Judaism is both a religion and a people. As Cowan put it, there are many people who consider themselves ethnically Jewish "even though they have no palpable religious commitment," a concept that can be supported by Jewish religious teaching.[50] By contrast, theologically, ethnic Christianity does not exist. Rather than being Christian because one's mother was a Christian, "one is a Christian because one has been baptized and seeks to live out the meaning of the baptismal covenant."[51] Christianity thus becomes, for Cowan, solely a creedal force, whose traditions and history carry no importance because they are not reinscribed by Christian theological traditions. The traditions of Judaism, which Cowan rooted in Jewish religious thought, therefore should take greater weight in the deliberations of interfaith couples.

Cowan locates psychological asymmetry in the historical relationship between Judaism and Christianity and the contemporary experience of living in a minority culture versus living in a majority culture. Problems occur as a result, often around the "December Dilemma"—the debate about how to navigate Christmas and Hanukkah. Jewish partners find themselves unwilling to have a Christmas tree in the house, but also feel guilty, because their Christian partner has embraced Jewish traditions. No matter how clearly they understand that "the tree [is] part of a Yuletide experience that is filled with happy memories," the tree "make[s] them feel like aliens in Christian America."[52] That said, the strength of their own reactions often surprises them. Cowan argues that it is their ethnic identity as a marginalized people that makes the Jewish partners in interfaith marriage unable to participate in Christmas festivities with the enjoyment that their Christian spouses find in Jewish ritual life.

According to Cowan's experiences with interfaith couples, in these situations the Christian partner often understands the Jewish partner as "stubborn." They see their Jewish partner as equal Americans rather than as part of an oppressed and "self-conscious minority group," and therefore expect them to have interior worlds similar to their own. Because they experience Jewish holidays as "enrich[ing] their lives, not threaten[ing] their identities," they neither see their holidays as potentially threatening to the Jewish spouse nor could they understand why their Jewish partner is not as accepting of Christian holidays as they are of Jewish ones. They would not necessarily see Christianity as theologically alien and ethnically threatening to their spouses, triggering for the Jewish partners a sense of being a cultural outsider as well as a stronger identification with Jews who have been persecuted by Christians.

Because of these three imbalances, Cowan argues, interfaith families function best as Jewish families. If the Christian spouse is a person of faith, she would be able to subscribe to all parts of her children's religious education, even if she personally believes in Jesus. If neither partner is a person of faith, the Jew still has a culture to impart whereas the Christian does not. In this understanding, ethnicity is culture: but ethnicities associated with Christianity do not create Christian culture. Lastly, the Christian partner could comfortably inhabit Judaism, while the Jew could not be at ease in a Christian setting.

Andrea King used her own experiences to make a similar argument about Jewish households being more successful because Christianity was a private set of beliefs while Judaism was a culture. King, an Episcopalian, and her Jewish husband selected Judaism for much the same reasons that Cowan delineated—King's husband wanted his child to identify as a Jew and was uncomfortable with the thought of a Christian family. King "felt that the Jewish worldview, with its emphasis on justice, freedom, and responsible action, would provide a solid moral foundation for raising a child."[53] She also found it acceptable that her child would not be Christian because she saw Christianity as a "private religious creed" and felt "no compelling need to bequeath [it] to [her] child."[54] In making this argument, she collapsed all of Christianity, including Catholicism and Orthodox Christianity, into Protestantism by framing it as a private religious creed, a matter of personal choice. The fact that she did not feel the need to pass her beliefs on to her child suggests that she does not connect belief to salvation. Her avoidance of strong truth claims is in line with the liberal end of the Protestant mainline, but is not a universal Christian viewpoint. Though reluctant, her husband rejoined organized Jewish life after their child was born, while King ceased to celebrate Christian holidays in her home, later telling her son that she celebrated Christmas privately, in her heart.

This version of Christianity, as a personal faith whose traditions one could sacrifice in the interests of family harmony, resonates throughout her advice manual. In this way, Christianity, which King refers to as her religion, is constructed exclusively as personal belief. One can be a Christian without participation in community or ritual. It is also deeply ecumenical, in that King's belief does not make such strong truth claims that she feels a need to share them with her child. Though King associated Christianity with beliefs, she did not explain the nature of her ecumenism. While there are a variety of Christian approaches to the idea of salvation apart from faith in Christ, King does not detail how she reconciled any theological understandings of concepts such as salvation or baptism with raising her son outside of the Church, a move that results in a depiction of Christianity simply as a set of personal tastes, rather than as a robust theological system, and one that suggests her own lack of education in the history and theology of Christianity.

Some of the sacrifices that King hints at in her own experience are reflected in her model Jewish interfaith family. While her composite husband, Sam Cohen, was not sure that he wanted his children to have a "religious background," he did want them to be Jewish.[55] "I want the boys to appreciate their cultural heritage, to know about Jewish ideas and history, to feel a part of that," King writes in the voice of Sam. "Since we don't live in a Jewish neighborhood, we're active in the temple. It gives the boys a sense of Jewish community. We also do many things to introduce them to Jewish traditions at home."[56] Jewish identity was marked by the inclusion of specific ritual acts such as circumcision for their sons and some Shabbat practice.

While Sam was ambivalent about religion, Kathy, the composite mother, had a strong relationship with Christianity. She continued to belong to a church for several years after they were married and, in small ways, continued her Christian practice. She kept a small live Christmas tree on their porch, even though it made Sam uncomfortable, and when the tree died, he asked her not to replace it. Sam's discomfort with Christianity and Kathy's belief that Judaism could provide her children with "meaningful traditions, holidays, ceremonies" and to feel that they "belonged to a religious community"[57] led the couple to decide that their family would be Jewish.

"I had to face the fact that raising the kids as Jews meant giving up my traditions and adopting Sam's," Kathy explained. "Since we wanted our kids to understand fully that they were Jewish, they had to live in a Jewish home. That meant no baptisms, no Christmas tree, no Easter eggs. I knew that we would not succeed in raising our children Jewish if I observed a different set of rituals and holidays than they did."[58] It also meant that she had to understand "that my kids would be different from me. It meant that there are things that I had been brought up with that I would never share with my kids." She had to "think about that for a long time before [she] could get comfortable with that idea,"[59] but in the end she did. Kathy remembered some initial sadness at giving up her traditions.

While the couple pointed to their solution as a compromise, with Sam taking on more Jewish practice than he might have preferred, his discomfort over Kathy's tree was seen as a reason not to replace the tree, whereas her sadness over the loss of Christmas and raising her children without her own traditions were losses that she was depicted as accepting. Like Cowan, King did not address the gendered aspects of her example. That said, in her "successful" interfaith family, she portrayed a woman who was willing to sacrifice her own traditions to prevent her husband's discomfort and because she felt it would be best for her children. Positing this difference in terms of Christianity as solely a religion, in this case, a belief system whose cultural elements were unimportant, in contrast to Judaism, defined as both religion and culture, helped to disguise the deeply gendered assumptions in Cowan's and King's accounts, both of which depict a traditional picture of a women's self-sacrifice for the good of her family.

Portraying Judaism both as faith and as a people and Christianity as a creed alone gave Cowan and King a rationale for creating Jewish interfaith families, but they were also simply reinscribing conventional wisdom that linked Christian expression to its faith claims alone. This view of the two religions has a set archaeology that enforced the idea that Judaism was an all-encompassing civilization while Christianity was acceptance of a particular religious belief. While these understandings of Christianity and Judaism animate Cowan's and King's works, they actually flip the power imbalance, arguing that in a secular world, Christianity's theology is meaningless, whereas the cultural and ethnic aspects of Judaism's civilization remain worth preserving.

Though seeing Judaism as a civilization and Christianity as a chosen belief system alone is a frequent distinction, it fails to capture much of Christian lived religion. Both Cowan's and King's treatments of Christmas reveal how nontheological practices shaped Christian experience and had the potential to shape interfaith family life, despite the authors' claims. The question of the Christmas tree served as a litmus test in debates about whether an interfaith family was "Jewish enough." For instance, often when an interfaith couple promised to maintain a Jewish home as a condition of having a Jewish wedding, the rabbi required that they promise not to observe Christmas at home. As already noted, Cowan supports this experience, using cultural asymmetry to suggest that a tree in the living room could make a Jew feel like an alien in his own home.[60] In his description of Jewish spouses celebrating Christmas with their future in-laws, Cowan writes, "They realize that they may be about to marry into a *religious culture* which could make their children feel Christian, not Jewish."[61] If a Christian spouse maintained aspects of their former tradition, that "religious culture" could create Christian children, not necessarily because those children accepted Jesus Christ as their Lord and Savior, but because of their attachment to holidays and other aspects of practice.

When combined with understandings about the transmission of culture, the unrealized idea of Christian culture, rather than creedal Christianity, complicates some of the solutions for negotiating Jewish identity formation in the interfaith family setting. As noted earlier, one marker of a Jewish home remarked upon when couples were arranging to be married by a rabbi was to forgo domestic celebrations of Christmas. Rabbis and other Jewish communal leaders suggested that interfaith families celebrate the holiday with Christian family members instead. King's advice manual demonstrates this approach. However, when the Cohen family decided to be Jews, that decision did not mean entirely rejecting either Kathy's tradition or her family.

King does not interrogate what it means to participate in family rituals from outside of the tradition. Rather, she suggests that linguistic separations would serve to establish separation between the Jewish children and the Christian practice. As the younger Cohen son, Zeke, explained, "I like Christmas at Grandma and Grandpa's house. . . . They have a Christmas tree, and we get presents, and Mom takes presents for everyone, even though it is not our holiday. Mom said it's like when we went to my friend Tai Wong's house for Chinese New Year. We can go to his house and help him celebrate his holiday, even if it is not ours."[62] In the Cohen family, there were clear demarcations of identity that even the children could articulate. As Zeke put it, we help them celebrate, but it is not ours. The issue at hand for the Cohens is related to practice; when they celebrate Christmas, they do so away from home, as guests of their children's grandparents. King essentially argues that the children could anticipate an annual ritual of Christmas in a family setting without it shaping their religious identity any more than sharing a friend's tradition, such as Chinese New Year, would. This was achieved by making linguistic distinctions, such as "we help [them] celebrate" and "it is not our holiday." These markers are ways of noting that participation in the ritual of a family Christmas celebration does not make the family Christian. This approach stands in sharp contrast to a number of children's books explored in the next chapter, which frame celebrating holidays with both families as part of the child's identity.

Nonetheless, there is no guarantee that the Cohen parents' depictions of Christmas as "not theirs" will prevent the kinds of "happy Yuletide memories" that Cowan attributes to the Christian spouses who do not want to give up the cultural, if not creedal, aspects of their childhood religious culture. While the text names Christianity as a set of potentially private beliefs, what the formerly Christian spouses recalled were the practices of their Christian lives.[63] When their children spend a holiday with their Christian grandparents, they, too, are participating in the practices even if the practices are not explicitly tied to a Christian theological system. Participating in practices shapes habitus (an individual's field of cultural play), but one cannot guarantee how the practices will shape the individual. An interfaith couple raising Jewish children cannot guarantee that, by framing Christmas as *other*, the children will experience it as other.[64]

Children's Books and the Jewish Interfaith Family

If the majority of advice manuals for adults were designed to convince interfaith couples to maintain Jewish homes, Jewish-owned presses also created a range of children's books to support Jewish children with Christian extended families. By and large, these books underscore the child's Jewish identity, while providing them with a framework to understand the non-Jewish members of their interfaith families, or the fact that one of their parents may not have shared the same Jewish identity. Books like *Mommy Never Went to Hebrew School* (1989), *Papa Jethro* (2007), and *Nonna's Hanukkah Surprise* (2015) demonstrate that these books had a long-standing market speaking to children of interfaith families, demonstrating that they could have meaningful relationships with their non-Jewish family members, while remaining firmly ensconced in Jewish identity.[65]

Mommy Never Went to Hebrew School, the earliest of the books, was written by Mindy Avra Portnoy, a Reform rabbi and published by Kar-Ben Copies, a press with the mission of publishing "high quality children's titles with Jewish content."[66] In 2017, they explicitly stated that their line includes titles that "reflect the rich cultural diversity of today's Jewish family." *Mommy Never Went to Hebrew School* presents a boy named David discovering that, when she was a little girl, his mother was Presbyterian. He learns about Mommy's conversion to Judaism, which is framed as something that happened for her, even though it happened in the context of marrying Daddy. Moreover, David learns that he is not the only person in his world whose family included conversion. "I wondered if I was the only kid whose mom wasn't always Jewish.

Then I found out that Aaron's dad is also Jewish by choice, and Sharon's mom is too."[67] Not only does David's world include adults who are Jews by choice, but kids can be as well. "My friend Sarah told me that she went to the *mikveh* when she was a baby, because she was adopted by Jewish parents." Furthermore, David learns that Jews by choice have an important role to play in Jewish history, as necessary and honored members of the community. "Ruth in the Bible had chosen to become Jewish. Ruth was the great-grandmother of King David."[68]

The messages in *Mommy Went to Hebrew School* served the Reform agenda, set out by Alexander Schindler, which depicts the "problem" of interfaith marriage as easily solved through conversion and suggests that Jews by choice are seamlessly blended into Jewish community. As a children's book, *Mommy Never Went to Hebrew School* skirts any hint of conflict at all, surrounding Mommy's conversion, her parents' feelings about it, or her acceptance into the Jewish community. Instead, it serves to reassure children of Jews by choice that they are fully Jewish in ways that are important and accepted in the Jewish community.

Papa Jethro and *Nonna's Hanukkah Surprise* are much more recent books, the first also written by a Reform rabbi and the second written by a Jewish woman in tribute to her Christian mother-in-law.[69] These books do not explore the child's nuclear family story, which could either be interfaith or conversionary, focusing instead on their relationships with their non-Jewish grandparents. In *Papa Jethro*, Grandpa Nick visits his granddaughter Rachel. As they play together, he tells her a story about Gershom, son of Moses, and his grandfather Jethro, the Midianite priest. Gershom teaches Jethro about being Jewish, just like Rachel teaches Grandpa Nick. While Papa Jethro and Grandpa Nick share themselves with their grandchildren, they do so using sweets and, in Jethro's case, language—things that can be shared without challenging a Jewish religious identity. *Nonna's Hanukkah Surprise* features another main character named Rachel, this time one who visits her Italian grandmother for Christmas. Rachel is looking forward to sharing Hanukkah with Nonna, but she accidently leaves her hanukkiah, or menorah, on the airplane. Nonna comes to the rescue, making a new one out of perfume bottles.

In these books, grandparents find ways to share of themselves with their grandchildren, while supporting and learning about their grandchildren's Jewish identities. The message of these books is one of uncomplicated love between grandparent and grandchild, in which their differences can actually bring them closer. The child's strong, uncomplicated, and not at all hybrid Jewish identity also gives the message that children of interfaith extended (and sometimes nuclear) families can have a singular, Jewish identity. These children's books, then, written over a span of twenty years, articulate a very similar message to that of Cowan's and King's advice manuals. A singular religion is a possible and desirable option for the children of interfaith marriages.

Since 2005, an organization called PJ (short for pajama) Library has distributed free books and music to Jewish and interfaith families. The organization, founded by Harold Grinspoon, partners with synagogues, Jewish federations, and Jewish community centers to encourage families to sign up and receive their books and music, with the ultimate goal of strengthening "individual families' connections to Jewish organizations, and [nurturing] family members' perception of themselves as part of an imagined Jewish community."[70] According to Rachel Gross, PJ Library is "one of the most influential Jewish organizations in North America" and focuses on making selections that will draw unengaged families into Jewish life.[71] PJ Library's assessments of their own programming have found that 90 percent of the families who receive their books are very satisfied with their materials and that the majority of their participants have experienced increased engagement with their Jewish heritage and practice as a result of their participation. Fewer families (30 percent) say that they have become more engaged with Jewish communal life, though that may not be surprising because most participants connect with PJ Library through some form of Jewish organization and therefore were already participating in the community to at least some degree. Significantly, the majority of participants also argue that their family feels more positive about their Jewish identity through their involvement with PJ Library.[72]

While PJ Library targets families that are not highly engaged members of Jewish life, whether or not both parents are Jewish, about 20 percent of the people they serve are in interfaith marriages, and PJ Library has been generally responsive to the requests of their "constituents."[73] As they do so, they have moved from representing primarily white families with two Jewish parents to a much more racially diverse Jewish landscape, covering adoption and interfaith extended families, with the message that the children in these families are Jews.[74] PJ Library includes reading guides and activities to accompany their books, both of which can assist non-Jewish parents in explaining Jewish practice or heritage to their children, and the positive feelings toward Jewishness that the books engender may have actually resulted in some non-Jewish parents converting.[75] While PJ Library, then, reaches out to all Jewish and interfaith families with a Jewish parent, they do so in part to underscore the Jewish potential of those interfaith families, increasing both their sense of themselves as Jewish and, likely, their acceptance as Jewish by the larger community.

Conclusion

Through the course of my research, I have been told the same joke, usually in interviews but also while mingling after formal presentations. A young Jewish man goes off to college. "Have a wonderful time," his father says. "Experience life! Just do not marry a *shiksa*!" At some point, the young man comes home and says, "Dad, I love college. And I have met a wonderful woman. She isn't Jewish, but she says that she will convert. So it is okay, isn't it?" The father loves his son, and the young woman is willing to convert, so what can he do? He says okay. A few years later, the young couple has returned to live in the husband's hometown and one day his father calls him. "Son, I just got the most amazing seats for the game this Friday night. I'll pick you up at 7." "Dad, I can't go to a game on a Friday night. It's Shabbos—we have people coming for dinner." To which his father responds, "Son, I told you not to marry a *shiksa*!"

This joke, just like Charlotte's banning of the Mets game from her Shabbat dinner, underscores a common perception of interfaith marriage: a non-Jewish woman will agree to raise Jewish children, but she will insist, with the fervor of a convert, that they be far more observant than the husband or his family would have been otherwise. In part, the adherence to religious practice is something under the control of the convert (or the still-Christian mother raising Jewish children) and therefore something she could use to be accepted by the family's Jewish community. Acquiring ethnic identity, however, was much more elusive, if not impossible. Women often rely on this ritual- and religious community–oriented conversion in part to make up for what they have lost—both Rachel Cowan and Kathy, King's composite mother, reflect on how the loss of their own traditions matters less as they come to love the Jewish traditions of the family that they have created. They also emphasize those practices because "religious conversion" is possible in a way that cultural conversion is not. One can fulfill the ritual requirements to become a Jew and live some degree of Jewish life, but one cannot erase one's own early formation or acquire a grandmother with a family recipe for gefilte fish. To make this dynamic successful, the Reform leadership and, in certain ways, the authors of the advice manuals frame Judaism as a religion to which one could convert and adopt through taking on set Jewish practices, an attitude espoused by the Reform leadership, but not necessarily by members of

Reform communities. In this sense, then, non-Jewish women who became Jewish (or agreed to raise Jewish children) did so with an understanding of Jewishness that does not necessarily match the expectations of their spouses. Also, because of the tightly prescribed descriptions given of Judaism and Christianity, they could not help but bring elements of a Christian background into their homes, despite their best efforts to the contrary.

While books for adults tackle the problems that the Reform movement identified as occurring in interfaith marriages, books for children emphasized that, despite having parents who were not Jewish or who had not grown up Jewish, the children could have uncomplicated Jewish identities. These books encouraged loving grandparents across religious differences—and even finding those differences to be interesting—while underscoring the support of Christian grandparents for their grandchildren's Judaism. The children's books do not tackle the questions or challenges handled in the advice manuals, but do suggest space for a diversity of families in Jewish life.

The official position of the Reform movement and the position articulated by advice manuals and children's books produced in concert with the Reform leadership spell out concerns both about the religious fate of the children of interfaith marriage and about Jewish survival. They argue that such families should choose one religion, Judaism, for their households. The ability to do so, or even to define what made someone Jewish, remains fluid even in discussions about how to create such families. Increasingly, Jewish identity is defined according to institutional involvement, such as participation in Jewish education or religious services. Families are also encouraged to incorporate some Jewish practice into their home lives. Jewish identity, however, is as marked as much by the *absence* of Christian practice in the home as it was by the *presence* of Jewish practice.

Religion, culture, and ethnicity were unstable terms in the debates about interfaith marriage in the 1980s and early 1990s. For those claiming that it was both possible and desirable for an interfaith marriage to result in a Jewish home, two competing definitions of Judaism held strong currency. On the one hand, it made sense to establish Judaism both as a religion (implicitly defined by Cowan and King as a system of beliefs and a defined set of practices, located largely in synagogues, but also including Shabbat dinner and sometimes kashrut) and as a culture (implicitly defined as membership in the Jewish people with a sense of European Jewish history and marginalization within the broader culture) and to contrast that definition with one of Christianity as based exclusively in belief. Those definitions allowed for the construction of compelling arguments for choosing Judaism as the household religion.

At the same time that one line of argument fused Jewish religion and Jewish culture, the Reform movement had compelling reasons to create a definition that rested heavily on Judaism as rooted in participation in Jewish communal life. Both of these arguments had internal inconsistencies and created tensions in other aspects of the Jewish community. Nevertheless, they were definitions that served a particular need: they offered a way to expand Judaism to include the intermarried, but with very specific, and often ideologically driven, definitions of what an "intermarried" household should look like as it maintained the authority of Jewish leaders and institutional religion.

These definitions did not incorporate the full range of interfaith family discourse, even for people who chose Jewish affiliation for their families. Patrilineally Jewish children of intermarriage were accepted by the Reform and Reconstructionist movements, but not by other branches of Judaism, a tension that destabilized strong Jewish identity among those who might cross movements. Jewishly affiliated interfaith families who barred Christian practices from their homes often created family traditions that involved celebrating those banned holidays with other family members, as their religious leadership suggested. Other families formally affiliated with Jewish communities while hiding the fact that they also celebrated Christmas at home. While Christian practices were removed from the home, they were not removed from the familial experience of the children. In effect, then, the understandings of Judaism and Christianity articulated in the Reform leadership's attempts to address interfaith marriage were strategic, designed to encourage Jewish homes, but were not necessarily descriptive of lived experiences, either of Jewish or Christian identity or practice.

CHAPTER FOUR

They Sure Will Be of Minority Groups
Interreligious, Interracial, Multiethnic Jewish Families

In a letter to the writer Alice Walker, the woman he would soon marry, Mel Leventhal wrote, "I have sent you, via first class mail, a surprise. . . . *The Collected Poems of P. L. Dunbar.* You mentioned to me that you would like such a book and so I decided to buy it for YOU, me, and THE CHILDREN. We must have books like this readily available for their scrutiny or casual glances. Ain't no one goin' to tell my children that they ain't got no heritage, except for Mammy. I think that we shall have to get some more Jewish stuff also and also some books on American Indians—If there is anything they shall not be ashamed of it is their black and indian and jewish blood. (I must admit it: they sure will be of minority groups.)"[1] Within this simple missive lies a complex dynamic of interfaith family life: the multifaceted conversation among the subjects of race, ethnicity, gender, and religion at play when an interfaith family is also an interracial one. For Leventhal, this dynamic involved embracing his potential children's status as "double minorities," African American and Jewish at the same time. This attempt to blend distinct racial, religious, and ethnic identities raises profound questions about the definitions of those terms.[2] Indeed, for interfaith families of color, at least one identity remains written on the children's skin. Yet, even when these families formally identify as Jewish, they must determine how to acknowledge a second minority heritage or status in the family's life.

As the previous chapter noted, starting in the 1970s, the Jewish communal response to intermarriage, spearheaded initially by the Commission on Reform Jewish Outreach, had been to encourage interfaith couples to live Jewish lives. Most rabbis willing to perform interfaith marriages did so on the condition that the couple maintain a Jewish home and, should they have children, educate them as Jews. While there was no broad consensus as to what constituted raising children as Jews and maintaining a Jewish home, the definition most often rested on Jewish education for children and on the exclusion of Christian practice. Rabbis and Jewish educators explained that children would absorb the dominant culture of American Christianity from their environs and that because Judaism was the minority culture, parents needed to create a Jewish home to nurture a specifically defined Jewish identity. While

Jewish couples were free to choose their level of observance or assimilation, interfaith couples were often required to maintain "good" Jewish homes.

The narrative models that Jewish institutions developed to incorporate white interfaith families into Jewish communal life often did not work well for interracial families for reasons that differed from the tensions faced by "traditional" interfaith couples. First, in the United States, the dominant image of Jews is of Ashkenazi—white, Eastern European Jews. As a result, Jews of color, including children of interracial, interfaith families, find their status as "real Jews" questioned both within and outside of the Jewish community. Second, the black and Latino children of these interfaith, interethnic families need skills to exist as people of color in a racist society. Families often tried to supply these skills by drawing on the family culture from the non-Jewish side of the family, but the resulting family cultures sometimes placed the family at odds with the parenting norms of their chosen and predominantly white Jewish communities.

Most importantly, the argument for a singularly Jewish home rested strongly on the minority status of the Jewish spouse. Because the Jewish spouse had to live life outside of the home under the yoke of the dominant culture, it was, these advocates argued, unfair to take away the home as a refuge from Christian life. Someone faced with Christmas trees and carols in public should not have to contend with them at home. For interfaith families in which the Christian spouse was not white, however, the Ashkenazi Jewish parent often lost the status as the singular religious or ethnic minority in the family. Instead, that person became the parent with the racial privilege of being considered "white" in the United States. In an attempt to raise children who were Jewish but also equipped to survive as black or Latino, families often bent the rules of what it meant to be an "acceptable" interfaith family—ensuring that their children were literate members of both parents' ethnic and sometimes religious communities. While Jewish communities were not always perfectly receptive to the needs and choices of interracial families, they recognized the minority status of black or Latino parents and allowed the interracial families more flexibility in how to combine traditions than they would for white interfaith families. Ultimately, these interracial families redefined and reshaped what the terms "race," "ethnicity," and "religion" mean in an increasingly multicultural American landscape.

Two Religions, One Race: The White Interfaith Family in Jewish Community

In my interviews with interfaith couples, I spoke with many couples in the model of interfaith family most often depicted in advice literature: Ashkenazi

Jewish men married to white Christian women. Jewish husbands often insist on maintaining a Jewish home, but then they not only expect their wives to do the work entailed in creating such a home but also demonstrate an ambivalence about Jewish practice. Their Christian (or post-Christian) wives therefore find themselves trying to guess what aspects of Jewish life might matter to their husbands while attempting to navigate Jewish life with less support from their husbands than they might prefer. These women found themselves responsible for life-cycle events such as brises and b'nai mitzvah, without fully understanding what had happened at the events or why their husbands and in-laws valued the events.

Similarly, Jewish husbands were deeply uncomfortable having Christmas trees in their homes or allowing their children to participate in Easter egg hunts. This reluctance frustrated their Christian wives, who understood that these practices were associated with Christian holidays, but saw them as essentially nonreligious cultural practices. The women noted that bunnies and eggs have nothing to do with the Resurrection and that Christmas trees are similarly disconnected from Christian theology. Their husbands still expressed concern that the presence of these practices would, in some way, make their children Christian, or at the very least, less Jewish. Experiences like those of the couples I interviewed are well documented, partly in scholarship and partly in journalistic accounts of interfaith family life.[3]

In *Jewish on Their Own Terms*, Jennifer Thompson explains that this dynamic occurs in part because the Jewish partners understand being Jewish in terms of "what you are," rather than in terms of "what you believe."[4] Jewish practices do not matter because of what they mean, but because they provide Jewish experiences; therefore, while the men valued their children participating in Jewish rituals, they had a hard time articulating to their wives what those rituals meant or why they were important. Similarly, for these men, being Jewish depends in part on abstaining from Christian rituals, whether or not those rituals are connected to theology. Thompson's point—that for these men Jewish identity depends on experiences, rather than belief—helps to explain both some of their own ambivalence about and their reluctance to have seemingly Christian rituals in their homes. At the same time, she points out that these interfaith couples, like many other Americans, feel free to select individual practices and shape their own paths through their Jewish identities. These differing perspectives added to the tensions created by the gender dynamics of Christian mothers doing the work of raising Jewish children.

Gender is a dominant factor in shaping the experiences of interfaith families. By and large, when Jewish communal institutions have reached out to interfaith families, they have done so by offering support to couples like the ones that I described—white Christian women married to Jewish men. While sometimes I interviewed couples together, I usually spoke with the husband and wife separately. These conversations revealed some of the tensions inherent in a gender dynamic in which the Christian women are doing the work of raising Jewish children, in order to fulfill an agreement with their Jewish husbands. Certainly, the women chose to raise Jewish children, but they are often then surprised that their Jewish husbands are not active participants in the project. Many women expressed dissatisfaction with their husbands' levels of involvement in maintaining Jewish homes, and many of the husbands wondered about their wives' motivations in complying. While they were pleased that they had agreed to raise Jewish children, they worried that the commitment would not last or that their wives might try to "slip some Christianity in" to their homes. Sometimes the husbands expressed gratitude for the work that their wives did to maintain Jewish homes, but some of the husbands also occasionally expressed frustration that their wives did not do more to create meaningful Jewish experiences for their children.

For a variety of reasons, scholarship has tended to focus on families in which Christian women and Jewish men are raising children, though Keren McGinity has written about Jewish women and how their interfaith marriages shape their self-understanding as Jews.[5] For that reason, I want to turn now to interfaith couples in which the wife/mother is Jewish and the husband/father is Christian, or, as was more often the case in my sample, had grown up Christian. This is not always the case, of course, but in the vast majority of the families that I interviewed in which the mother was Jewish and the father had Christian heritage, the husband/father was no longer a practicing or believing Christian when he met and married his Jewish wife. Some men noted real anger or resentment about their upbringing; for instance, during one interview, one formerly Catholic father asked why on earth he would ever expose his children to the dangers of the Catholic Church, referring to the Catholic sex abuse scandals. These men were happy to cede the raising of their children to their Jewish wives.

Many of the men I spoke with, however, did not particularly resent their Christian upbringings. Some men came from families who had not been particularly defined by their Christianity—several people talked about the sense that the family went to church so that the children would have some Sunday school, but the church community was not central to the family identity and faith was not foundational for their lives. For others, Christianity was a powerful force in their childhoods, both in terms of the church community and as an orienting belief structure. As they grew into adulthood, however, these men found themselves moving away from the communities and beliefs that they were raised with and becoming unaffiliated Americans. They did not necessarily wholeheartedly reject their upbringings—they went home for Christmas with their families. They went to church for weddings and funerals. They may even have assumed that they, too, would take their children to Sunday school if they ever had any. They did not, however, tend to go to church, and their religious beliefs were largely extraneous to their lives, if they existed at all.

These families, in which Jewish women were raising Jewish children with support from men who were nominally Christian or who no longer identified as Christian, noted that they were expected to raise children who seamlessly blended into the Jewish context. Often, that was not difficult for them to do. Rachel noted that her scientist husband, Paul, had not seemed strongly attached to having his children connected to Christianity. Before they were married, when they talked about children, she agreed that the children would have his last name; he agreed that their children would be Jewish. Because his own parents divorced after he grew up, Christmas made Paul sad and he did not want to commemorate the holiday in their home. As the cook in the family, he was happy to make traditional foods for Jewish holidays, and he supported his wife in a family Shabbat tradition of challah and a special dessert from their local bakery followed by family movie night.

When she and I first spoke about the nature of their interfaith family life, she wistfully reflected that it would be nice if he shared in the Jewish part of her life, but observed that there was no tension about having their children be Jewish, rather than Christian. It was just that Paul was not interested in organized religion or in participating in religious community. As a result, she felt that her engagement in the community disrupted their time together as a family. She did not like sitting alone in the synagogue on holidays. She did not like feeling like she was dragging him along, reluctant, not about Judaism but about religion.

Over the course of my field work, however, the dynamic in that family changed. Paul found a community in the synagogue and became deeply involved in their music program. At their daughter's bat mitzvah, he observed to their assembled guests (including many of his Presbyterian relatives), "When we married, I agreed that Rachel could raise our children Jewish. I thought that would probably be a good thing. I also thought she would be primarily responsible for it. I guess I thought I would offer them discourses on chemistry. But this has become something we do as a family, and I am so glad to have become a part of it." Rachel and Paul's family had become, essentially, a Jewish family. They occasionally spent Christian holidays with members of Paul's family, but for a constellation of reasons, including commitment to Judaism and Paul's family history, there were no moments of Christian cultural practice in their home.

Alyssa Wolin Jackson, the education director at a liberal synagogue and the child of a Jewish father and Christian mother, converted to Judaism when she married her non-Jewish husband. After growing up in a religiously unaffiliated home, she embraced Judaism as an adult, but also fell in love with a non-Jewish man. Like Rachel and Paul, Alyssa and Matt came to an agreement involving a negotiation of religion and names. Alyssa did not particularly want to change her last name, but Matt, who is from Texas, felt very strongly that everyone in the family should have the same last name. Alyssa agreed to change her name, and in trade, Matt agreed that the children would be raised Jewish. In order to secure their Jewish identity, Alyssa converted so as to, in the best way possible, secure her status as a Jewish mother.

Alyssa and Matt are actively involved in Jewish communal life—she through the education program and he through the music program. Their home is kosher, though sometimes, for Matt's birthday, Alyssa picks up bacon at a takeout breakfast place, and he eats the bacon on the back porch. Their children attend Hebrew school, have modern Israeli names, and say the Shema every night before bed. Since they do not celebrate Christian holidays in their house, the family travels for Christmas, alternately going to Texas to join Matt's parents or to the Northeast, with Alyssa's Christmas-celebrating interfaith family.

Their home is infused with Jewish life, and their community is largely the Jewish community. Still, Alyssa and Matt wonder how much to let their children experience mainstream Christian culture. The Charlie Brown TV shows were very important to Alyssa and her sisters while they were growing up—a huge piece of family culture. The year that she first showed her son *It's the Great Pumpkin, Charlie Brown*, Alyssa wondered whether they should avoid *A Charlie Brown Christmas*, with its scrawny Christmas tree and recitation of sections of the Gospel of Luke. Matt deferred to her: "You are the Jewish parent," he said. And, on the day after Thanksgiving, she popped the DVD in the DVD player. But she also noted that, as a religious education director, she knows that she struggled with the question of whether or not to let her children have access to Christian popular culture far more than the Jewish parents in the congregation did—and, to a certain extent, more than interfaith couples who were not "second-generation interfaith." Indeed, while I was doing field work, the Jackson daughter made me a birthday card for my January birthday, and Alyssa was clearly a bit embarrassed that the card had a Christmas tree.

Matt noted that their son, in particular, is very interested in Judaism and also in big questions about the nature of the world, about life and death, and about the supernatural. He realized how different their son's mental world is from his own. They were in Texas at Christmastime, and they went to a drive-in nativity with Matt's father and stepmother. The nativity told the story of Christ's birth, and it continued past the Christmas story to some key Gospel moments and the Resurrection. Matt's son, Ari, who was six years old, was very curious about who Jesus was. Matt and Alyssa told him that Jesus was a man who lived a long time ago, and who was an important teacher. As they drove away, Ari looked out the back window and waved. "Goodbye, man!" he called. It was, Matt reflected, really quite odd to realize that that his son, who knew countless prayers in Hebrew, who was aware of Rabbi Akiva, who played puppets pretending to be the rabbi and the cantor of their congregation, did not know who Jesus was. It was even more striking because they live in the South, surrounded by Christians. While Matt and Alyssa did not set out to hide Jesus from their son, they had intentionally created such an exclusively Jewish world for their children that they did not know basic elements of their father's heritage—like the identity of Jesus.

For families like Rachel and Paul's, the commitment to Jewish life grew organically in their family, in part because Rachel was in charge of the household's Jewish life and had grown up in a Jewish context. For Alyssa and Matt, the process was more deliberate—Alyssa found herself actively selecting which aspects of her own upbringing seemed acceptable in her Jewish home, perhaps especially considering that she ultimately became a Jewish professional. Her example is not uncommon. Increasingly, the "Jewish parent" in an interfaith marriage is herself the child of an interfaith marriage. (While my qualitative research did not generate a large enough sample to make demographic claims, I found many more examples of women raised by interfaith parents affiliating with Judaism in adulthood, despite their own interfaith marriages.) These families find themselves more actively policing the presence of Christian practices in their homes, even when they are not in interfaith marriages.

Lillian grew up celebrating Christmas in her mother's home, even though her Jewish mother and Catholic father were no longer married to each other.

(Her mother did not want their "broken home" to cost her daughters a beloved celebration.) As an adult, Lillian continued to have a Christmas tree, despite the fact that she identified as a Jew and married a Jewish man. To her, the tree was not a symbol of assimilation—it was a connection with her childhood and her Catholic father. Lillian only stopped putting up the tree when her children's Hebrew school director told her that she needed to stop celebrating Christmas because doing so would confuse her children. Lillian was troubled by this explanation—she did not feel that her Jewish identity had been compromised by celebrating Christmas. At the same time, she did not want to cross the Hebrew school, or the standards of the community that she had joined, and so she got rid of her tree.

Jewish communities interact with interfaith families in a broad range of ways, but certainly they often discourage including Christian practices (specifically tied to Christmas) in Jewish-affiliated homes. Repeatedly, when I talked to interfaith families who chose to remove Christianity from their homes, they did so out of concern about acceptance in Jewish communal life. They worried about how the other children in Hebrew school would react if their children had Christmas trees or Easter baskets. They strove to create children who could blend into Jewish communal life, and, perhaps more importantly, other members of their families and communities supported these choices.

Whether or not it is true that interfaith families can seamlessly assimilate into Jewish contexts (and both my work and Thompson's suggest that the presence of interfaith families changes what Jewish communities look like), the perception is that these families can blend in—that the white, Jewish children created by interfaith families can become Jewish on the terms of the community, rather than, in Thompson's phrase, Jewish on their own terms. This logic is further supported by the sense that Judaism is the minority tradition. Its minority status both causes people to argue that Judaism needs protection from the Christian majority in order to thrive and that the Jewish partner needs to have a space to retreat from life as a minority in a dominant Christian culture. Keeping the house free from elements of a spouse's Christianity allows the home to provide that space.

As a result, white interfaith families who choose to affiliate with Judaism are less likely to have access to multicultural models of interfaith family life. As it turns out, however, interfaith couples who are also interracial find themselves more able to assert Jewish identity, while combining that identity with aspects of the Christian parent's tradition.

Why Do They Call My Afro a Jew-fro?
Black and Jewish in the American South

When William became a bar mitzvah, his Torah portion, *Chayei Sarah*, contained a depiction of slavery. As William's rabbi put it, writing for the Ritual Well website,[6] "As a young Southern Jewish African-American, [William] wondered what it meant to enter into Jewish adulthood with a Torah that embraced, accepted and, perhaps, even advocated for slavery."[7] William is the child of an interfaith marriage between his Jewish, Ashkenazi mother and his Baptist-raised, African-American father. His parents agreed from the start that he would be raised Jewish, but for them, the boundaries between Judaism and William's father's background are more porous than for many interfaith families. The family is very aware that, Jewish or not, the world will perceive William as black; that, being black, he will find himself fielding the realities of American racism; and that while there certainly are other African-American Jews, racism will be as present within the Jewish community as outside of it. In addition, the family is aware that there is a power imbalance, informed by race as much as by religion, through which their families might read their choices. Because of race, this power dynamic is different than that of the more "expected" interfaith family.

Helen Wilson and Andrew both framed their backgrounds in terms of class and food culture as much as race or religion. Helen comes from the industrial northeast and explained that her own parents were Reform, and her father was quite involved in the Reform temple—he taught Sunday school and took the kids on most Friday nights. Her maternal grandfather was the son of a Jewish scholar in Russia. According to the family story, he became Nathan Starr because they could see billboards for Nathan's hot dogs and Starr hot dogs from Ellis Island. He married an American Jew, Helen's grandmother, and together they were members of an Orthodox synagogue. Her paternal grandfather was the son of a Polish tailor, who worked in a Jewish deli and as a tailor. Her paternal grandmother came to the United States with her siblings, fleeing the Holocaust. Neither of Helen's paternal grandparents were members of synagogues.

The family's interactions with food were indicative of the role that Judaism played in their daily lives. Helen observes that all of her grandparents were "Jewish through food."[8] They appreciated specifically Ashkenazi food, such as matzoh ball soup, and knew where to buy good deli items. Growing up, Helen's parents' household was not kosher, though they did not bring pork or shellfish into the house. They did, however, trap lobster and dig clams off the Massachusetts coast, but those things would be eaten on the beach or on the porch. Chinese food was eaten on the couch, rather than at the table, and Helen had her first pork chop after meeting her husband. The food practices that Helen is describing demonstrate how Jewish identity can be maintained through practices that reference, rather than strictly adhere to, Jewish law. Helen's family did not keep kosher in the strictest sense of the term—they ate shellfish and pork-heavy Chinese food, but they restricted where such food could exist. It was not eaten at the dining-room table. In doing so, the food was marked as something to be kept apart from the daily meals, and pork was not eaten as part of the routine family diet. In these ways, the inclusion of Jewish dishes, and the boundaries placed around the consumption of *treyf*, the family used food to underscore Jewish identity. Later, in her interfaith marriage, Helen would exhibit similar flexibility.

Helen's family had a history of interfaith relationships. According to Helen, for forty years, her paternal grandfather lived with her parents, and her paternal grandmother lived with a non-Jewish man, to whom she pretended to rent a room. He moved out only to go to an assisted living community, at which point Helen's grandmother visited him every day. He was, Helen explained, "the love of her life." In describing her grandmother's attitude toward romantic relationships with non-Jews, Helen reflected, "When I was in college and had a Chinese boyfriend who my nana really liked, she told me to live with him but not to disgrace the family by marrying him. She was ahead of her time but could never imagine a world where I would marry a black man and my sister a Guatemalan man, both of whom would commit to raising Jewish children."

Helen grew up in a working-class, urban family with two children; Andrew grew up on a hog farm in the rural South, one of the youngest in a large African-American family. He had been a bookish child and had sometimes been accused, by family members, of "acting white" when he showed an interest in school. Going to college and getting a graduate degree had further distanced him from his family. When I asked him if he was worried that it would be hard for his son to be black and Jewish, he responded that he was more worried that it would be hard for William to be black and smart. He hoped that in a Jewish social environment, William would be encouraged to work hard in school and to be smart. These contrasting stereotypes, of African Americans not valuing education and of Jews being focused on education, reflected Andrew's own experience of growing up in a community that had internalized aspects of its own oppression and his hope that the Jewish community could support William in becoming a smart, well-educated, black, Jewish man.

Andrew's family attended an independent, spirit-filled Baptist church. Very involved as a teen, Andrew developed a personal relationship with Jesus and a talent for preaching. He was called to preach and was ordained at eighteen. Church and community gave him a sense of purpose and pride. Nonetheless, in his early twenties, Andrew came to question many of his beliefs and moved away from his religious background. Rather than becoming a more liberal Christian, he found himself connecting to God and spirituality through nature. He talked about going to commune with nature by climbing a mountain near his home, appreciating quiet time outside. Rather than deriving purpose from his role in a religious community, he came to find meaning in his work as a social worker and educator.

Even before their marriage, Andrew and Helen carefully found ways to braid their traditions together. They met at a soup kitchen and homeless shelter that was run out of a synagogue. Helen, a teacher and new transplant to the city, went to volunteer and (possibly) meet Jewish men. There she met Andrew, a graduate student in social work who was working as the shelter's director. The shelter received support from all of the synagogues in town, and Andrew knew many of them. When they decided to marry in a Jewish ceremony, she told him to pick the rabbi. He chose, knowing, he claimed, that she would in the end join the synagogue in which they were married. The couple was married by an out lesbian, the rabbi of a gay-founded synagogue. When the synagogue opened its doors to straight families, they attracted many interfaith families and a number of mixed-race couples. Between the mixed-race couples and adoptions, both foreign and domestic, the Hebrew school was about one-quarter young Jews of color. Andrew explained that he chose the rabbi of a synagogue whose values matched his own most closely, focused on social justice and radical inclusion. He knew he would be comfortable there, even though he is not Jewish. It was a place where he felt he could comfortably participate in the raising of a Jewish child.

From the start, the couple was committed to creating a home that honored both of their cultures. They stood under a *chuppah* that they made to reflect themselves and their heritages (see figure 3). The fabric itself was an African-American story quilt, with blocks dedicated to their respective families and heritages, as well as the things they share: their books and their commitment to social justice. In the early years of their marriage, they added squares that reflected who they were together—the last image shows them standing together, Helen hugely pregnant. She laughs and explains that for some strange reason, since then there has not been time to add to the quilt, which hangs over their bed.[9]

FIGURE 3 African-American story-quilt chuppah. Image courtesy of Heidi Whatley.

In my examples thus far, there has been no contradiction between an African-American identity and a Jewish one, but the family points to specific places in which they have accommodated their Jewish practice to fit Andrew's family's rituals and customs into their lives, and in which blackness matters. This family aims for their own form of hybridity rather than exclusivity. For instance, they ensure that William attends church with his grandmother in part because, in Helen's words, "If you love Grandma, you need to know what Grandma loves," but also because they want to make sure that he has experience with black churches and worship styles. As Andrew said, "I was a preacher when I was young. And that was a huge part of my life. And while it is not part of my faith life now, the experience shaped me." Andrew and Helen want William to be Jewish, but they also want him to be familiar with the religious tradition that shaped his father and continues to shape his father's family. Helen pointed out that weddings and funerals for the Wilson side of the family take place in a Baptist church. She wants her son to be familiar enough with that setting that, when his grandmother dies, he can find comfort, rather than alienation, in her funeral.

In addition, Andrew and Helen consider black church culture to be an important part of African-American experience. When William learns about the civil rights movement and takes a field trip to Martin Luther King, Jr.'s birthplace and to Ebenezer Baptist Church, they want him to feel connected to that history. Certainly, they do not want him to feel alienated from African-American history, or activism, when it is located in Christian settings and contexts. Rather than suggesting that being exclusively Jewish means being shielded from the other parent's religion of origin, Helen and Andrew have been careful to make sure William has the cultural capital that they believe is essential to black cultural competence.

Additionally, they are very aware that excluding Andrew's traditions for the sake of Jewish purity could be read by his family as an attempt, not to protect a Jewish minority identity, but to escape racial and economic disadvantage by blending into what they perceived as Helen's white, middle-class identity. Andrew noted that this perception was funny, because Helen was from a working-class family, if a northern, urban one. Still, his family saw Jews as people with money and certainly saw Helen as a white woman who happened to be religiously Jewish, not as an ethnic minority. Andrew and Helen did directly connect their insistence that William understand his father's African-American heritage to rejecting the practices of "passing."[10] Their concern that Andrew's family would see the elimination of his family's traditions as erasing blackness, rather than protecting a Jewish home from Christian influence, is part of a legacy of passing. Their repeated insistence that William must know both of his heritages, and their refusal to do anything that might appear as disrespectful of his father's family, is prioritizing an "anti-passing" politics over a home with a particular notion of Jewish purity.

The ramifications of making sure his family was respected can best be seen in their Passover/Easter arrangements. Andrew grew up on a hog farm in South Georgia where Easter dinner is a feast, involving ham, biscuits, chicken and dumplings, and many kinds of pie. It is the kind of country cooking common in southern farm kitchens, black and white. Helen explains that when Passover and Easter overlap, they keep kosher for Passover until they leave Hebrew school on Sunday morning to drive to Grandma's for Easter dinner. From the moment they walk in the door, all of the food is permissible. In addition, while they privilege Hebrew school attendance over being present for church on Easter morning, they attend church with Grandma when it does not conflict with Hebrew school, for instance, during visits over the summer.[11]

It is important to note that many of Andrew's family's traditions are not specific to African-American culture, at least not in the way that the couple's story-quilt *chuppah* was a clearly a fusion of two specific traditions. The Easter tradition is a deeply local tradition—it is about farm life in the rural South and is central to Andrew's family culture, though the extent to which the food traditions are specifically or exclusively African American is a subject of some scholarly and cultural debate.[12] The point, for the Wilsons, was not to privilege a racially based set of practices, but to realize the political and psychological need to respect Andrew's family's practices, even as they maintained a Jewish home.

This process was not always smooth. One challenge came up in planning William's post–bar mitzvah Kiddush lunch. Part of the price of belonging to the "hippie synagogue" in town is that synagogue policy stipulates that all meals be dairy-free/vegetarian, with more of an emphasis on the dairy-free than the vegetarian. For Andrew's family, however, a meal and an important celebration must involve meat. Helen was very stressed out that her in-laws would feel that they were bad hosts and was angry that the synagogue did not understand that cultural sensitivity demanded bending the policy. She accepted that she needed to host a meal for the community, and that she could do as she chose at the party that night, but she felt that the only solution was to host a lunch at the synagogue and then a second, later lunch for her guests. She was, however, frustrated, even angry, and felt that if the synagogue really wanted to reach out to interfaith families, they needed to be willing to make exceptions to ritual policy when necessary.

Helen also found herself compromising her own boundaries. In 2013, when Hanukkah fell unusually early, it overlapped with Thanksgiving rather than Christmas. That year, Helen helped her husband and child decorate the house for Christmas, as she does every year, but the Hanukkah decorations had already been put away. Rather than a tree, they have a Norfolk Island pine, festooned with a six-pointed star made out of tongue depressors that William made when he was three, and a stocking hung on the door next to their mezuzah. Despite Helen's militant championing of the need to include the traditions that "Grandma loves" in her child's life, and her awareness that her husband had willingly participated in her Jewish life, she did experience some discomfort about Christmas, similar to what Paul Cowan discussed in chapter 3. The same woman who had preserved her son's Christmas tree topper for a decade found herself, this year, "feeling sad that Hanukkah is over and now it is all Christmas all the time. [I] just need to keep reminding myself: trees are pretty, trees make people happy, trees are not meant to exclude."[13] She, and some of the others raising Jewish children with the support of Christian spouses and coparents, pointed out that marriage is compromise and felt that agreeing to a tree was small when compared to the larger issues around religious education and community.

The Wilson family, then, deviated from the advice that religious leaders tended to give to Jewish-identified families in previous decades. While they see themselves as a religiously Jewish family, they do celebrate Christmas. The celebration matters to Andrew—he enjoys the decorations and celebrations, even if he is no longer a professing Christian. Helen, meanwhile, is not concerned that a Christmas celebration will undermine William's Jewish identity in the face of their community involvement and his Hebrew school education. While they are aware that celebrating Christmas would not be accepted in all Jewish communities (and has not always been accepted in their community), they do not feel judged for their choices. As Helen well knows from her time as a Hebrew school teacher, they are not the only interfaith family in the community to celebrate Christmas. As a result, though she would probably prefer that they not celebrate, she realizes Andrew has been supportive of raising a Jewish child, and she feels that it would not be right to deny him some of his own celebration in his home.

Helen reflected on what she thinks it is like for William to be simultaneously African American and Jewish, and whether his situation is different from that of her sister's children, whose father is from Latin America. She notes that William has to "come out" to people as Jewish, whereas his cousins can "pass for white" and therefore are not questioned as Jews, if people do not look too closely. William now wears a mezuzah as a pendant, a bar mitzvah gift from his Jewish uncle, but he still often has to explain his Jewishness. (She notes that her niece and nephew are not trying to pass for white—they live near their paternal grandparents, eat dinner there frequently, and speak exclusively Spanish in their grandparents' home. That said, they also do not stand out as sharply in Jewish community settings.) At thirteen, however, William does not seem to find it difficult to navigate his dual identities. He was recently a panelist in a community conversation about Jews of color. When he was asked if it was difficult to be black and Jewish, the same kid who at six once asked "Why do they call my Afro a Jew-fro?" explained to an audience that he thinks it is "pretty much hard for everyone to be a good Jew."

That said, William has experienced moments of racism at synagogue, and as a teenager, he has sometimes told his mother that "being Jewish is your thing, not mine." Both of his parents think that most of his rejection of

Judaism is adolescent rebellion. His mother reflected, "I think some was rebellion against me. I think part of the natural 'you don't get me' gets tangled up in the world doesn't get me because of the rampant racism and injustice everywhere." As a result, moments of racism in the community can exacerbate his frustrations and he does not enjoy being black in a primarily white environment. For instance, when he has been an assistant teacher at the Hebrew school, children have challenged the idea that you can be black and Jewish at the same time. According to his mother, he experiences these comments as racism and while William does not mind educating the children about the fact that he is both black and Jewish, their comments do serve as a reminder that the Jewish experience in the contemporary United States is primarily a white experience.

These moments of tension are not only the terrain of the children. When William gave his bar mitzvah *d'var*, he talked about being both Jewish and African American. Afterward, one of the Hebrew school teachers asked Helen why he calls himself black. She answered, "Well, because he is." She noted that while it was a "weird" question, it was also asked "with love and a desire to become more knowledgeable" and reflected that they feel a lot of love and acceptance from the community.[14] Helen's comment might, on some level, reflect a white spouse and parent dismissing some of the racial complexities of her community—for all Andrew supports her taking William to the synagogue, he does not attend frequently himself. Andrew, meanwhile, noted that he chose their Jewish community specifically because it was the most diverse and liberal Jewish community available to them, but not because it was perfect. That said, they agreed that, even though William sometimes resisted attending synagogue, he always seemed glad to have gone and that he needs to learn to navigate communities in their imperfections.

This family therefore demonstrates a conscious attempt at hybridity even within a distinctly Jewish home. It is very clear, when the couple was planning their story quilt, that they were intentionally blending African-American heritage into their family. Their insistence that William be comfortable in his grandmother's black Baptist church is partly about love and respect for relatives, and would probably be true if the relatives in question were white, but it is also about a sense that, at least in their family, the church is a large part of what blackness means, and they want their son to have the cultural competency he needs to move through that part of his world. These moments of compromise— the Easter dinner, the bar mitzvah lunch—are less clearly about race. The food cultures are the cultures of the rural South, black and white, but their sense that they need to respect the family's culture, rather than asking the family to conform to Jewish norms, is based in the power dynamics of race. Helen is very aware that she is not just a Jewish woman, asking her Christian in-laws to respect her minority religious culture. She is also a white woman who should not devalue the traditions of her black in-laws. So whether or not the traditions are specifically African American, the minority culture/majority culture dynamic imagined for interfaith marriages was disrupted in this case by the racial dynamic.

A Little Latin, a Lot Jewish

The Cordero family further complicates the categories of race, religion, and ethnicity—a family that, unlike the Wilsons, can to a certain extent "choose" to perform their ethnic and racially mixed identity, or belie it.[15] Malka Singer Cordero grew up in San Antonio, Texas, where the Jewish community is small and closely connected. Her parents are both Ashkenazi Jews from the northeastern United States who relocated for her father's academic career. Malka's family was very focused on education—she noted that her sense of self was derived from academic achievement. She describes Judaism as central to her self-understanding, in part because the Jewish community was very small and very academically focused, full of transplanted Yankees. Her family belonged to an Orthodox synagogue; she notes there were three synagogues in town, and her parents had selected the nicest rabbi, though they themselves were not at all religious people. As a result, Malka observed that her Jewish education, which she described as taking place in a "musty, old men drinking schnapps" kind of environment, did not match her home life in any way. Her grandmother, however, had lived in Palestine in the 1930s, spoke Hebrew, and was very much a Zionist. She took Malka and her older brother to Israel and gave Malka a strong sense of Jewish identity. By the time Malka met Juan, however, she was working in civil rights and public service law in a large southern city. She explained that she was often on the road, working with prisoners, and was not part of a Jewish community. She went to the local Reconstructionist synagogue for High Holiday services when she was available, but her entire life was her work and the friends and community that it inspired. Looking for activities outside of work, Malka decided to take kung fu, and it was there that she met Juan.

Like Malka's, Juan's family was in San Antonio, but he had grown up in Puerto Rico. He attended Catholic boys' schools for his entire education. He described his family as "doing what they are supposed to do as Catholics: going to mass, taking First Communion," but it was in his Jesuit high school that he started to explore religion more deeply. The Jesuits, he said, "broke him open to the wonder of religion in the world." He talked about going on retreat and doing yoga on the beach, of being asked and encouraged to engage with a broad range of religious traditions and philosophies. "In a way," he joked, "that was the Jesuits' mistake. They did not make me hate religion. They made me see that there are ways in which it is all true. And then it was hard to stick, faithfully, to the Catholic Church." Juan explained that while he knows that there are dark spots in the Church's history, and certainly terrible things have happened more recently, he never had a bad experience with the Church. The Jesuits who were his teachers were young men who advocated for him and inspired him. Rather, he left the Church because he started to doubt Christ's divinity; and, as he put it, "It is hard to call yourself a Christian if you doubt Christ's divinity, and if you can't call yourself Christian, how can you call yourself Catholic?"

Juan joined the navy, married his first wife, a woman with a similar loose affiliation with the Catholic Church, and had a son and two daughters. They divorced when the children were young and he largely raised them as a single father. While neither he nor his ex-wife invested deeply in giving his children a Catholic identity, for the children's early years, he and the children lived near his parents. As a result, Juan's parents provided the children with some education in both the Catholic Church and Puerto Rican culture. Now, as adults, none of the children identify strongly as Catholic, existing somewhere between "lapsed Catholic" and "religious none." When Juan's children were teenagers, they were very involved in a kung fu studio where he would eventually meet Malka. As a result, Malka has known his children for as long as she has known Juan.

Together, Juan and Malka had two more children, Shayna and Pablo. In talking about their decision to raise the children as Jews, Juan commented that he did not think there had been any uncertainty about it at all: it was clear to him that Malka wanted her children to be Jewish. Malka said that, because Juan was ten years her senior and already had three children, the question really was whether he was willing to have more children—it was important to her that the possibility, at least, existed. If there were children, however, it was clear that they would be Jewish. "That," Malka explained, "would be something that I know—in my heart—that it would be very hard for me to compromise on; whether that is fair or not is a different conversation, but certainly, it would have been hard for me."

Malka revealed that, in the end, there was little that Juan wanted to bring with him from his Jesuit background, and so she does not feel that compromise was necessary. He said, instead, what to her was the perfect answer: "It is fine if you teach them about Judaism, as long as you teach me, too." Juan, still imbued with the curiosity about religion that he got from his Jesuit education, was perfectly willing to learn about the Judaism that Malka would share with the children, though she observed that the kind of Jewish life she wants for the children is a big commitment and so perhaps he should have asked what was involved!

At the time of my interviews, the family marked Shabbat with dinner and sometimes Malka left work early to get out the nice tablecloth, candles, challah, and wine. They noted that it is hard for them to get to services on Friday night, with work, dinner, and traffic, so they make sure to go to Hebrew school on Sunday. They had near-perfect attendance at Hebrew school, missing it only for major events. In part, they go for the education, but also because the family *minyan* is the main time that they have for the children to develop affinity for the prayers. Malka noted, though, that in a family where both parents work and where the children play sports and are scouts, giving up a Sunday morning is a huge commitment. Having been raised in a small Jewish community, however, she feels strongly that if you do not actively cultivate a Jewish identity, it does not grow automatically. They attend most of the family-oriented events at the synagogue and are also affiliated with an independent minyan of interfaith families raising children as Jews. Malka explains that they would not be likely to celebrate Shavuot or Sukkot on their own, but they appreciate having communities to make Jewish life happen.

They observed that their daughter, Shayna, loves being Jewish. In an identity poem in third grade, she wrote about being Jewish. She likes the Hebrew school kids, and she loves the ritual. Juan and Malka suggested a family trip to Israel coordinated around her bat mitzvah and "she has not let [them] forget it"—they are not sure why Shayna has such a strong sense of Jewish identity or whether Pablo will develop one, but they are clearly pleased that she has it.

When Juan and Malka met and married, his children from his first marriage were teenagers. His girls in particular loved decorating their Christmas tree. Both Juan and Malka talked about how, though neither of his adult daughters thinks of herself as Christian, the tree and the gifts are very important to them. As long as they lived at home, there was a tree—it was clear that Malka had no desire to deny her stepdaughters their own tradition and celebration. Juan explained that he had to get them a tree, and Malka emphasized the joy that they found in the tree and gifts. When they left home, however, the Corderos stopped having a tree unless the girls planned to come home. It was not important to Juan. Malka reflected, "I have no judgment about Jewish families, interfaith families, who have a tree—if it is important to one partner, religiously, culturally, historically, or whatever, and they want to share it with their kids. But for Juan, it was not." The major winter holiday became Hanukkah. But Christmas is, Malka points out, a special time in the United States. There is no school and Juan cooks a traditional Puerto Rican holiday meal on Christmas Eve, with roast pork and rice and pigeon peas, plantains, and flan. They often invite Jewish friends to their dinner.

Malka does not mind the pork-oriented Christmas dinner. She commented, "Juan has been so supportive of raising our children as Jews. I want them to know and appreciate Latin culture. And it is neither like I grew up keeping kosher nor like he advocated for an American commercial Christmas." The inclusion of the Christmas holiday is not completely consistent year to year, and it is not a big deal in the family. It is also often coupled with Chinese food for lunch and a movie matinee. Is it there because they are a religiously blended family or is it a time to honor Latin heritage? Neither parent is certain, though Malka notes that the fact that Christmas is central to Puerto Rican culture is part of why it is easy for her to encourage the special meal on years when her stepchildren are not around.

As very small children, Shayna and Pablo both explored what it meant to be Jewish and Puerto Rican. Their parents recounted them saying, "Daddy is Puerto Rican, and so we are Puerto Rican. And Mommy is Jewish, and so we are Jewish. Daddy could become Jewish. Can Mommy become Puerto Rican?" In this teasing out of what it means to be Jewish and Puerto Rican, they started to get to the differences between religious identity and ethnic identity, in which no amount of knowledge of island culture or Spanish language would make Mommy Puerto Rican, and that while Daddy could become Jewish, he was not. "He just likes to come with us." Indeed, while Juan has enjoyed his own journey into Judaism, he feels no need to convert—he prefers to see the value in all traditions, rather than to commit to one. The children understand that Judaism is a religion that one can take on through conversion as much as by birth, whereas ethnicity or race is not something that their mother can adopt.

Juan was delighted to raise his children as Jews, pointing out that he had always had positive experiences of religion. He underscored, more than once, "Nothing happens in that synagogue to which I am not happy to subscribe. Nothing happens in the Hebrew school that does not please me." Both sets of grandparents have been deeply supportive of their marriage. While Juan's mother is devoutly Catholic herself, she is so delighted so see some form of religion in his life, or at least in his home, that she has been fully supportive.

She sends New Year's cards and takes apples and honey to Malka's parents at Rosh Hashanah. Meanwhile, when the couple took a trip for interfaith families to Israel, Malka's parents called, concerned: Was the point of this trip to pressure non-Jewish spouses to convert? Malka needed to respect Juan's own path and religion!

Otherwise, the conversation in the Cordero house was a bit different than the one in the Wilson house. Their daughter, Shayna, has a Latin last name, but an identifiably Jewish first name. They are not really worried about how she will be received in the Jewish world—she understands herself to be Jewish, is proud to be Jewish, and has figured out that maternal descent means that no one can argue about whether she is Jewish. Pablo is younger, and while he was named according to Jewish tradition, named for Malka's grandfather Paul, he has an entirely Latin name. Malka worries that in school, teachers will respond to him with negative stereotypes of Latinos, expecting him to be disruptive, macho, and not academically inclined, and that those assumptions could hurt him. He is still very young, and the concern is largely about the future, but both she and Juan are aware that Shayna will be able to "pass" as white and Pablo probably will not. Their major concerns are twofold: they do not want Shayna to choose to pass, and they do not want her brother to see her get "skin privilege" to which he does not have access. While they have put quite a bit of energy into making the children Jewish, Malka wishes that Juan had been more serious about teaching them Spanish. He agrees—it was a mistake. But despite their worries about Pablo, neither Juan nor Malka feels that they need to prepare their children for Latino life in quite the same way that the Wilsons are clear that William will need to interact with the world as a young black man.

Making the comparison to African-American/Jewish families, Malka suggested that the situation was different. If they wanted their children to speak Spanish or to identify as Puerto Rican, especially far away from family and community, they would have had to make the same concerted effort that they had made to have their children feel Jewish. They have not made such an effort—Juan points out that he is quite assimilated (not anti-island in any way, just assimilated)—and that none of his nieces and nephews with two Puerto Rican parents can speak Spanish. The parents contrast this experience to that of children with one black parent and one Jewish parent. Their blackness is "a fact," not something that has to be cultivated, but something written on their bodies, "about which the world will make assumptions, good or bad." For the Latino, Jewish children, racial or ethnic identity becomes a choice rather than a default, something that they can or might choose or, at least to a certain extent, cast aside.

Conclusion

In both of these case studies, the dynamic between the parental traditions was set up by a different power differential than was imagined by the Jewish communal groups in the previous chapter. The Christian spouse had a strong family and cultural identity that was not a mainstream American Christian identity. As such, it was not the culture with which American Judaism exists in a majority/minority relationship. That dynamic probably made it easier for the Jewish spouse to accept and accommodate the non-Jewish culture in the home. It also, however, destabilized the majority/minority power dynamic, creating a situation in which the two cultures had to interact with each other on a more equal footing. Jewishness lost the deference that it often receives as the minority culture as it made room for another minority culture, albeit Christian.

In part because of the political liberalism of many Jewish communities, these families found themselves with more freedom to assert multiple identities for their children than their white counterparts. Ashkenazi Jewish communities were more willing to acknowledge the need to include African-American or Latin American culture in these interracial, interfaith families than they were to acknowledge the validity of including the Christian practices of white interfaith families. Some readers have noted that both the Wilsons and the Corderos reflect much lower levels of conflict than among many of their white, Jewish-identified interfaith families. Several potential reasons present themselves. First, often, the preferred Jewish narrative for white interfaith families involves the Christian spouse (or the spouse of Christian heritage) sacrificing his or her own traditions and identities for those of the spouse. Given that these expectations could also result in Christian women sacrificing their own traditions and then doing the bulk of the work to raise Jewish children, this imbalance had the potential to cause tension. Because the interracial, interfaith families were more likely to pull from both heritages, and to have some communal support for doing so, they experienced less of this potential resentment. Second, often white interfaith families were blindsided by some of the differences that they experienced. As largely secular Jews and post-Protestant/lapsed Catholics, these couples did not always anticipate the challenges of their interfaith homes and so did not always communicate about their differences in advance. The interracial couples were keenly aware of their differences and so were more likely to have discussed how they wanted to approach those differences during their courtships. The religious differences were braided into the conversations and compromises around other racial and cultural differences. Lastly, it is possible that the couples with whom I spoke consciously or unconsciously felt the need to present themselves as model families who had figured out how to successfully navigate their interracial and interfaith lives.

This is not to say that these families have had a seamless experience within Jewish communities. Years after I did my initial interviews, Helen Wilson contacted me. She had been invited to give the d'var, or sermon, at her synagogue's Rosh Hashanah services, in front of almost one thousand people. She spoke about the challenges of raising a black man in a liberal Jewish community. In her d'var, she wrote, "We chose to join [the community] because of how we were welcomed. . . . Despite people's surprise, we continue to come to services after William's bar mitzvah because connection to community is important and that is still harder for a family like ours. This is not something we could find just anywhere. As a multiracial, interfaith family we cannot take this for granted. We have to work for it."[16] As profoundly grateful as she was for that welcome, backed up with examples of how the community, and specifically the rabbi, had reached out to her son, Helen observed that the community did not always understand the challenges of a racially blended family. Speaking in the fall of 2015, after a year of highly publicized police violence against black people, she spoke of the need to teach her son the respect and manners that are necessary for, but no guarantee of, his safety as a black man in a community. "We live in a system, a city, a country where people 'mess' with black boys—and it is different. Like other black men, my son will likely be stopped by police more frequently, targeted unfairly, and endangered," she reminded the community. While she called on them to join antiracism activities as a community, she was actually getting at a far more personal concern: "As a soon-to-be black man, my son needs to be able to regulate his emotions. There are situations in the world where folks might kill him if they perceive a threat. He could be another story on the news. If you meet William, he will look you in the eye, smile and shake your hand. He must do this to create a positive impression. We taught him this. This polite, seemingly extra-formal behavior is literally a matter of life and death."[17] Helen's reference to William's "seemingly extra-formal behavior" was particularly striking in their community setting. The synagogue in question was the kind of liberal, progressive community that would join in antiracism work and that would overtly attempt to welcome interfaith families, same-sex families, mixed-race families, and Jews of color. That political attitude was coupled with relaxed parenting among many of the families. Children were encouraged to honor their emotions, more than to regulate them. The community tended to value creative expression over formality, manners, or (often) a sense of the "appropriate." Helen wanted them to remember that those attitudes were the result of privilege that her child did not share. She called on the community to learn to educate children about the differences among them without "guilt or defensiveness."[18]

According to Helen, the community received her comments well, and she received many compliments. Indeed, the very fact that she was invited to speak about race in such a public context demonstrates the synagogue leadership's desire to confront racism both in the broader world and inside the community. Her need to speak, however, demonstrated that no matter how welcomed multiracial, interfaith families were in her community, they were still in a position of needing to teach about their experience—of interpreting for their larger, whiter community. Ironically, the progressive aspects and attitudes of the community were, in some ways, both precisely the ones that made them welcome and precisely the ones that reflected the most difference in household culture.

The Wilsons and the Corderos share the same liberal Jewish community and the differences in their experiences highlight the reality that the mixed-race dynamic is, in these communities, much more fraught than other dynamics. As the Corderos point out, their daughter, Shayna, can pass (and while their son cannot pass as white, Pablo can read, in certain contexts, as a Sephardic Jew). As a result, their presence in Jewish community is not questioned in the way that William's has been.

That said, interracial, interfaith families who choose to affiliate Jewishly are unable to blend as seamlessly into Jewish communities as their white counterparts do. At the same time, their communities offer them considerably more flexibility in combining traditions and heritages than they do for the white interfaith families who chose Judaism as a primary religious identity.

CHAPTER FIVE

Chrismukkah

Millennial Multiculturalism

The first few years of the new millennium witnessed the birth of a new holi-day: Chrismukkah. While Christian and Jewish interfaith families have long negotiated their respective traditions, this holiday marked a departure from older models of interfaith family practice. Rather than emphasizing religious community and potential conflict, it reflected a new era of comfort with a consumer model of religious and multicultural identity. Fittingly, Chrismukkah was born on Fox's hit show *The OC*.[1] Seth Cohen, one of the main characters, claims to have come up with the idea for the holiday at the age of six: eight days of presents and one day of "many, many" presents. After lighting the me-norah and exchanging gifts for the eight days of Hanukkah, the family, with its Jewish father and Protestant mother, then celebrates a home-based Christ-mas with stockings, gifts, and tree but combines it with elements of "Jewish Christmas" by ordering take-out Chinese food and watching a family movie. After *The OC*'s first Chrismukkah episode aired in 2003, Ron and Michelle Gompertz, an interfaith couple from Bozeman, Montana, launched www .chrismukkah.com, followed by a Chrismukkah cookbook. Chrismukkah immediately attracted notice. In 2004, it was listed on *Time Magazine*'s list of buzzwords for the year.[2] *USA Today* referred to it as a revenue-generating "faux holiday," suggesting that it had garnered enough cultural recognition to be a money maker.[3]

Chrismukkah and its increased public presence marked a shift in the pub-lic discourse around Christian-Jewish interfaith families in the United States at the turn of the millennium. In children's literature, greeting cards, humor books, television shows, and blogs, interfaith families who practiced ele-ments of both Christianity and Judaism worked within a public discourse that depicted a multicultural, interfaith identity constructed through the stra-tegic use and reframing of practices from both backgrounds. Rather than un-derstanding this identity as based in a failure to choose one religious practice over another, multicultural interfaith families argued that their blended prac-tices both reflected an unavoidable reality and offered distinct advantages and a moral formation to their families. "Religion," as used by these multicul-tural families, becomes the domain of religious institutions, with membership lists and competing truth claims. "Culture," their preferred term, suggests practices that are equivalent and can exist simultaneously in the lives of families and individuals. While scholars such as Henry Goldschmidt describe the space between religious and cultural definitions of practice as creating an unbridgeable gap for the communities that he studies, my research demonstrates that by framing practices as "cultural," interfaith families practicing both traditions create a space for such choices to be framed as morally cohesive through the language of multiculturalism.[4]

Two trends allowed interfaith families to draw selectively from their Christian and Jewish backgrounds in order to create a mosaic of household practices that formed new, hybrid identities: the development of a "seeker" mode of religion and the rise of multiculturalism as a theoretical and lived concept intersected with a consumer-based mode of identity formation to create new possibilities for interfaith families. Specifically, the seeker religion model enabled a shift between religious traditions that combined practices from multiple religious traditions, a religious reality that was deeply shaped by consumption. Multiculturalism thus allowed individuals and families to participate in practices that shaped their connections to select ethnicities and placed them over and above any single belief system. Some interfaith families created and advocated for blended Christian-Jewish multicultural identities through consuming both Christian and Jewish practices and objects while creating new, hybrid practices and objects to consume. Indeed, these families participated in a form of consumption that added new elements of meaning, even while reshaping more traditional practices. The scholars Leigh Eric Schmidt and Andrew Heinze point to the myriad ways in which this form of consumption reformulates religious ritual, practice, and identity. Schmidt underscores the role of consumption in family Christmas celebrations, a central piece of the logic of Chrismukkah. Similarly, Heinze points to the rise in importance of American Hanukkah celebrations and underscores their parallels with child-focused Christmas celebrations. Chrismukkah itself, then, serves as a (sometimes minimally) reconfigured holiday that points to "cultural" heritages rather than "religious" truths, allowing interfaith families to shape a family-based, multicultural practice.[5]

These new multicultural interfaith families made sharp distinctions between Christianity's and Judaism's religious traditions linked to "official" theologies and what they termed culture or traditions (i.e., food, storytelling, and home-based ritual). This rhetorical distinction between religion and culture allowed proponents of dual-practice households to move the conversation away from competing truth claims and religious affiliations and toward a multicultural approach to identity increasingly popular in the 1990s.[6] This chapter will thus historicize the emergence of a distinctly "multicultural" interfaith holiday celebration, grounded largely in practices of consumption, and illuminate its implications for the meanings of religion and culture in American popular culture. It draws parallels between the use of consumption by interfaith families and an emphasis on multiculturalism through consumption in American society.

By the time the invented holiday of Chrismukkah emerged, multicultural interfaith families already had a decade of cultural material—which emphasized maintaining both traditions by distancing them from religion—from which they could draw. Chrismukkah, then, represents one of the most popular depictions of Christian and Jewish cultural practices that could be combined in interfaith family life. At the same time, interfaith families both built upon and reconstructed a moral system that was connected to other dominant trends in late twentieth-century America and that carried emotionally evocative meaning.

Interfaith Marriage and Millennial Multiculturalism: Historical and Theoretical Contexts

The development of an interfaith holiday like Chrismukkah must be understood in the context of several important trends. The decades on either side of the millennium were characterized by high rates of intermarriage and an increased flexibility around both ethnic identity and certain kinds of religious practice. Together, these cultural shifts afforded spaces for blended families whose family religious practice drew from both Christianity and Judaism. As Robert Putnam and David Campbell point out, in the 1990s, 50 percent of all American marriages began as interfaith marriages, with 30 percent of the marriages remaining mixed and 20 percent becoming religiously homogeneous through conversion or the selection of a third religion.[7] More particularly, they note that over 50 percent of American Jews entered into interfaith marriages, about half of which remained interfaith.[8] Perhaps because these marriages remained a controversial issue, particularly in the Jewish community, a disproportionate selection of the resources for interfaith families focused on Christian-Jewish marriages and families.

In the early 2000s, however, advocates for blending Christian and Jewish elements began to articulate a new version of interfaith family life. Using a consumption-inflected definition of multiculturalism, they framed Christianity and Judaism as cultures from which a family could draw to create their own pastiche of traditions. In this approach to interfaith family life, a dual-religion home stemmed not from an inability to choose an identity, but from a distinct set of values, including the refusal to privilege one parent's identity over the other's. This popular form of multiculturalism celebrated diversity as a rich array of cultural resources while downplaying the possibility of conflict or power imbalance resulting from difference. Instead, this form of multiculturalism calls on individuals to strive to "break down barriers" and "build mutual understanding across our differences."[9] Interfaith families, proponents argued, were an excellent place for children to be fundamentally shaped as multicultural citizens who would be able to reach across difference, because their very familial relationships would equip them to act as cultural brokers. For example, in her blog, *On Being Both*, Susan Katz Miller argues that the "interfaith identity label, the label more and more of us have chosen for our children, has unique benefits and positive associations."[10] She also suggests that a dual-religious heritage gives her daughter the ability to "ponder the mystery of the universe in two languages. She is primed for deep empathy, building bridges, resisting intolerance."[11] Raising children to be interfaith is modeled here as raising them to have a particular, beneficial, skill set for life.

Multicultural interfaith families result in part from movements that came to exist earlier in the twentieth century, specifically multiculturalism and seeker religion. The rhetoric of multiculturalism first arose in the 1960s and 1970s, in a conversation that placed the category of "culture" in the center of American civic life. In 1967, *Loving v. Virginia* struck down antimiscegenation laws on the federal level, both bringing already-existing racially and ethnically blended American families into the public eye and laying the groundwork for an increasing acceptance of diversity within families. In 1965, Congress passed the Immigration and Nationality Act, ending a heavily weighted quota system and creating a new group of immigrants who could not be fully integrated into the black and white racial binary of American society. This change, combined with the rise of political movements like Black Pride and the American Indian Movement, created a new interest in understanding one's ethnic and racial history and context. Though at first this genealogical and cultural interest was the territory of people of color, it also reshaped the ways in which white Americans connected with their ethnic heritages, creating space for their cultural backgrounds to be performed in public settings.[12] Jews and "ethnic" Catholics had given up much of their ethnic distinctiveness in the process of becoming considered as white socially, and this multicultural turn allowed for a reclamation of a range of discarded practices. The values of multiculturalism shaped particular strands of the social sciences, which influenced public policy and best practices in fields such as education.[13] The trend toward multiculturalism became so strong that by 1990, most white Americans identified themselves with an ethnic group on the U.S. Census, rather than as simply "American," a notable change from just twenty years before.[14]

This multicultural understanding of culture sharply differs from the anthropological definition of culture and cultural constructs. Many anthropologists understand culture as "a fluid and contentious process that transgresses the boundaries of clearly defined communities."[15] For multiculturalists, "culture" is a stable force that can be distilled into "static objects," including holidays, foods, and specific items that can be made or purchased.[16] In a cultural framework, an object that might have theological significance in another system of meaning—a menorah or a crèche—instead comes to represent membership in uniform "cultural" groups. This trend in multicultural logic as applied to religion, appeared, for instance, in the Supreme Court case of *Lynch v. Donnelly*, in which the Court defined the crèche displayed as part of Pawtucket, Rhode Island's holiday display not as a religious symbol, but as "sponsored by the city to celebrate the Holiday and to depict the origins of that Holiday."[17] When previously religious objects—like a menorah or a crèche—become cultural, they then become equivalent, within and across groups. Eating gefilte fish becomes as much a marker of Jewishness as lighting Shabbat candles, and each holds the same weight, though from a Jewish legal standpoint one is a food resulting from economic necessity and the other fulfills a commandment from God. Within the economy of multiculturalism, these practices are now equivalent to Christian practices of dying Easter eggs or singing Christmas carols referencing the Christ child. The process of remaking these practices as cultural did not mean that they necessarily mattered less; rather, they were conceptualized differently and divorced from a meaning that referred back to commandments from God or signifiers of faith and piety. In a multicultural understanding, one is Jewish because one eats matzoh ball soup; one is Italian Catholic because one abstains from meat until after midnight on Christmas Eve, a process that blurs the lines between religious and ethnic identity. This means that various units within one tradition become translatable through the logic of equivalence; they are separated from their particular cultural and religious traditions in order to be understood through the abstracting and universalizing language of multiculturalism, which irons out historical and cultural differences and translates it into equivalence.

If, in a multicultural system of identity formation, identity becomes tied to certain practices, those practices are inherently tied to consumption. European-Americans in particular tend to express ethnic identity through the consumption of material and nonmaterial commodities such as "Kiss Me, I'm Irish" aprons, klezmer music, and vacation packages to visit the homeland, the old country, or—in the case of American Jews—Israel. This market exploded in the late twentieth and early twenty-first centuries and resulted in what Marilyn Halter describes as an "occasional" or "optional" ethnicity. As long as they were white, consumers could play up or play down their ethnic identities by increasing or decreasing culturally marked consumption. One could also combine ethnicities, either participating in multiple forms of consumption or in forms that themselves merged heritages.[18] The identities remain "optional" precisely because, at least for white Americans, they can be combined, put on, or taken off largely at will. Halter notes that "offspring of parents with different ethnic backgrounds are particularly receptive to the possibilities of this more occasional ethnicity, focusing on the wealth and multiplicity of cultural resources on which they can draw."[19] If institutions and other sources of authority defined religion by affiliation, truth claims, and strict understandings of peoplehood, the language of ethnicity allowed more flexibility for combining traditions than did the language of religious choice; it created space for a pastiche of practices to be viewed as yet another form of multiculturalism.

At the same time, multicultural interfaith families have grounded their choices in the moral framework and religious practices of both therapeutic and seeker culture. American therapeutic culture places the psychological development of the individual potentially over and above the needs of the group. Because therapeutic culture values the spiritual growth of the individual and rhetorically empowers that individual with the ability to select and evaluate religious practices, it has created the potential for interfaith families to apply a consumer model to their religious practices.

By the beginning of the twentieth century, Americans had begun to imagine what T. J. Jackson Lears refers to as "a self that was neither simple nor genuine, but fragmented and socially constructed.[20] In the emerging therapeutic society, the ultimate goal of the self was to seek, despite its fragmentation, self-actualization through experience. While the experience could be controlled or spontaneous, "commitments outside the self shrank to meet the seeker's immediate emotional requirements."[21] This development of the self puts the needs of the individual above the needs of the community or family, such that by "urging unending personal growth," proponents of this thera-peutic ethos "devalu[ed] the customs and traditions designed to preserve cul-tural memory," and ultimately devalued "the personal memory enshrined in family continuity."[22] The self-realized individual of modern psychotherapeu-tic culture is, then, unrestricted by, but also unmoored from, the demands of traditional community structures.

The postwar form of this American therapeutic culture came in the form of humanist psychology, which understood people to be "creative, self-fulfilling creature[s]" and which drew heavily from both Protestant and Jewish thought at the same time that its developments, in many cases, led Protestants and Jews away from churches and synagogues in their search for fulfillment.[23]

If many baby boomers ceased to religiously affiliate, what did they do in-stead? Though the dominant mode of postwar religion involved "dwelling" in one's religious community for the bulk of one's lifetime, in the 1960s, many baby boomers became seekers, moving from one religious tradition to an-other or borrowing from a variety of religions. If many boomers turned away from religious institutions, they "grappled hard in search of a holistic, all-encompassing vision of life."[24] In doing so, they saw religion as "whatever one chose as one's own." For some, then, religion became an intensely personal journey rather than a shared, communal activity, while for others, fidelity to a religious tradition remained important, though they added practices such as meditation or yoga. Focusing on what best served the individual's needs, boomers drew their practices from a variety of traditions, combining multiple traditions in a "pastiche-style of spirituality."[25] Despite the rootless quality of boomer religious life, they often valued deep spiritual engagement whether or not they connected such engagement to institutions. They therefore passed to their children a belief that religious practice and tradition exist to enhance the individual's spiritual life over and above any communal obligation.[26] In the 1990s, boomer religion set the dominant cultural tone outside of religious institutions, opening up space for religious patterns to operate in the same paradigm of choice as ethnic models. Individuals selected religious practices and material culture pragmatically rather than as dictated by religious com-munities or traditions.[27]

The possibility of combining religious practices did not immediately in-crease the options for Christian-Jewish interfaith families, however, because seekers tended either to leave their religion of origin altogether or to add practices derived from Hinduism and Buddhism (e.g., yoga and/or medita-tion) to their Christian or Jewish practices and identity. Seeker models of re-ligion did not, in most cases, allow for the combination of dominant forms of

Christianity with dominant forms of Judaism. The context of multicultu
ism allowed Christian and Jewish practices to be cast as ethnic practices
rather than as historically competing and sometimes antagonistic religious
traditions. As the salience of theological difference declined because people
of Christian or Jewish heritage were increasingly likely to espouse the views
of secular Americans, engaging in both religions' practices became not only
possible but also desirable. For some, this tendency meant a turn away from
religion altogether. Others were increasingly likely to understand the particu-
lars of their tradition's beliefs as metaphors or as an approach to understanding greater universal truths, but not as the one truth path. This combination
of multiculturalism and institutionally unbounded spiritual seeking, present
in the 1990s and early 2000s, offered interfaith families new freedom to create
hybrid identities for themselves. These blended identities sat easily in an
emerging popular culture that accepted and often celebrated blended identities. Multicultural interfaith families understand the traditions in which the
parents were raised—in this case Christianity and Judaism—as constellations
of practices and identity rather than as manifestations of belief or affiliation.
Advocates of such families emphasize "tradition" and "culture" in contrast to
a definition of "religion," which, for them, implies affiliation with organized
communities or dedication to a specific theology. According to their understanding, religions are under the control of religious institutions and authorities, who may police boundaries as they see fit. While the Jewish movements
each use different criteria to establish "who is a Jew," they tend to require
either matrilineal descent or Jewish education provided by a Jewish institution. Although various forms of Christianity police their boundaries differently, baptism or faith commitments often serve as a yardstick. Multicultural
interfaith families use cultural identification to sidestep formal institutional
requirements. In doing so, these blended, interfaith families draw a distinction that scholars such as Henry Goldschmidt argue is essential to a multicultural project. When practices are tied to truth claims or genetics, viewed as
either reflections of piety or holy commandments, they cease to be equivalent and cannot be blended.[28] As a result, advocates of multicultural interfaith
families tend to co-opt "tradition" and "culture" to describe (predominantly
home-based) practices maintained outside of the context of affiliation with a
single tradition. They demonstrate a blending of traditions precisely by eliding difference. Just as the multicultural understanding of culture does not
match the definition held by anthropologists, the term "religion" in this context does not match definitions of the term used in religious studies. From a
religious studies standpoint, the range of practices employed by multicultural

interfaith families carry many of the characteristics of the religious, in that they are often "tied together emotionally and cognitively, but also spiritually and materially by vital rituals, living myths, indescribable experiences, moral values, shared memories, and other commonly recognized features of religious life."[29] Around the turn of the millennium, however, more evidence arose of a "culture and community" of interfaith families in American society more broadly. These formal and informal networks came to embrace complex identities, cultivate an ability to move between religious cultures, and explore hybrid practices. In addition to a more fluid definition of Jewishness or Christianness, the sources here reflect a relational understanding of practice that roots meaning in family heritage. Robert Orsi articulates an understanding of "religion as a network of relationships between heaven and earth involving humans of all ages and many sacred figures together."[30] The Christian and Jewish practices reflected in children's literature and in adult resources for an explicitly blended culture demonstrate that they provide powerful ways of expressing these relationships across culture, heritage, and practice. For interfaith families, drawing from a range of practices such as the cooking of family recipes or the displaying of heirlooms offers ways to maintain sacred relationships with relatives and communities from both sides of the family and to shape a unique individual and familial moral universe.

Popular Depictions of Culturally Christian and Jewish Families

Multiculturalism, optional ethnicity, and boomer-style religious sensibilities created a new approach to articulating interfaith religious identity in the 1990s and 2000s. In conversations surrounding interfaith families (one-faith family versus blended family), the terms "religion" and "culture" have garnered specific definitions. Religion has become the territory of established communities. Culture has become a place where syncretism can occur. Sources as diverse as children's literature and novelty books connect religiously blended households to the traits of cultural flexibility and respect for difference. These traits function as moral virtues in the value system of multicultural America. In addition to depicting a set of values, these sources depict a set of practices gaining in meaning because of their association with family and heritage. Through the connections to family and heritage, the very practices that the sources seek to describe as cultural take on a deep and pervasive meaning that scholars often see as religious, even as participants carefully eschew the term.

Proponents of multicultural interfaith families address the fears about interfaith family identity with a simple message for children: it is normal for children to have two religions in one home, a normalcy that they often underscore through their depictions of parallel celebrations of Christmas and Hanukkah. In this light, in 1999, Scholastic published Margaret Moorman's *Light the Lights!*, a beautifully illustrated celebration of the holiday season centered on the lights of both the menorah and the Christmas tree. With her parents and her family, the main character prepares for the many days of Hanukkah. When Hanukkah ends, they put away the menorah and decorate for Christmas. Both parents are involved in both celebrations, the holidays flowing into each other to create a holiday season emphasizing the parallel practices of holiday lights, family, and food; no practice is flagged as religious, and the practice is in no way problematic. *Light the Lights!* is typical of many books supporting both Christian and Jewish practices. They can make these claims because they avoid questions of theologically structured belief and affiliation, places where the religious identities come into conflict.

A year later, Effin Older's *My Two Grandmothers* emphasizes festivities and foodways over the theological differences. Older sidesteps the religious differences of Christianity and Judaism by presenting those identities as familial "traditions," combinable as long as the families show mutual respect for each other, rather than merely tolerating conflicting religious beliefs and practices. For Older, "traditional" becomes a term that flags a practice, an identity-constituting action that can exist outside of the networks of meaning ascribed by contemporary American Christianities and Judaisms. She, and other authors like her, depict families in which mutual respect allows diverse practices to coexist in a household and therefore point to a positively inflected multicultural life for interfaith families.

Older emphasizes the different familial relationships by tying religious identities to particular relatives. *My Two Grandmothers* was, unlike many other books aimed at children of interfaith marriage, published by Harcourt, a major, for-profit publisher. It depicts food as a primary element of familial identity, passed matrilineally through the generations. The story frames food as a tradition and values the food practices of the Christian farm family and the Jewish urban family equally, considering them both to be culturally specific. This balance acknowledges the cultural specificity of the dominant culture as well as the minority culture.

My Two Grandmothers is the story of a little girl named Lily who likes to visit her grandmothers: Grammy Lane, who lives on a farm in the country, and Bubbe Silver, who lives in a tall apartment building in the city. Lily visits her grandmothers several times a year, describing the fun things she does with each of them. Each grandmother shares aspects of who she is with Lily throughout the year, and many of those aspects have to do with food. After a cold winter day of snowshoeing in the woods, Grammy Lane suggests red flannel hash to warm them up. "Flannel? Like my pajamas?" Lily responds. "Heavens, no!" Grammy Lane says. "Flannel because it warms you up. My mother, your great-grandmother, taught me how to make it. I'll teach you someday, too. It's a Lane tradition." When Lily next sees Bubbe Silver, she tells her about red flannel hash, and Bubbe responds, "Sounds like my gefilte fish. . . . My mother, your great-grandmother, taught me how to make it. It is a Silver tradition." Like Grammy Lane, Bubbe Silver promises to pass on the tradition. Even the food choices that Older chose underscore that Grammy and Bubbe are not so different—hash and gefilte fish are both recipes for using up leftover bits of meat by people who did not have the luxury of wasting anything. The word "tradition" defines the recipes, connecting Lily to her ancestors.

Later in the story, the narrative underscores that Grammy Lane is Christian and Bubbe Silver is Jewish when Lily spends Christmas with the one and Hanukkah with the other. While the family says a blessing as they light the menorah and sing "Away in the Manger," the dominant picture is of family, togetherness, and consumption, of both presents and food. The holidays show Lily surrounded by her extended family, Jewish and Christian, fully participating in their celebrations. Demonstrating that she belongs with both families, when Lily describes each holiday meal, she explains, "We Lanes love pie!" and "We Silvers love latkes!"

The story concludes when Lily wants to introduce each grandmother to some of the other's traditions. She invites both of her grandmothers to a party at her house. "Please bring something traditional," she writes and, indeed, Grammy Lane brings apple pie and red flannel hash and Bubbe Silver brings gefilte fish and horseradish. The grandmothers, who clearly get along, smile at each other. "She's just like a Silver," Bubbe says to Grammy, who responds, "Every inch a Lane." In the world of the children's book, Lily can be both a Lane and a Silver, and since, as readers, we never learn Lily's last name, we do not know whether she is actually a Lane or a Silver. Similarly, we never see her in her own home, engaging with the practices forged or neglected by her parents. While it is clear that Grammy Lane is Christmas and the all-American farm and that Bubbe Silver is Hanukkah and the big city, Lily herself remains without context.

While Lily can be both a Silver and a Lane, she does so in the multicultural mode of consumption that is sequential and episodic. Nonetheless, her consumption of her family traditions connects Lily to a matriarchal lineage and defines her identity in terms of her family. The work of the historian Elizabeth Pleck offers further insight into the specifically familial ways that food rituals create a sense of identity. She argues that food rituals give Americans a sense of who they are and where they came from that serve "to define one's identity but also indicate changes in identity."[31] In teaching Lily the recipes that their own mothers taught them, Grammy Lane and Bubbe Silver are replicating this creation of family meaning—tightly tying Lily to both her Christian and Jewish family heritages. In doing so, they connect Lily to a relational network of female kin, grandmothers and great-grandmothers. The potential conflicts between a Christian identity and a Jewish identity are elided in favor of a family identity.

Most of the children's books that depicted children engaging in both their Christian and Jewish heritage took the approach of *Light the Lights!* and *My Two Grandmothers*, highlighting family celebrations and stripping away overtly theological content. Very few children's books delve into differences and potential incompatibilities between the traditions.[32] Independently published, *Bubbe and Gram: My Two Grandmothers* did tackle questions of prayer and belief. It won awards in 1997 and 1998, the Publisher's Marketing Association's Benjamin Franklin Silver Medal Award for excellence in independent publishing, and the Church and Synagogue Library Association's Helen Keating Ott Award for Outstanding Contribution to Children's Literature, respectively. It was written by Joan C. Hawxhurst, the first executive director of the Dovetail Institute, a nonaffiliated institution designed to support interfaith families in living out both religious traditions in one home.

Hawxhurst did not shy away from differences in the beliefs and truth claims of Christianity and Judaism, and *Bubbe and Gram* addresses some of the differing theological tenets of Christianity and Judaism. Unlike other books, it depicts the mezuzah on Bubbe's door and the Lord's Prayer with a picture of Jesus on Gram's wall, implicitly hinting at tensions between the traditions, with the prayer in the mezuzah proclaiming the oneness of God and the picture of Jesus gesturing toward the Trinity. Hawxhurst mentions prayers as part of both Bubbe's Shabbat dinner and Gram's Sunday dinner. Descriptions of Passover, Easter, Christmas, and Hanukkah focus as much on their particular claims about Moses, Christ's resurrection, the manger, and the Maccabees as on the festivities of the holidays. While the religious content of *Bubbe and Gram* is out of step with the other texts, it is produced by an organization that is explicitly open to actively raising children in multiple traditions, and the organization affirms that interfaith parents should address competing truth claims. Most importantly, though, the book's fundamental message is the same as that of the books that focus less explicitly on theology: the grandmothers deeply respect each other and each fully supports the other's attempts to pass on aspects of her tradition. The narrator notes, "There are lots of things that are different about Bubbe and Gram. Sometimes Bubbe doesn't understand the things I tell her about Gram's house. She says that's because she grew up practicing a different religion. But she always tells me that it's good to learn about being a Christian." On the next page, the conversation is repeated with the Christian grandmother.

Even in this more religiously oriented manual, the grandmothers are happy to have the grandchild learn about both traditions, including the importance of religious figures. Like the more secularly oriented books, the grandparent-focused books leave the religious traditions in the grandparents' homes. The grandchild remains a participant observer, taking part in the traditions without a sense that the traditions are being instilled in the child.

While these books tend to downplay theological and institutional particularity, they emphasize close familial bonds. Children share in the religious celebrations of their family members and draw meaning from the relationships that the children have with the adults in their families. The traditions depicted in loving detail in books like *Light the Lights!* are tied to family and friends—gelt in an uncle's pocket, an annual tree-decorating party. The family traditions in these stories are in fact shared practices that connect the main characters of the children's books to their parents, grandparents, and family history.[33] These familial practices also connect the main characters into the relational networks coming from their Christian and Jewish contexts, locating the children in both matrices of meaning.

While proponents of multicultural interfaith families gave small children messages that it was acceptable to celebrate dual holidays and share traditions with family members, older children tackle more complex themes of identity. They therefore delve into existential topics about the meaning of "halfness," that is, the meaning of a blended Christian-Jewish self. In 2000, Virginia Euwer Wolff published *The Mozart Season*, a young adult novel about Allegra, an adolescent violinist with a Jewish father and a "not Jewish at all" mother from Kansas. At the end of the book, Allegra reaffirms an understanding of her identity that has threaded through the text: "You can be half Jewish. Maybe whole Jews or whole Gentiles wouldn't understand. But you can be. I am."[34] "Halfness," here, does not equate with erasure.[35]

Allegra's closing words stand in sharp contrast to Margaret's closing thoughts on her dual religious heritage in *Are You There, God? It's Me, Margaret*, published in 1970. Thirty years before Wolff created Allegra, Judy Blume's Margaret connects Christianity and Judaism to churches and synagogues. Despite an absence of institutional belonging, however, Margaret has a personal relationship with God. She feels His presence and confides in Him frequently.[36] When she fails to find Him in any religious institution, she feels betrayed and angry, believing that if she had been raised within a tradition, she would have been able to find God within religious structures. Margaret's social setting makes her lack of religious identity a problem: while Margaret told her readers that not being any religion was fine in New York, in her New Jersey suburb, every child has a religious home, be it Protestant, Catholic, or Jewish.

Allegra, by contrast, lives in a community in which church or synagogue is rarely (if ever) mentioned. Her blended heritage does not trouble the people in her daily life. Though presumably Jewish himself, her violin teacher and confidante, Mr. Kaplan, is unconcerned with Allegra's halfness. Her older brother, Bro David, tells her that she cannot be made all Jewish, supporting her in understanding herself as half and half. Only her grandmother, Bubbe Raisa, in far-away (and Jewishly coded) New York, is concerned about Allegra's Jewishness. Though Allegra feels sympathy for Bubbe Raisa, her concerns do not shake Allegra's sense of herself.

The difference between Allegra's and Margaret's experiences of their blended backgrounds demonstrates the changing impact of multiculturalism over time. Margaret is troubled by her blended heritage, believing that because she is both, she is nothing and is surrounded by people who are depicted as fitting neatly into religious categories: Jew, Presbyterian, Methodist, Catholic. Allegra acknowledges that not everyone believes that she can be half-Jewish but maintains that despite those opinions, she is both halves and proud to be so: "One, if you are half and half, you're lucky because each kind has some really good things about it. Gentiles are good at building things, cathedrals and huge barns and things. Jews have courage to wander all around the world getting abused and killed and still go on having the Torah. . . . Two, if you're half and half, you're the thing that can't be. You can't be half Jewish. So you go through your life being something that can't be."[37] Though Allegra suggests that it is a disadvantage to be "something that can't be," she uses the framework of multiculturalism to compare herself to her friend Jessica, who is half African American and half Chinese, to point out that blending is possible. Just as Jessica both identifies with her black family's role in American history and attends Chinese school, both halves of Allegra's heritage are fully present in her life as well. Her mother, she reflected, could cook both Kansas food (corncakes and eggplant pudding) and Jewish food (latkes and pecan haroset). On her bed is a patchwork quilt, under which the quiltmaker, her Kansas great-grandmother, had died. On the wall in her dining room is a picture of her Jewish great-grandmother, Elter Bubbe Leah, for whom she was named and who died at Treblinka. As Allegra moves through the main dramatic arc of the story, their lives and deaths lend gravitas to the moral questions that she faces.

The difference between Margaret's experience in the late 1960s and Allegra's in the 1990s suggests a shift not in attitudes toward interfaith families, but rather in the social worlds that those families entered. *The Mozart Season* simply painted a girl growing up in a fairly cosmopolitan, secular segment of America. Though secular, her society used the arts to access both moral meaning and community. Religious and ethnic identity, by contrast, defined neither social and family life, nor identity. Judy Blume based Margaret's religiously segregated social world on her own memories of New Jersey in the 1950s, the decade with the highest religious affiliation of the twentieth century. For Blume's Margaret, her family's lack of institutional membership puts her outside of the cultural mainstream and differentiates her from her peer group.

By contrast, religion is not a dominant feature of 1990s Portland, Oregon, in which Wolff locates *The Mozart Season*. Neither Allegra's friends nor her parents nor their friends discuss religious community; the discussions of morality and empathy that recur throughout the book do not take place in markedly Christian or Jewish language. Instead, they form their communities and morality in other contexts, namely in the arts and in the compassionate consideration of the lives of others. In the novel, Allegra and her family wrestle not only with the stories of her great-grandmothers, but also with the histories and humanities of a homeless family friend and other young musicians in her concerto competition. The text leaves no doubt that the members of Allegra's community struggle with large questions and experience transcendence through the arts. They do so without the presence of traditionally defined Christianity and Judaism.

The differences between the worlds of *The Mozart Season* and *Are You There, God? It's Me, Margaret* reflect broader social patterns: the twentieth century saw fewer Americans affiliating with organized religion. Indeed, a large part of Margaret's discomfort with her lack of religious identity came from community expectations of religious belonging. In Margaret's suburban

OUR RUG
TENT
SALE

175 BLOOMINGDALE RD

SAVE UP TO 80%*

ON OVER 5,000 AMAZING RUGS

INCLUDING TRADITIONAL, CONTEMPORARY, PERSIAN & MANY MORE

HURRY IN FOR THE BEST SELECTION

MONDAY-SATURDAY, 10AM-8:30PM, SUNDAY, 11AM-7PM

PRIVATE PREVIEW
JUNE 20-21

SAVINGS OFF OF ORIGINAL PRICES

bloomingdale's

BLOOMINGDALE'S
175 BLOOMINGDALE RD
WHITE PLAINS, NY 10605
(914) 684-6300

SHOW THIS POSTCARD FOR AN ADDITIONAL 20% OFF!

ONE-OF-A-KIND RUGS

*Sale ends July 7, 2019. Savings are off original prices. Reg./Orig. prices reflect offering prices. Savings may not be based on actual sales, intermediate markdowns may have been taken. All sizes are approximate. Rug savings cannot be combined with any other discount, promotion or certificate. Photos are representative only. Limited quantities. Prices, savings and selection may differ on bloomingdales.com. See bloomingdales.com to order or check merchandise, or check merchandise availability in your local store. For home merchandise availability, please visit bloomingdales.com/homemerchandise. Warranty information is available at department register or by writing to: Bloomingdale's 1000 Third Avenue, New York, NY 10022. Attn: Risk management Department, 10th Floor. Return policy: No returns on final clearance. Discount offer is for rug tent merchandise only.

***********ECRWSS**C360   9787

Roger Gerber
26 Sage Ter
Scarsdale NY 10583-2045

PRIVATE PREVIEW

JUNE 20 - 21

SAVE
UP TO
80%*

on our entire selection of one-of-a-kind, hand-knotted, rugs.

Thousands of rugs to choose from in every shape, size, color and style

This is a limited time event so hurry in for the best selection.

world of the late 1960s, belonging required a concrete religious identity. In Allegra's fictional Portland, Oregon, in the 1990s, a religious identity was simply not necessary. These shifts created more room for interfaith families to build lives and communities outside of the confines of organized religion.

While proponents of multicultural interfaith families address children in the earnest language of support, their outreach to adults assumes a much sharper tone. In 2000, an interfaith couple, Daniel Klein and Freke Vuijst, produced *The Half-Jewish Book: A Celebration*, which advocates for interfaith and intentionally blended family cultures. They argue, first, for half-Jews as providing a normative Jewish experience in the late twentieth century, and they celebrate a set of characteristics nurtured in an intentionally interfaith home, including tolerance and an ability to act as cultural brokers. These traits, presented as valuable moral goods, echo the values of a multicultural, millennial society.

The western Massachusetts couple opened by announcing that "we are living in the era of the half-Jew" as the majority of American Jews marry non-Jews and "the number of American half-Jews under the age of eleven now exceeds the number of American full Jews under eleven."[38] In short, they call for an acknowledgment that the half-Jewish experience has come to dominate the American Jewish landscape and for the celebration of that reality. The couple interviewed and surveyed over one hundred half-Jews and collected data on half-Jewish celebrities, historical figures, and artists, as well as resources for half-Jews. On the basis of this research, they claim that rather than being a "fractional" identity, being half-Jewish could be a "double" identity. In other words, they oppose the denigration of half-Jewish identity by suggesting it as a "cultural, intellectual, and aesthetic mix that is . . . greater than the sum of its parts."[39]

Belying any sense of religious connection or practice, Klein and Vuijst take a broad definition of what makes one half-Jewish: "a person is half-Jewish if half of her genetic or cultural make up is Jewish and half is not. That is it."[40] As a result, they suggest that because the home could, and inevitably would, contain elements of both cultures, raising a child to acknowledge that bicultural reality was the most honest approach. Thus, even in a single-religion household, Klein and Vuijst maintain a multicultural approach. Children in such a home might be religiously Catholic, Methodist, or Jewish, but culturally, they are unequivocally half-Jewish. Again, their rhetoric of blending is maintained in part by separating Christian and Jewish beliefs or formal affiliation from what they refer to as their "cultural, intellectual, and aesthetic" elements.

Klein and Vuijst frame the formation that occurs in interfaith families as a moral good by arguing that children of interfaith marriages are more successful than average in multicultural, millennial America. They therefore spend much of their book using famous half-Jews to tease out the traits created by the double perspective that they believe blended homes foster. They suggest that though Gloria Steinem "insists that her talent for fitting in with any group is simply the outgrowth of being a woman . . . Steinem's excelling at this talent may also be accounted for by her insider/outsider status as a half-Jew."[41] Klein and Vuijst then tied Steinem's success to a flexibility bred of hybridity.

While Klein and Vuijst work hard to sell the positive traits that they associate with the half-Jewish identity, the celebratory aspect of their work depends on their assertion that the newly fused whole is actually better than the sum of its parts. This assertion rests on a new set of assumptions. First, the authors consider individuals more important than religious communities. No mention is made of the impact of intermarriage on either the Jewish people or Jewish community in *Half-Jewish*. Rather, the authors critique organized Judaism (writ large) for its failure to support patrilineal Jews, whose last names expose them to anti-Semitism but whose patrilineal status exclude them from communal belonging. Second, Klein and Vuijst do not understand growing up outside of institutional religious life to be of inherently less worth than a religiously shaped childhood. They express no concern about salvation, nor do they assume a lack of moral formation or tradition in those with a dual heritage and a secular life. Rather, they believe that interacting with two cultures fosters versatility and cross-cultural understanding. The valuing of these traits, like the repeated use of the word "multicultural," demonstrates a shift in attitude directly tied to the late 1990s enthusiasm for a deeply syncretic popular multiculturalism. The message contrasts sharply with the assumption that raising children without a single religious tradition will confuse them; indeed, Christianity and Judaism are not even framed as religious identities. Framing these traditions as cultural, Klein and Vuijst insist that combining them creates new, valuable multicultural identities.

While Klein and Vuijst differentiate Jewish and Christian cultural identities, it is important to note that they see a distinct moral advantage to the traits that they associate with an expanded set of cultural dispositions. They also point to the ability of half-Jewish children to find comfort in the religious practices of both traditions, despite the competing truth claims. In Klein and Vuijst's worldview, then, minimal, if any, tension (comic or otherwise) exists for the child of two traditions in the ways outlined in the children's books just discussed. Instead, this new "half" identity supersedes all traditions that came before it.

Chrismukkah: A Multicultural Romp

Two years later, Ron Gompertz published *Chrismukkah: Everything You Need to Know to Celebrate the Hybrid Holiday*. The blurbs on the back of Gompertz's book came from such elevated sources as the *New York Times*, which raved, "The double-barreled holiday offers an excuse to eat mashed potatoes and potato latkes in the same sitting, with candy canes and chocolate gelt for dessert." The *Wall Street Journal* observed, "Chrismukkah puts a name to something millions of families are already celebrating."[42] The reviews of *Chrismukkah* signal a sharp break with the cultural environment of the 1970s and 1980s, when the mainstream media reacted to rising rates of interfaith marriage with stories about Jewish groups' concerns.

Gompertz frames the celebration of Chrismukkah as a multicultural romp, suggesting that the holiday celebrations could be unmoored from the story of the Christ child or the miracle of long-lasting oil (or, perhaps more importantly, the story of Jewish survival against oppression and assimilation). People who loved their heritage but did not believe in the truth claims of their traditions could enjoy Chrismukkah. He presents the practices of Chrismukkah in an ironic tone, using retro images with kitschy titles, as well as the occasional snatch of sarcasm or insult. Gompertz's use of irony allows him to humorously defuse tensions associated with blending Christian and Jewish practice in order to articulate strongly held convictions about interfaith life. Indeed, for most interfaith families, he insists, truth claims and institutional religion are not relevant to their lives in the first place.

Gompertz argues that Chrismukkah already existed in many interfaith homes, but he also clearly felt the need to introduce it on a more popular scale. "I need to admit something up front. Chrismukkah is pretend. It doesn't exist. It's made up. Wishful thinking. A holiday hoax." He points out that it would not "get you in good with God" or "bring you spiritual enlightenment." It is, however, a way to have fun during the holiday season by letting go of the "December Dilemma" of Hanukkah or Christmas in favor of enjoying both. With this perspective, he argues, Chrismukkah could be a "'merry mish-mash' season as real as Santa Claus, Hanukkah Harry and the notion of 'peace on earth and good will toward men.'"[43] Chrismukkah, Gompertz argues, provides a chance for couples to create their own American melting-pot traditions out of whatever aspects of their plural heritages they wish to preserve. These traditions are selected in a form of millennial capitalism in which the act of consumption becomes part of a "discourse of possibility," in this case, possibilities for claiming and shaping complicated constellations of practices.[44]

While Chrismukkah itself is a celebration for American families containing Christians and Jews, Gompertz told National Public Radio (NPR) that he hoped it would inspire other kinds of interfaith families to create their own holiday fusions.[45]

Chrismukkah solves what Gompertz sees as a distinctly modern American problem. He explains that "like most interfaith couples," he and his wife were not religious but remained proud of their cultural heritages and curious about their spouse's tradition. While aware of the notion that celebrating both religions confused children, they wanted to "respect and honor" both sets of traditions and raise their daughter to be "informed, tolerant, and balanced." He also argues that, as "a multicultural family, we are part of a growing demographic trend in America that is a by-product of our country's melting pot history. From this perspective, Chrismukkah is more than just a pretend holiday about two incompatible religions." Indeed, seen with the long view of history, Chrismukkah becomes part of "an evolutionary continuum as old as Judaism and Christianity."[46] Gompertz's use of the word "evolutionary" suggests that his secular and blended holiday is part of the inevitable forward march of progress in American society. He therefore makes a case for normative multiculturalism as the overarching, unifying value system for a certain type of self-identified nonreligious interfaith families.

Despite his momentary earnestness, the rest of the text is tongue-in-cheek, a joyously ironic celebration of all things kitsch, using a tone that is a persuasive cultural marker meant to imply savvy and sophistication. The book contains goofy recipes for combining traditions, such as the matzoh bread house, which is unconcerned that matzoh is food for Passover food, not Hanukkah. A similar tone arises in the recipe section, which names a Long Island Iced Tea recipe the "Passion of the Iced." This play on the Passion of the Christ skirts the fact that the Passion story is associated with Holy Week and Easter, rather than Christmas. It also avoids the fact that Passion plays have, historically, increased tensions between Christians and Jews, often resulting in anti-Semitic violence during Holy Week. Gompertz, then, employs satiric irony (intentionally or not) in order to sidestep some of the historic and theological tensions between Christians and Jews.

Gompertz's book describes customs that fuse elements of Christian and Jewish foodways and traditions in a lighthearted style that offers the interfaith family a smorgasbord of new family traditions and potential practices. His (no longer extant) website sold the accoutrements of the holiday. In 2010, the site listed a kit for the matzoh house, blue and white Christmas tree ornaments decorated with menorahs, and Chrismukkah cards. The site, with a soundtrack of Christmas carols played by a klezmer band, remained live for over seven years. Gompertz explains that Chrismukkah is "about throwing everything up. As garish, as busy, as multicultural as we could make it." He does so in response to a perceived need of interfaith families and is rewarded with media attention and popularity.

Chrismukkah exploits a largely unspoken fact: many interfaith families celebrate holidays from both sides of the family. "It is a bit of a spoof, a bit of a satire, but it's something that is very, very real for those of us who are in mixed marriages and have to battle the feelings of our spouses, the feelings of our in-laws," Gompertz said in a 2006 NPR interview. "And when things get too heavy, it's a good time to make light."[47] "Making light" involves sidestepping or making light of theology, focusing instead on nostalgia and fun, a move that Gompertz repeatedly asserts is typical of what most interfaith families do and want.

Though he embraces a move away from theologically oriented holidays, Gompertz allows that his spoof could go too far. For instance, in his NPR interview, he noted that he created the new holiday food of "gefilte goose" because "gefilte ham" seemed fundamentally disrespectful to Jewish tradition. This distinction is interesting in part because so much of Gompertz's celebration already thoroughly offends both the Catholic hierarchy and the Jewish Board of Rabbis. In December 2004, the two groups responded to Chrismukkah on the Catholic League's website, saying, "We . . . want to see the spiritual integrity of all faiths fully protected. Chanukah and Christmas celebrated during the same period should not be fused into some cultural combination that does not recognize the spiritual identity of our respective faiths. Copying the tradition of another faith and calling it by another name is a form of shameful plagiarism we cannot condone."[48] As shying away from the gefilte ham indicates, Gompertz indeed means no offense. He does not, however, share the perspective that Christmas and Hanukkah were the "traditions of another faith." Rather, he contends that he and his wife could maintain the traditional Christian and Jewish practices in their own families while remaining "not religious."[49] Gompertz regards both his cultural Judaism and his intermarriage as a natural cultural progression—one that could, with a healthy touch of irony, be celebrated.

Gompertz claims that he enthusiastically supports other holiday combinations, both with other religions and other Christian and Jewish celebrations, although he created Chrismukkah, not "Eastover." As both Christian and Jewish cultural critics have long pointed out, there is a largely secular and very materialistic component to both Christmas and Hanukkah, hence the cries of "put the Christ back in Christmas" on the part of some Christian clergy and objections to lavish Hanukkah celebrations as inherently part of Jewish assimilation to American culture (since Hanukkah is traditionally a minor holiday in the Jewish liturgical year). Because many Americans locate Christmas and Hanukkah primarily in the cultural terrain of holiday parties and holiday shopping, they lend themselves to fusion, and at times, confusion, with each other.

Christmas and Hanukkah are both holidays with complex historical relationships to the market. As Leigh Eric Schmidt points out, the early twentieth-century Christmas was so "enmeshed in consumer culture" that "amid the shopping, the cards, the Toyland Santa Clauses, the packages, and the lights, the festival of winter seemed once again to allow only marginal room for Christ."[50] When Gompertz draws on Christmas apart from Christ to create Chrismukkah, he is pulling from an array of traditions that are tied to the market and already enjoyed by Americans—including many whose families, though historically Catholic or Protestant, no longer consider themselves Christian. Similarly, by the turn of the millennium, American Hanukkah came with an array of traditions tied to market trends. Andrew Heinze names consumption as the common denominator of Christmas and Hanukkah, a way for "American practice and attitude" to infuse the traditional form of Hanukkah. That said, he also maintains that it ceased to be a holiday about the rededication of the Temple.[51] American society, then, has long had celebrations of Christmas and Hanukkah that play down the theological import of the holidays in favor of their consumer and festive elements. Chrismukkah largely draws from these established and overlapping trends.

December Holidays in Practice

Chrismukkah, as Gompertz and *The OC* pitch it, is a source of media frenzy, but not necessarily an indication of how interfaith families, attuned to the questions of identity posed in the young adult novels, might celebrate it. Material culture and ethnography offer insight into those familial practices. While Gompertz marketed Chrismukkah cards on his website, the early twenty-first century also saw such cards available in mainstream grocery stores in New York City, Atlanta, Chicago, Seattle, and their suburbs. The cards serve a niche (primarily urban) market and are more likely to appear in grocery stores in Jewish neighborhoods. They tend to be grouped along the border between the Christmas cards and the Hanukkah cards. Made by two of the major greeting-card companies in the United States, American

FIGURE 4 Whimsical
Chrismukkah card.

Greetings and Hallmark, the cards are sold individually, rather than in packages of eight or ten. As shown in figures four and five, they range in tone from the sentimental to the comic, but all of them create common ground by denuding the holidays of one kind of religious content—references to Christ or Judah Maccabee—and replacing it with a new set of religious values: family, tolerance, friendship, joy, and unspecified wonder.

The sentimental cards mention the "miracles of the season" or stress other kinds of themes, such as what all people share: "We celebrate two different stories with different traditions, but one hope we all have in common—a world filled with comfort and care." Some of the cards refer specifically to the practices of Judaism and Christianity: "A menorah in the window and an evergreen wreath on the door show that holiday feelings are filling our homes and loving good times are in store. The joy and beauty of this time of year remind us of the wonderful people in our lives. People like you." If the more sedate cards lean toward neutral colors, ornaments, evergreens, and menorahs,

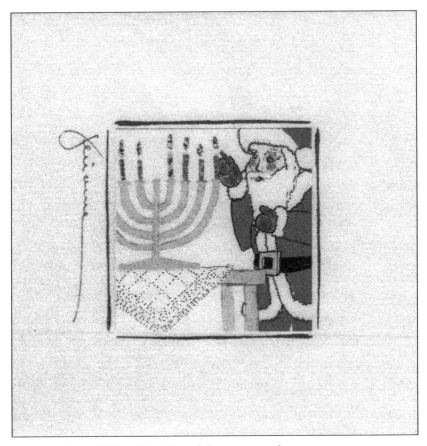

FIGURE 5 Chrismukkah card with Santa lighting a menorah.

the humorous cards often feature brightly colored homages to Santa humor. One card pictures Santa sitting on a snowy rooftop, sharing a drink with his friend the Fiddler on the Roof. The caption inside reads "Tis the season, whatever the reason!" Another Santa card depicts an elf wearing a yarmulke and calling out to his team of reindeer, "On Isaac! On Izzy! On Eli! On Abe! On Levi!" Inside, it reads, "Merry Hanukkah!"

While these cards target interfaith friends as much as interfaith families, they indicate a shift in attitudes toward both the winter holidays and the relationship between Christians and Jews. The early twenty-first-century American culture that produces these cards sees Christians and Jews as friends and neighbors, people who would acknowledge and participate in each other's celebrations. The cards downplay particular holidays' distinctiveness, with phrases like "tis the season, whatever the reason" and suggestions that trees and menorahs are simply accessories to the same themes of peace on earth, friendship, gifts, and merrymaking.

In several ways, this broader merging of specific holidays into the holiday season lends cultural support to the merging of the holidays in interfaith homes. First, it ritualizes and formalizes the social world that gives rise to interfaith families, one in which holiday greetings are sent across religious lines. They make it possible to buy one set of cards to send to both sides of interfaith families. Lastly, Christmas and Hanukkah are depicted side by side, their juxtaposition underscoring the holidays' shared messages of festivity, cheer, friendship, and family. "Is it Chanumas or Chrismakkah?" asked one of many cards marketable to interfaith families. "What word would best de-scribe bringing together two different traditions to enjoy food, lights, and laughter all under one roof?"

If only a small percentage of the cards directly reference a dual celebration in one family, all of them participate in a syncretic multiculturalism that blends Christmas and Hanukkah and posits that the essential meaning of both holi-days is neither the birth of a savior nor the miracle of oil, but rather peace, friendship, and merriment. The fusing of the holidays appears perfectly normal and fun, not a cause for concern. While not all religious communities approve of Chrismukkah, Hallmark and American Greetings are happy to sell it, sug-gesting they expect the cards to be profitable in at least some markets.

Conclusion

This new millennial discourse around interfaith family life is carried out in part in the American marketplace, with children's and young adult books published by major publishing houses and self-published for sale on Amazon .com, novelty book celebrations of interfaith family life, and mass-market greeting cards. These popular depictions of the interfaith family advocate for combining the practices, but in keeping with a rhetorical hesitancy about combining Christian and Jewish religious practices and, using the ethnic in-flections of multiculturalism, draw a distinction between "religion" and "culture." By locating the resulting mosaic of practices firmly in the "cultural" terrain (a terrain marked by an absence of affiliations, truth claims, or life passages), these sources advocate for the possibility of creating a multicultural Christian-Jewish home, just as one might create an Indian-Irish home.

While the conversation around the intentionally blended interfaith family carefully draws distinctions between the practices that they combine and "re-ligion" (or practices that might conventionally be seen as religious), it also has an overarching moral message. Multicultural interfaith families are, these sources suggest, a moral good because they embody values that the authors suggest are key to a diverse society, namely tolerance and respect. In addition, they create children who, because of the blended settings in which they were raised, are better able to move between cultures and act as mediators across social difference, traits that the authors equate with success. As we have seen, then, multiculturalism provides a lens through which to understand a moral logic for shaping the selection of practice and for the framing of blended identity at the turn of the millennium.

CHAPTER SIX

Living the Interfaith Family Life
Dual Religious Heritages Shaping Family Cultures

This is not a handbook. I bought all the handbooks. I devoured them. I threw them all away. . . . I want to write a book that will shelter and give people comfort and keep people company as they face the difficult choices entailed in interfaith family life.

Why? Truly, truly, one reason is because the books out there suck. They are dry little guidebooks with reasonable flat dialogues between invented interfaith couples . . . , people you would never want to meet in this life. . . . These husbands say things like "What Kathy does on Sunday is her business." These wives say things like, "Why must Sam be upset about having a Christmas tree?" . . . Tell the truth, I want to wag my finger at the rabbi who invented [them] as an excuse to hear himself give pat answers.

—Jennifer Kimball

This epigraph is drawn from personal writings shared with me by Jennifer Kimball, a scholar, blogger, Mormon feminist, and interfaith parent.[1] She wrote out of frustration with the ways in which manuals for interfaith families address the issues of interfaith family life, and she argued that the books are often produced by Jewish publishing houses and written out of a fear that Judaism will be destroyed by intermarriage. It is that fear, she suggested, that produced "flat characters, with their scripted ignorance and their see-through dissatisfaction." She argued that while many Jewish institutions voice this concern—that a child with both a baptism and a bris will ultimately recognize that his parents lacked follow-through in both traditions—it is a red herring. Rather, Kimball suggested that for the authors of these books, a central concern is the future of the Jewish people, not the daily lives of interfaith families.

On some level, the fears found in these books were grounded in a statistical reality. The 2013 Pew Research Center for Religion and Public Life study "*A Portrait of Jewish Americans*" noted that 79 percent of married "Jews of no religion," as they called secular or cultural Jews, and 36 percent of "Jews by religion" were married to non-Jews.[2] Of those people in interfaith marriages, 20 percent said they were raising their children Jewish, 25 percent say they were raising their children partially Jewish, and 37 percent say they were not raising their children Jewish at all.[3]

When these statistics are combined with the consistently rising interfaith marriage rate, evidence that children of interfaith marriage are less likely to be raised Jews fueled anxiety about Jewish continuity in many Jewish communal organizations. While the nonpartisan research arm of the Pew Charitable Trust produced "A Portrait of Jewish Americans," some of its funding came from the Neubauer Family Foundation, which is invested in the Jewish community and its preservation. It also followed more than a generation of sociological research, often paid for by Jewish think tanks or organizations.[4] This earlier research both documented the growing trend of interfaith marriages and the correlation of interfaith marriage with a failure to affiliate with synagogues and to raise Jewish children. I use the word "failure" intentionally here, because this research focused on the effect of interfaith marriage on Jewish communal life and on the perpetuation of the Jewish people and Jewish religion, as measured by affiliation with Jewish institutions. As a result, the research was generally predisposed against interfaith marriage, which it framed as a threat to Jewish survival. It focused on the families' failure (or disinclination) to join synagogues or seek out Jewish education for their children and with their tendency to celebrate Christmas, suggesting that the former came from an internalized anti-Semitism and the latter from a desire to assimilate.

As this research was largely designed to study and solve the "problem" of interfaith marriage, it did not explore the lived religion of interfaith families themselves. This chapter uses case studies to explore the lived religion of the families that Pew describes as raising children "partially Jewish," though that is not a term any of the families would choose themselves. In doing so, it places these families inside a growing American trend of hybrid identities and syncretic religious practices. These four families were selected from my broader sample of more than thirty interviews with families who "do both" largely because they were exceptional in how articulate they were. They were not, however, particularly unusual in their practice or their approach. Since I initially conducted these interviews, Susan Katz Miller has gone on to publish a book that addresses interfaith marriages.[5] As a result, I have used her name, with her permission. The other families have pseudonyms.

Most importantly, interfaith families are part of a number of broader trends. Some of those trends were explored in chapter 5, but, importantly, interfaith marriage is growing among all Americans, not just American Jews, as is a failure to affiliate with religious institutions and a tendency to combine religious traditions. According to the Pew Foundation, American religious

FIGURE 6 Bridal couple with rabbi and Franciscan friar. Image courtesy of wedding couple.

life is far from stable—rather, they go so far as to characterize it as being in "constant movement."[6] Their numbers, from surveys done in 2007, placed the rate of interfaith marriage in the United States at 37 percent (counting Protestants who married across Protestant family groups).[7] In addition, 28 percent of Americans had left the religious tradition of their childhoods, either for a different tradition or to become unaffiliated.[8] Fully one-third of Americans "regularly" attended religious services at more than one place, with another quarter doing so occasionally. Americans were not simply attending multiple houses of worship within their own traditions—one-fourth of them "sometimes" attended religious services of a faith other than their own for reasons other than weddings or funerals—while members of interfaith marriages are less likely to attend religious services than those married to co-religionists. Those who did attend services at least yearly, however, are more likely to attend services of more than one religious tradition (again, exempting attendance for life-cycle events).[9] Pew's research suggested that these numbers were likely to get larger, not smaller, moving forward.

Americans were not only crossing over into each other's worship spaces, but also incorporating beliefs across religious boundaries. Twenty-two percent of self-identifying Christians believed in reincarnation, and 23 percent believed in astrology. Similar proportions of the general population believed in yoga as spiritual practice (and not just exercise) and in spiritual energy located in physical things.[10] The Pew Foundation broke these statistics down further, by race, educational level, and Christian denomination (notably, though the survey included non–Christian Americans, they did not include Jews or other religious groups in their data breakdowns). Most importantly, for an examination of interfaith families, the Pew Foundation found that "older people (those over 65) consistently express lower levels of acceptance of these kinds of beliefs compared with other people."[11]

Acceptance of the practice of drawing beliefs from multiple religious systems, then, increased with the baby boom and subsequent generations. None of the Pew studies addressed whether religiously mixed marriages (one's own or one's parents') makes one more (or less) likely to draw from a multiplicity of beliefs than the rest of the American population. What it does indicate is that when interfaith families combine practices or include practices from multiple traditions, they were part of broader patterns in American religion. So while Christian-Jewish families had unique motivations for blending traditions, they were not unique in doing so. As a result, explorations of how they recast religious practices or navigate contradictory belief systems may provide insight into how other Americans were living their religious lives in the early twenty-first century.

Interfaith families often had slightly different motivations than the majority of Americans living with blended religious lives. The parents in interfaith families may or may not have been drawn to their spouse's tradition. They may, or may not, have been able to be open about their multiple religious practices when speaking with their communities. However, an American taking up Buddhist meditation or yoga could often do so while remaining disconnected from the history and community of that belief system, and therefore could focus on aspects of the tradition that felt positive or beneficial. Interfaith families do not have this luxury, as they contend, in a myriad of ways, with the histories and communities that shape the traditions they seek to hold in their lives, especially as those histories are manifest in the attitudes and opinions of family members.

Rather than finding such families unmoored from religious practice and moral formation, I found, through my research, that Christian-Jewish blended families often developed a cohesive family narrative or sense of who they were together as a family beyond denominational constraints. Instead of supporting the idea that a bireligious household was inherently confusing to the children, a separate set of values took center stage in the family's life, producing a strong story of the family's identity. The religious or cultural rituals of Christianity and Judaism remained present in these families, only insofar as they supported internal narratives of family identity.

As chapter 5 explored, however, multiculturalism offered interfaith families a way to combine practices from a multiplicity of heritages while uniting them with a set of moral values and assumptions rooted in concepts of respect, tolerance, and diversity. In the previous chapter, some interfaith family advocates proposed intentionally hybrid and morally inflected identities, combining practices in a multicultural model of identity instead of privileging one religious identity or set of beliefs. Here, this model is borne out through the example of four families who, in very different yet related ways, redefined their religious lives in parallel with some aspects of the multicultural model. These families sought to create new boundaries and parameters of belief and practice. Importantly, however, if the multicultural model avoided questions of contradictory theologies by bracketing those questions, either by ignoring them or through a profession of secularism, some of the families explored here explicitly used language of faith and mystery to explore their fused identities.

An Interfaith Homestead: A Christian-Jewish Alternative Lifestyle

Cultivated fields, at a farm in her hometown, surrounded Hannah Kaplan's wedding. The food was mostly locally sourced, one of the bride's junior high school teachers led the band, and the bride's sisters baked the multitiered wedding cake. The values of simplicity and self-sufficiency, not because there was no other choice but because doing so had inherent meaning, animated the planning and execution of the wedding. Nods to Jewish culture—the groom's effort to get his new father-in-law to dance by playing the *hora* and the bride's mother's Yiddish congratulations—blended with nods to Christianity, such as a ceremonial structure drawn from the Book of Common Prayer, though the couple removed God from the ceremony out of respect for the many belief systems present among the guests. The couple introduced a moment of silence by saying, "We offer this silence for your own contemplation and, if you like, prayer, and for people everywhere in our world who are not themselves able to enjoy the freedom of marriage," underscoring a commitment to equal rights in their celebratory moment. The couple performed their own ceremony in part because, like many young couples, they did not have a strong relationship with a member of the clergy of any religion.

Dan Kaplan and Kathy Brewster, Hannah's parents, forged for themselves a third path: a back-to-the-land ethos, which they viewed as part of a central moral universe for the family as well as practice of their lives.[12] Dan and Kathy initially went back to the land to escape from a "technological and consumption-oriented culture that they found to be spiritually and ethically lacking," not because they were trying to solve dilemmas posed by their interfaith marriage.[13] They strove to find solutions to those problems in what Rebecca Kneald Gould has defined as the central tenets of homesteading, an "ethic of simple living, of being a producer more than a consumer, and letting nature set the terms for one's daily chores."[14] This ethos provided a central family identity, trumping both Kathy's Christian and Dan's Jewish heritages. As parents, when Dan and Kathy measured their success in imparting their values, it was by a commitment to simple living rather than to Jewish or Christian traditions. While their daughters had attachment to some Christian rituals, such as the family's celebration of Christmas, they did not consider themselves Christian and had differing senses of Jewish identity. None of the daughters has made their parents' scale of commitment to the land; however, they all echo those values in their own lifestyles.[15]

Kathy was born in 1950 and brought up in a New England college town where her father was a United Church of Christ minister and seminary professor. As a child, Kathy watched her father go south as a freedom rider and listened to stories of his being jailed in Alabama in the company of liberal activist and Yale University Chaplain William Sloane Coffin. In high school, she attended Coffin's services at Yale and went to college fired up by the possibility of what Christianity could be. When she got to college, however, she found that there were many people who shared her social justice orientation, and "they were not necessarily Christian at all."[16]

Two years older than Kathy, Dan grew up in a middle-class Jewish family in a mid-Atlantic suburb. As a teenager, Dan became deeply frustrated by his childhood congregation's failure to engage with civil rights, the Vietnam War, and other pressing social issues. When he wrote a confirmation speech that critiqued the congregation, the rabbi would not let him deliver it, and he was forced to deliver a "censored" version. Dan left for college intent on re-creating himself and leaving organized Judaism forever.

Dan and Kathy met at a small liberal arts college in the late 1960s. The environment was infused with liberal, counterculture values addressing the war in Vietnam, the planet, and gender roles. When Kathy graduated from college, they were married and drove away in their VW microbus for a honeymoon. They bought farmland, living in the bus while they built their own house. They had very little money, but were self-reliant, raising, slaughtering, and preserving their own food. Neither of them gave weight to their differing religious backgrounds in light of their shared political and lifestyle commitments.

Though ultimately Dan became a doctor and Kathy a teacher, they continued to farm and raise animals, though on a smaller scale. For their daughters, Dan and Kathy's early years took on the quality of family lore. Hannah, their eldest daughter, focused on the creation of that first farm: "They were these two twenty-somethings from the suburbs. They learned how to build a house, do electrical wiring, all of those things, from books and from summer volunteer projects. I can't imagine doing that myself." That early self-reliance provided a central family story for their daughters, though they also understood and respected their parents' decision to enter professions. "They really do value living off the land. Look at this place," Rebecca gestured to her parents' farmhouse and the eleven acres outside the window. "But they also valued other things that they could not give us as full-time farmers. I don't think it was a compromise of values, just a shifting of which values were getting prioritized." Their homesteading ethos—living simply, producing over consuming, and the natural rhythms of farming—remained central to Dan's and Kathy's lives, and to the environment in which they raised their daughters.

Living in rural settings limited the available religious communities. Kathy rarely found communities that combined all of the elements of Christianity that she desired: liberal theology, excellent preaching, and a strong music program. Judaism was simply unavailable. Hannah and Rebecca spoke warmly of a Methodist Sunday school, but the parents had more mixed memories of the church. In Appalachia, the family was part of a neighborhood Sunday school, along with two Catholic families, a Baptist family, and a Methodist family. In a letter to his Christian theologian father-in-law, written in the early 1980s, Dan expressed their concerns in the following way: "The things they have covered, far too literally for me, include Noah's ark and the flood and the creation story. Rereading these, I was again horrified at the violence, the demeaning position of women, and the wrathful and vengeful nature of God. How do you feel about this kind of biblical history?" Dan, the Jewish parent in the family, did not express concern with the Christian religious environment that they had helped create for their children. Rather, he was concerned with the literal interpretation of the biblical stories. While literal readings of the Bible are connected to certain strains of conservative

Christianity, the fact that Dan went to his Christian minister father-in-law for advice suggests that his concern was not the Christianity of the group, but, as he states, their literalism, and the violence, sexism, and vengeance embedded in the Bible stories. He worried about the impact of those stories on his five- and three-year-old girls, who he hoped would develop feminist sensibilities. Dan and Kathy chose to emphasize feminist, nonviolent moral and psychological development over Christian or Jewish identity formation.

In their home, the parents explained that there are many religions, all of which "are all or can all be okay." They made a point of lighting the menorah every year, although the family's big holidays were Thanksgiving and Christmas, and Kathy herself had never attended a Passover seder. The daughters' descriptions of Christmas reveal a celebration that owed as much of its ritual to homesteading as to Christianity. The family opened stockings upon waking, but then spent the morning feeding animals, making and eating a special breakfast, and getting Christmas dinner prepared. The family listened to a reading of the Christmas story, as told in the Gospel of Luke, and gathered around the piano for Christmas carols, both at Kathy's prompting. Rebecca played Christmas carols on the piano and Hannah read the Gospel of Luke, but both report doing so to please their mother rather than because they found meaning in the practices. The family then opened the often home-made presents, one at a time, so that they could be admired. Kathy encouraged everyone to save the wrapping paper for next year. The holiday, Hannah noted, "is highly ritualized."

Visiting the family home the weekend before Thanksgiving, I realized that Dan, the Jewish father, was the one most excited about Christmas. He had celebrated Christmas growing up, so he did not share in the sense of being an outsider in America during the Christmas season that some other Jews have articulated. Rather, he reflected that he has always loved Christmas, particularly gifts, which he considers "love made tangible." The entire family talked about the importance of making or selecting special gifts. Every year, Dan makes stained glass for his daughters, and Kathy gives them hand-knitted items, a tradition they have expanded to include handcrafts gathered on travels. In recent years, Hannah has given handmade ornaments, Rebecca has compiled a family cookbook, and Rebecca's toddler gave everyone her preschool artwork. Activities were also popular family gifts and are a tradition that has extended beyond the nuclear family. Hannah gave her husband a "hike of the month" club as a birthday present, in which each month they go on a hike in a local park together. For all of the emphasis on presents, the family framed the gifts as "nonmaterialistic," in keeping with the family ethos of simple living. Both Hannah and Rebecca pointed to the importance of the homemade gifts as representing time, thought, and creativity.

Hannah's and Rebecca's descriptions of Christmas underscore the ways in which homesteading practices rather than Christian ones took on meaning for them. First, though the chores delayed the festivities far more than the Bible reading, both sisters took them as a matter of course. More significantly, while both daughters framed the Christian elements of the holiday as meaningful to their mother, the homemade gifts and activities were clearly also important to them. Not only have they brought homemade gifts into their own nuclear families but they also have framed the homemade gifts as more meaningful and valuable than things that can be bought.

When I asked Kathy and Dan how they hoped their daughters would move through the world, Kathy spoke of freedom from materialism and a love of nature, work ethic, family, and friends. Dan, echoing her, commented that family endeavors like putting up hay together are, to him, religious experiences because they promote bonding and an appreciation for hard work. Every summer, the family harvested the hay, laying each cutting in the sun to dry; should it rain, the hay needs to be given time to dry again, a process that gave the Kaplan daughters firsthand experience with the "difficulty, chance, and careful planning" that goes into farming. "I do not enjoy the process at all, but I respect that it is hard to do, and we all did it together. We did it because of sustainability and self-sufficiency," reflected Hannah. "They could have bought hay, but since they have the land, they feel like they should grow it themselves. So it is really part of how we do things, or did things, as a family." The ritual of putting up hay was deeply entrenched in homesteading values, as well as being grounded in a connection to the land and family, ultimate concerns and values that theologians such as Paul Tillich have deemed religious.[17]

Kathy talked a great deal about her concern for transmitting values to her children. She saw specific obstacles to her success in what she described as the increasing materialism of American culture and, to a certain extent, the ways in which her daughters' life choices differed from her own. She worried that contemporary American culture includes a sense of entitlement she felt was not part of her generation's experience. How does one balance helping and supporting one's children, she worried, while giving them a sense of how important hard work is? Can a simple family life counteract society's materialism through example? While she joked about one child's love of shopping, her comments reflected an undercurrent of concern about engagement with consumer culture. While social justice was verbally emphasized in their home, the realities of raising three children while sustaining a farm meant it was not frequently modeled. Were those values transmitted? Kathy's concerns were not directly connected to the absence of religious community in her daughters' lives, but rather to her uncertainty about how, or if, her values translated into a nonhomesteading lifestyle. Hannah has been an urban dweller since graduating from college; Rebecca lived in a large city and a small town before returning to her hometown after getting divorced; and their younger sister, Judy, is also living in a city. None of the daughters live off the land or are as committed to the simple living of their parents.

The daughters' ethical commitments were lived out differently than in their parents' lives, but the connections are apparent. All three of their daughters remained committed to sustainable agriculture and organic foods. In almost every home, Judy maintained a vegetable garden. Both Hannah and Rebecca shopped at farmer's markets and engaged with community-supported agriculture before locavore culture became broadly fashionable, and for many years Hannah was also part of a food cooperative, in which members order in bulk, do the work of managing a communal "store," and shop on the honor system. Hannah was very involved in homelessness issues in college, Rebecca carefully restored an old house, and Judy has worked as a doula, participating in the natural childbirth culture that is tied to the feminist and counterculture values of the family. Some practices have shifted in the daughters' lives: rather than growing their own food, Hannah and Rebecca are, in Rebecca's words, "committed to buying directly from farmers whenever possible." In other cases, the specific practices, for instance, the gift-giving customs, continued to shape aspects of the daughters' lives. Hannah and Rebecca presented their choices as growing out of the family culture nurtured by Kathy and Dan, despite the very different structures of their adult lives.

Kathy and Dan did regret missing out on a community of like-minded people, which felt like a notable gap in their lives. While Kathy mentioned the absence of church, the couple seemed to miss community in general, not simply religious community. Living in rural areas that both tended to be politically conservative and to have a lower median level of education, Kathy and Dan felt they often lacked a community of similarly educated, like-minded peers. While they had chosen their current location in part because it is a college town, they felt that, as university outsiders, the community is largely closed to them.

Additionally, Christianity had been of central importance to Kathy's parents, and Dan worried that he had let his in-laws down in failing to show his daughters the value that religion could have. Because there "have been Brewster ministers in America for as long as there has been an America," Dan worried that his father-in-law had been disappointed to be the last Brewster minister. In that moment, Dan, the only member of the family to explicitly use religious labels to describe farming, drew a sharp distinction between homesteading and Protestantism, a distinction that perhaps was tied to the ways in which his father-in-law in particular found comfort and moral compass in faith and also to the sustenance provided by their religious community.

Rebecca suggested that she would have liked a stronger religious orientation. While she took a certain pride in her Judaism, she did not know much about Judaism or have a strong sense of Jewish tradition. Similarly, while Christian traditions, particularly her family's celebrations around Christmas, felt deeply important, they did not connect to a moral or transcendent framework in her mind. Rebecca wondered if religious community and worship practices would add depth to her life.

Hannah reflected on her identity, largely around the question of Jewishness. She recounted an incident that she refers to as the "first public assigning of her as Jewish." When she was in ninth grade, one of her classmates found out that her father was Jewish and said, "I knew you were Jewish because of how you look." Hannah was furious, not because it would be bad to be Jewish, but because she was appalled at the suggestion that "you can tell a person's religion by her appearance." Her college's robust Jewish community helped Hannah understand the idea of ethnic Jewishness, but it did not increase her own identification as a Jew. Rather, she decided that despite being named Hannah Kaplan, she was not Jewish. Living in a city with a large Jewish population, she often experienced other people's expectations of her Jewishness. As a result, she was most comfortable discussing her identity with Orthodox Jews, because when she explained that her father is the Jewish parent, they could together agree that while she has a Jewish name and "looks Jewish," she is not, in fact, Jewish. That said, despite her "wistfulness" about religious community, her agnosticism kept her from joining a church.

The Kaplan-Brewster family did not, with the one exception of Dan's comment about haying, frame homesteading in religious terms. They did, however, provide practices and values that underscored the children's growing up and offered them a touchstone of how to be in the world. As a result, while one could observe the lack of formal religious affiliation, the largely cultural Christianity, and the absence of Judaism in the Kaplan-Brewster home in terms of what Sylvia Barack Fishman would describe as "nothing," a vibrant moral life was being imagined in the Kaplan-Brewster home.[18] Like the family in Wolff's *The Mozart Season* (discussed in chapter 5), the Kaplan-Brewster family drew their moral system from the parts of their life that the parents shared: for the Shapiros, music; for the Kaplan-Brewsters, homesteading.

In some ways, the moral life that the Kaplan-Brewster family created bore commonalities with the concept of multiculturalism as it applies to interfaith families. The family created a moral system that reflected the egalitarianism and feminist potential that multiculturalism espoused. Unlike the multiculturalists, however, the Kaplan-Brewster family did not make strong ethnic or cultural claims around Christianity or Judaism. Hannah's teenage horror at being told she looked Jewish demonstrates this framing of Christian and Jewish identity as religious identity, and religious identity as something individual and chosen.

Unitarian Universalists for Jewish Awareness:
A Third Way in a Third Tradition

When I first contacted Audrey Groff to ask if I could interview her as part of my work on interfaith families, she immediately corrected my terminology. "I dislike the term interfaith families," she explained, "I do not think that we are interfaith—we have the same faith and it is Unitarian Universalism. We are not interfaith. We are interreligious, because we have two religious traditions that lead us to our faith. But the faith is the same. And so I do not feel like we have compromised." In introducing herself to me, Audrey Groff deflected a fundamental criticism of Christian-Jewish couples who choose to raise their children as Unitarian Universalists: that they have achieved a lowest common denominator of religion, lacking the ethical, theological, and ritual distinctiveness of either Christianity or Judaism. The Groff family has, according to Audrey, created a vibrant and shared Unitarian Universalist identity that preserves the elements of Judaism that Audrey wants to share with her children and the beliefs and customs that her husband, James, brings to the table as well.

Audrey was raised in a Reform Jewish congregation in a wealthy southern suburb. Her parents "were more culturally Jewish than religiously Jewish, but . . . the whole Jewish legacy is important to them. History is important to them. Family is important to them. And that whole Jewish geography and culture is important to them. So for me to marry someone who was not Jewish was an adjustment." That said, her parents never pushed her to date Jewish boys or not to date Gentiles, nor did they suggest that she should not marry James Groff.

As a young woman, Audrey moved to the Midwest and met James, the man whom she would eventually marry. James came from a Missouri Synod Lutheran family, but he was not going to church when the couple met. They knew from the start that they might have problems reconciling their backgrounds and spent much time in the dating process talking about religion and identity. They found that they shared any number of values and worldviews. James realized that he no longer believed in the teachings of his church. Being Jewish remained important to Audrey, but she came to appreciate the depth of her connection to James, regardless of their different backgrounds. At the time, a self-described "young and hypersensitive" Audrey felt deeply uncomfortable in her in-laws' church in what she described as their rural, insular community. She said that while now she realizes that the preacher's exclusionary messages about non-Christians or the unsaved were for everyone, at that time, every week, she felt that they were aimed at her—as if the minister had known ahead of time that there would be a Jew in his pews and was reaching out to shame and frighten her into converting. She was the first Jewish person her future in-laws had ever met.

Ultimately, the young couple moved back to Audrey's home city and decided to be married in her parents' Reform synagogue. The rabbi had been very supportive of their relationship, talking to Audrey and lending her books, so the family was shocked when he explained that he could not perform the ceremony because synagogue policy, set by the lay board, forbade him to do so. "That just about crushed me," Audrey remembered. Ultimately, Audrey and James were married at another Reform congregation in which the rabbi permitted interfaith marriage if the couple attended a basic Judaism class and became members. Audrey's parents left her childhood congregation, joining the congregation with the more liberal policy toward interfaith marriage. Their search for an officiating rabbi left Audrey and James feeling supported by her parents, but conflicted about the Jewish community.

The young couple joined one of the synagogue's new *havurot* designed specifically for interfaith couples, where the conversation continually circled back to the importance of being Jewish.[19] As important as Judaism was to Audrey, neither of the Groffs was interested in pursuing an exclusively Jewish life. "All of [the *havurah's*] conversations were oriented toward that decision," she recalled, "explaining it to Christian parents, helping the Christian partners learn about Judaism, and managing the sense of loss that they felt at giving up their own traditions." Audrey felt odd about asking James to give up whatever aspects of his heritage he wished to retain, and ultimately, he objected to the tenor of the *havurah*. "I am not going to convert," he declared. Audrey, who had never asked him to convert, understood his need to find a community with more diversity.

As a result, by the time they had small children, Audrey and James had left the Reform congregation. During a walk one afternoon, a neighbor suggested that they try the Unitarian Universalist congregation. James came home filled with excitement, unable to believe that there was a religious community that shared his beliefs. He recounted that he heard his own post-Christian views reflected in the ethical messages of the Unitarian Universalist principles, which included belief in the "inherent worth and dignity of every person" and emphasized a "free and responsible search for truth and meaning."[20] Audrey's initial response was more moderate, but, as she continued to attend services, she frequently found the sermon moving her to the verge of tears. "The minister would be speaking to five hundred people but it would seem like somehow he knew just what I needed to hear. That is what I wanted for my family. I wanted the rituals to be what we needed, to have meaning apart from just maintaining rituals."

Audrey and James had read a number of advice manuals for interfaith couples, including the ones explored in chapter 3. I asked her what she thought of authors casting Unitarian Universalism as a compromise position. Her first response was to echo Jennifer Kimball's thoughts, suggesting that the authors of those manuals were interested in pushing Judaism as a solution to interfaith marriage, rather than actually aiding couples. "The Reform movement had to go through a process around interfaith families and those books see us [Unitarian Universalists] as competition," she asserted. "They don't know UUs well and they are trying to deflect competition." While she conceded that she knows many couples who experience Unitarian Universalism as a compromise, in her view the UU community may not truly be a good fit for those families. Her assessment is shared by Lee Barker, the president of Meadville Lombard, a Unitarian Universalist seminary in Chicago. In his experience, couples who join congregations because of the Unitarian Universalist message ended up finding lifelong community and spiritual growth within UU congregations. In contrast, those who come to it as a "middle ground" in which to raise children often do not become well integrated into the community. They rarely stay through their children's entire religious education and always leave the community after the children leave home.[21]

In contrast, the Groffs have found life as Unitarian Universalists very satisfying. They have created a place for her Jewish heritage in the congregation's life. Largely through Audrey's efforts, the congregation has developed a Rosh

Hashanah service, a Yom Kippur service, a Hanukkah party, and a community seder for Passover. Audrey has helped to write the congregation's Passover haggadah and coordinates the highly participatory High Holidays services. When the Jewish liturgical events are coupled with the Christian calendar that the Unitarian Universalist congregation had always maintained, the couple had a community for both of their holidays. They also had a staunch tradition to pass on to their own three children—for holidays, all holidays, they went together, as a family, to the Unitarian Universalist congregation, where the children saw both parents participate together, underscoring Audrey's contention that they have, in the end, a shared faith. Audrey sang with the choir and therefore performed in the Christmas services and at Easter. James always read for the High Holiday services. Their daughter chanted the four questions in Hebrew at the congregational seder on Passover.[22] The UU community anchored the family's religious practice, both Christian and Jewish, preventing the dual holiday calendar from feeling bifurcated.

The Groffs' particular UU community might be described as inherently interfaith, though Audrey saw it in a slightly different light. The Jewish celebrations that she and others have incorporated into the congregation's liturgical life have been warmly embraced by many non-Jewish persons in the congregation, leading Audrey to reflect that "something is happening here. These traditions and rituals are no longer exclusively Jewish. They are Unitarian Universalist as well." In this way, in Audrey's congregation, Unitarian Universalism took on many of the practices and ethical teachings of Judaism, creating an inherently hybrid tradition. Audrey found no conflict between the UU tradition in which she raised her children and the Jewish heritage that she wanted to transmit to them.

The meaning-driven understanding of practice in UU congregations fits well with how Audrey understood Jewish practice, and she rejoiced in seeing Jewish practice become meaningful to a broader community. In incorporating Jewish practices into UU liturgical life, Audrey and James reflected assumptions rooted in the very multicultural understandings of practices previously discussed. Just as, for participants in optional ethnicity, being of Irish lineage is not necessary in order to take Irish step dancing, find it meaningful, and incorporate it into one's identity, so for Audrey, being ethnically Jewish was not necessary for finding meaning in Jewish practice. When I attended the seder, led by Audrey and her congregation's two ministers and music director, many people explained that they had never been to a seder other than this one at their UU congregation, but it was integral to their annual liturgy and a source of inspiration and meaning. Furthermore, they were not necessarily interested in how their UU seder did or did not differ from seders in Jewish settings any more than they cared about how their post-Christian "flower" and "water" communions differed from Christian communion. The entire congregation was, at a few points during the year, optional Jews.

The Groffs were unusual in the extent to which their congregation supports their Jewish practice. One of their ministers, a Jewish UU herself, was very involved at the national level in the Unitarian Universalists for Jewish Awareness (UUJA) group. She provided support for lay-led initiatives, included Jewish themes in sermons and worship on Sunday mornings, and encouraged other clergy to do the same. The congregation was large, and while the extremely energetic Audrey spearheads much of the Jewish inclusion, she had help from others in the congregation, be they of Jewish heritage or not. As a result, Jewish life was braided into the communal and congregational life.

Unitarian Universalism, however, has congregational polity, which means that immense variation exists in the ritual lives of UU communities. A search of the UUJA listserv suggested that many Jews, some intermarried, some not, in UU communities were not as happy as Audrey Groff. Audrey's community has always called itself a congregation, rather than a church. For many Jews in UU communities, their community's self-description as a church, either officially or informally by members, felt exclusionary. Similarly, some Jewish UUs resented being responsible, as the "Jew in the congregation," for ensuring that Jewish holidays were observed. This subset of Jewish UUs would have preferred to see ministers shoulder responsibility for Jewish observance in the communal lives of congregations. Ministers, however, were sometimes reluctant to do so, out of concern around appropriation. While not all Jews in UU congregational settings shared such negative experiences, and Leah Hart-Landsberg, president of UUJA, saw increased Jewish ritual in UU congregational life, these responses demonstrate that because of both regional differences and congregational polity, not all Jewish spouses in interfaith marriages found UU communities to be supportive of maintaining and transmitting their Jewish identities.[23]

The Groff family celebrated both Christian and Jewish holidays at home and in their religious community, framing each holiday in terms that fit with their shared Unitarian Universalist ethos. Audrey explained two aspects of their family traditions: first, they focused on what she and James view to be the metaphoric meaning of the holidays. Hanukkah became a holiday of religious freedom, and Christmas was framed in typically UU terms: *every* night a child is born is a holy night, engendering the hope for peace on earth and goodwill toward men (and presents). Easter centered on rebirth and renewal. Passover focused on religious freedom and civil rights. This formulation of Passover struck the Groffs as very Unitarian Universalist but is, in point of fact, broadly accepted in mainstream Jewish communities; while the understanding of Easter is exclusively metaphoric, the metaphor itself is common in liberal Protestant contexts such as the United Church of Christ, where part of the import of Christ's resurrection is the ability to begin again one's daily life. The Groff children were well versed in biblical stories of all of the holidays and in Jewish blessings and Christmas carols.

Their religious calendar has created some tension, particularly with Audrey's relatives. Audrey's sister married a Jew from a more observant background than her own and left their Reform upbringing behind for Modern Orthodoxy. When the sisters got their families together for Passover, they disagreed over how to conduct the seder. Her sister and brother-in-law used a haggadah that was largely in Hebrew, with, according to Audrey, little translation or discussion of the underlying meaning of the holiday. The Groff children found their aunt and uncle's seder to be long, boring, and alienating. By contrast, when her sister's family came to seder at the Groff house, Audrey and James used the haggadah that Audrey wrote with her UUJA group. Audrey felt that her sister and brother-in-law were dismissive of her seder. She expressed frustration that her sister cannot say "Your way is not my way, but I respect it" and felt that they should alternate years and methods of doing the seders.

Similarly, the Groff celebration of Christmas caused tension with the same relatives. Audrey's sister refused to visit the Groff house while the Christmas tree was up, which meant that Audrey and James could not host a family Hanukkah party. That policy led to a temporary rupture between the families, when Audrey refused to talk to her sister's family. Eventually, she began clearing away the Christmas decorations before she hosted them for a New Year's lunch. "Yes, it is my house," she reflected, "but I don't need to make other people uncomfortable. Besides, James and I like to begin the new year with a clean slate, so I like to get the holiday things put away." While Audrey felt that her children had a strong Jewish heritage, her sister clearly disagreed. Audrey saw her sister's opinion as representative of the larger Jewish community. A feature on her UUJA group in the local Jewish newspaper pained Audrey because it treated her efforts as a betrayal of Jewish community rather than as a way of sustaining and broadening the reach of Judaism.

Beyond holidays, the Groffs have created their own family traditions. They made a point of lighting Shabbat candles at a family dinner on Friday nights, but they also lit a flaming chalice, the symbol of Unitarian Universalism, before every meal, often using chalices made by the children in Sunday school. Although Audrey did not articulate a meaning for the chalice lighting, it echoed the lighting of Shabbat candles, which the family did intentionally to maintain Jewish customs in the home. The family's chalice lighting rooted their shared UU faith in a communal and daily practice. While much less of James's family's theology and religious practices were present in their home, the foodways of his family remained meaningful to him, and Audrey carefully planned holiday meals to include the Midwestern recipes of his childhood. Food, she half-joked, was his religion, explaining that whenever they return to Missouri, his mother and aunts cook exactly the same meals—she can write out ahead of time what they will eat. While James left his family's theologies behind, by learning his family recipes and including them in special family dinners, Audrey has helped him to transmit to their children some of the special memories of his Lutheran childhood.[24]

Audrey and James were proud of the ways in which they have given their children a connection both to their values as a couple and to their families, although those familial connections have not been consistently smooth. Audrey believed her children feel secure in their identity and was pleased they sought out college religious communities. Their daughter was involved in the UU students' group at her college. As a freshman, their son went to the Jewish students' group for Hanukkah. He called home and said, "Mom, all of the kids said the blessings in Hebrew." "Did that bother you?" she asked. "No. I just said them in English. Some of them did not know what the Hebrew meant!" Encoded in that story was a sense of the Groff family values and their conviction that their way of doing things was better—they preferred their children to know the meaning than the Hebrew.

While the Groffs transmitted much of what mattered to Audrey about her Jewish heritage to their children, they did not do so by the terms of the broader Jewish community or in ways that were necessarily sustainable in other UU congregations. When we last spoke, it remained unclear whether her children would be comfortable in Jewish communal life or whether they would want to be in Jewish community rather than UU community: while they have knowledge of some Hebrew prayers, for instance, they were not familiar with Jewish liturgical or communal life. Should they want to become active in other UU communities, they may find that many communities lack the level of support for Jewish tradition of the one in which they were raised. Of course, the Groff children may not be bothered by UU congregations that do not offer High Holiday services, or, like their mother, they may take pride in contributing to and shaping a congregation's ritual life.

Like the Kaplan-Brewster family, the Groffs were clearly conscious of themselves as religiously blended, but they sought out a religious community and identity that were values-based, then marshaled the traditions and resources of their birth religions to support what they articulate as a shared faith. Sometimes that process required reinterpreting or reinventing traditions, which they were happy to do when necessary. If the Brewster-Kaplans followed a third way because it was more important to them than either of their traditions, the Groffs forged a third way that lifted up what they believe to be the best of their traditions. They found a way to do so in religious community, but they had to do much of the work of shaping the Jewish elements of their new community. Additionally, while that third way has many of the values and traditions that Audrey saw in Judaism, she was quick to note that by his choice, very little of James's Lutheran heritage had been preserved in their home, beyond a few recipes. She saw them as creating a Jewish Unitarian Universalist household, with Jewish holidays, Christian holidays, Shabbat candles, Missouri Synod foodways, and dinnertime chalice lighting, in which all of the practices were recast into a cohesive system of meaning drawing on UU thought. Though critics have considered UU communities as a lowest common denominator, for the Groffs, it proved a shared third path.

"People Who Walked Out of Egypt and Across the American Plains": A Mormon-Jewish Family Life

Every night, when Jennifer Kimball puts her four- and six-year-old daughters to bed, she gives them a choice of prayers: "Would you like to say the *Sh'ma?*" she asks, "or a Mormon prayer or a silent prayer?"[25] The Mormon prayer, from her own tradition, takes an epistolary form. Jennifer taught her daughters a feminist version, drawing upon Mormon theology of both a Heavenly Mother and a Heavenly Father, so her girls began "Dear Heavenly Father and Heavenly Mother" before offering thanks and requesting blessings. Jennifer also taught them the *Sh'ma*, traditionally the last prayer that Jews say before bed, from their father's tradition. She says that because it is the shortest of the prayers— the simple recitation, in Hebrew, of the statement "Hear, O Israel, the Lord is our God. The Lord is one"—it is often the one that she hopes for in the bedtime routine. Her oldest daughter made up the silent prayer herself and has explained to her mother that the silent prayer is a time when she asks God, without words, about things that really matter to her.

One night, after praying the *Sh'ma*, Jennifer and her four-year-old daughter had the following conversation, which synthesizes the family's interfaith approach:

"Mommy, how do you know the *Sh'ma*?"

"I learned it."

"Did Daddy teach you?"

"No. I love your Daddy and so I listened and I watched and I learned Jewish things."

"Does that make you Jewish?"

"I don't know. What do you think?"

"Hmm. I don't know. You know, sometimes when I have a question, I close my eyes and ask God in my heart." Amelia closed her eyes and thought, before continuing, "Okay. You have a Jewish God in your heart and a Mormon God in your heart. The Jewish God is the Daddy God and the Mormon God is the Mommy God and they are all the time together, sharing Jewish, sharing Mormon. And they have two children, a boy and a girl, who are Jewish and Mormon. And they are all of the time together, changing and changing, back and forth, back and forth."

"That is a lovely vision, Amelia."

"I have a song, Mom. Here it is: We are sharing our feelings, Mormon and Jewish. We are sharing together. If you are a kid, then you have both. The grown-ups only have one together, but if the daddy is Mormon, that's okay. And if the mom is Jewish, that's okay. They are sharing together, they are having fun together. That's the whole song. It is called 'Give and Do.'"

Jennifer shared these stories with me as a window into the minds of her children. Amelia's vision of sharing theologies, practices, and stories reflects Jennifer and Jacob's mode of interfaith parenting. The couple emphasizes building a repertoire of narratives for and with their daughters through which they can grapple with what Jennifer terms "mystery." Amelia's stories, much like her parents' approach, focus on the process of interfaith religious life rather than on the product of religious identity.

When Jennifer and Jacob met, she was living a "Jack," or unorthodox, Mormon lifestyle, having become disillusioned with the Church of Latter Day Saints (LDS) after a number of feminist and intellectual Mormons were fired from their teaching positions at Brigham Young University during her undergraduate years.[26] Jacob says that in hindsight, he was probably open to dating a Mormon because, as he explored Buddhism, he was practicing his own ability to be nonjudgmental. He added that he thought Jennifer was so beautiful and smart that he did not ask as many questions as he might have, and therefore did not quite realize at first what he was getting into by dating a Mormon. The couple dated for three years before marrying in what Jennifer refers to as the most blended wedding they could devise, with a Mormon officiant for the vows and a rabbi for the ring ceremony.

As a family, the household has a dual religious and liturgical life. At the time of my interviews, their daughters were ages four and six. Both had either attended or were attending Jewish preschool. The family had Shabbat dinner weekly and had recently become more frequent attendees of their local Mormon ward, though the parents noted that they normally just attended the children's parts of the service. While they had not been holding the traditional Mormon Monday night activity and religious study time known as "family home evening," their six-year-old had recently come home from Sunday school asking about it. Jennifer said that while her initial response was that they did not have time for family home evening, she had corrected herself to tell her daughter, "If family home evening is important to you, then we will celebrate it."

The family kept a modified but dual religious calendar. They attended High Holidays and *Simchat Torah* services at the local Reconstructionist Synagogue, where they also attend other child-centered events, including family and "Tot Shabbat" services for children. They had recently begun hosting a breakfast gathering after Yom Kippur, for all of their Jewish friends in the neighborhood, many of whom were also in interfaith marriages. They attended Jacob's parents' Passover Seder and a Hanukkah party with his extended family. Every year, they hosted their own holiday party with latkes, tamales, and a toy drive for the Native American reservation where Jacob, an anthropologist, did his research. They celebrated Christmas and Easter, though they do not have a Christmas tree and neither Santa nor the Easter Bunny visit the girls. Though they did not decorate with a tree, they did put up a crèche for Christmas. The couple explained that Jacob felt an instinctual "allergy" to both a tree and Jesus, and Jennifer felt that although Jesus was central to her faith and necessary in her family life, the tree was not central. As a result, Jacob lived with Jesus and Jennifer lived without a Christmas tree.

In their home, Jennifer and Jacob stressed "meta-conversations," or explicitly talking with the children about the implications of the differences of the two traditions, and understood that sometimes the children may be confused. "But," Jennifer explained, "life is confusing. So someone might cry a bit? Crying is part of choosing and searching, and finding a path." She pointed out that the religiously consistent message of her own upbringing did not prevent her from crying, and she did not expect her children's processes to be totally free from stress and confusion. The expectation that her children would grapple with Judaism and Mormonism demonstrated Jennifer's commitment to raise them as children who will engage deeply with traditions—their "bothness" was not intended to replace deep engagement with either tradition. If anything, Jennifer and Jacob hoped that the contrasting stories and messages will encourage deeper questioning and exploration of each heritage.

Jacob reflected that the primary tension for him around the dual heritage came from concern for his parents. "I am in a mental war with myself because I cringe at the possibility of my girls saying something from church, because I know the word Jesus is radioactive to [my parents]. I worry about what the girls learn at church coming out in front of my parents." In the end, he said that there was always the possibility that one of the girls would share aspects of their Mormon identity with his parents that would make the grandparents quite uncomfortable, "but then," he said, "my parents will need to deal." Jacob's concern revealed an awareness that the theoretical knowledge that their grandchildren are both Mormon and Jewish may feel very different to his parents than it would to be confronted with aspects of that reality, but he expected his parents to develop the flexibility necessary to help him and Jennifer nurture the girls in their dual identities.

Both Jennifer and Jacob hoped that they have provided the girls with a repertoire of stories and practices that would help them navigate their adult lives. As scholars of cultural studies, the couple was careful not to dichotomize the categories of religion and culture, suggesting instead that the practices and worldviews that they share with their daughters were all formative. Jennifer and Jacob both talked repeatedly about having meta-conversations with the girls, a process that Jennifer identified as part of her own "pet theory" about interfaith parenting. She believed that the more meta-conscious the family is, the better it works. The parents, then, reflected with their daughters about what it meant to tell narratives that were, at times, contradictory and to participate in multiple communities and practices. They were largely transparent with their daughters about the tensions inherent in those life choices.

Jacob, who agreed with Jennifer's theory, suggested that the couple's attitude came from their own scholarly work with American Indian culture, where the question of literal truth is less important. Jennifer agreed, saying that in her case, she was deliberately drawing from the way that native people understand their stories. "Native people do not deal with the questions of whether the story is true: this is the story that makes me who I am." In terms of her own life, she said, "I have resigned doctrinal certainty. But the narrative structure is important to me. I teach my children about God as Mother and Father. If they start out with literal understandings, that is okay. . . . But to me these are stories, and they are beautiful stories that hold me in place. This issue of 'literally true' is not as important." Resigning doctrinal certainty did not lessen the importance of the narratives in Jennifer's mind—they remained one of the primary media through which she experiences sacrality. Without doctrinal certainty, then, the act of telling the narratives, be they Mormon or Jewish, became a religious practice in and of itself. The narratives became metaphors of mystery, identity, and community; both the telling and the reflecting on the telling became family practices underpinning the process of religious exploration.

Jacob and Jennifer recognized that sometimes the messages of those theologically rooted stories were contradictory, but they were comfortable allowing the narratives to remain in tension, offering their daughters entry points into a mystery that is, Jennifer pointed out, confusing even without multiple theological stories. In this regard, the Mormon and Jewish stories existed for the Kimball-Geller daughters in the ways that, for children who grow up in religiously liberal homes with one tradition, creation stories exist alongside picture books explaining dinosaurs and evolution. In the Kimball-Geller home, however, there was an additional complement of narratives.

Jennifer suggested that the girls, especially their older daughter, are already separating the two religions according to the two families. She explained that she and Jacob elicit meta-commentary from the girls, exploring how they experience being both Mormon and Jewish. One day, she asked their older child what it is like to "do both" religions and their daughter, age six, responded, "I am never around both sets at once. I can do the Mormon thing when around Mormons and Jewish stuff when I am around Jews. But I have more of a taste for the Jewish stuff." At age six, Amelia experienced no conflict between the identities because they are modes of being that exist in contexts: Jewish with Jewish relatives and in Jewish spaces, Mormon with Mormon relatives and in Mormon spaces. She was, however, experimenting, both with the idea of having a preference and with sharing that preference with her Mormon mother.

Every now and then, Amelia slipped into the "wrong" context, and Jennifer realized that she can self-correct. Because Amelia was six and starting to learn about death, and because one of her grandfathers had a progressive illness, her parents had provided her with two different narratives for death. The Mormon narrative, as filtered through Jennifer, was "you are going to go be with your family; you are going to go be with your ancestors." Jennifer reflected that, for her, that claim had some "nonliteralistic bandwidth, because your ancestors might all be in the ground." Jennifer, however, found the idea very comforting and wanted her daughter to have that comfort. Amelia also knew the Reform Jewish belief that people stay alive in memory. In this framing, there is no resurrection to look forward to. The parents were open with the children that "we do not know what happens next, but these are two important ideas, the Mormon idea and the Jewish idea." One day, Jennifer explained that they were at the dinner table with a Jewish aunt, and they were talking about what happens when people die. "And I saw Amelia be very careful," Jennifer remembered, "and switch. She said that we will be with our ancestors. Then she stopped and corrected herself, to say we will be with them in our memories." Amelia had a clear sense that some of the stories in her repertoire are shared ground with her father's family and some are shared territory with her mother's, and she made attempts to keep those stories separate. Her own comment about "never having to be both at the same time" suggested that she is conscious and deliberate in separating those narratives, as did her willingness to self-correct.

Jennifer and Jacob were aware that the major questions of the next five years will be whether the girls will receive Mormon baptism, conventionally given at eight, and then whether, at thirteen, they will become b'nai mitzvah, literally, "children of the commandments," in the Jewish coming-of-age ceremony. Both rituals involved processes of study, though the Mormon process is a private, parent/child-focused study while the Jewish process is more formal and involves enrollment in religious education. When describing Amelia's baptism, which could occur in a year and a half, Jennifer emphasized the role of Amelia's own choice: it was most important to let her make her own decisions. Her parents spelled out the requirements for baptism, that she must read and discuss the Book of Mormon with Mommy every night before bed and then the bishop will ask her questions before baptism. Jennifer and Jacob were very clear that the Mormon sets of questions are not strict questions of doctrine. Amelia would not, if she chooses to be baptized, be asked if she accepts Jesus Christ as her Lord and Savior. Rather, she will be asked about her understanding of God and of baptism. Her parents joked a bit about what would happen if Amelia discussed Heavenly Father and Heavenly Mother, but neither offered a serious commentary in our conversations about what might happen when either of the girls shares her feminist Mormonism with authority figures like their bishop.

The next coming-of-age event after baptism would be Amelia's bat mitzvah. (Simone would be baptized in between, should she choose to be, but conversation focused on Amelia, who, as the oldest child, is the developmental and social pioneer of the family's religious journey.) While language of choice was prominently featured in the parental discussion of baptism, Jennifer and Jacob seemed more definite about the looming bat mitzvah. "We both see them becoming bat mitzvah. That is an 'out-loud' goal for us," said Jennifer. I asked whether they would be able to find a rabbi to give a bat mitzvah to a child who was a baptized Mormon. "That will be a real challenge," Jennifer acknowledged. Jacob responded more forcefully: "My response has always been this: It is none of their fucking business. 'I am paying for you. Bar mitzvah my goddamned kid.' I also feel like any rabbi who would say that to me is not a rabbi whom I would want to baptize, excuse me, bar mitzvah my kid in the first place. That if you cannot handle the complexity, then really, you are going to try to force that. . . . Here is my kid that wants to participate in Jewish life and you're going to tell them that because of something they did when they were younger, they can't? Well, eff you." Jennifer responded directly to Jacob, rather than to me, when she said, "Here is a third way: They made a good spiritual choice when they were eight. If we have no options, and we run into a rabbi and the rabbi who we think would be best to bat mitzvah them, who is most friendly to our situation, really feels like they can't do this because of Jewish law, then they have a *mikveh* and get baptized again. So they make another spiritual choice [later]. Our principles for raising them the whole way have been consistent. These are our two traditions. You have the power to make good choices. You need to make deliberate, thoughtful choices."

Jacob's depiction of the rabbi providing a commercial service underscored a fundamental assumption of the Kimball-Geller method: the religious traditions have wisdom to offer, but the religious leaders do not (or should not) have ultimate religious authority. The parents, and as they mature, the daughters, are the religious authorities—a failure to support their decisions becomes not a disagreement about approach so much as an inability to work with the family's complex reality. In this way, he echoed the multicultural approach explored in the previous chapter—identities can be taken on and taken off and are available in the religious marketplace. Jennifer's comments about spiritual choice, however, depicted the weight the couple gives the decisions and the efforts to which they go in order to address them. If baptism needed to be layered with *mikveh*, so be it. Another baptism was always possible later, if that choice seemed best.[27]

While Jacob suggested that he might be being naïve, he simply could not see their family being part of a synagogue that would deny his girls bat mitzvah training and celebrations because of previous choices to be baptized. Parents of interfaith children sometimes seek out religious ceremonies for their children in an attempt to gain communal acceptance for their children (as the interfaith blogger and interfaith parent Susan Katz Miller points out, having had a bar mitzvah helps interfaith children defend their Jewish identities).[28] The Kimball-Geller family is aware of those realities, but as can be seen here, Jennifer defined decisions surrounding baptism and bat mitzvah as spiritual choices for her daughters, choices that their father demonstrated, in his slippage between the terms, that he saw as inherently valuable and equivalent, for all of their differences.

The idea of choice intersected with the couple's understanding of the options presented by their traditions, though both seem to think that the girls will choose to be Jewish. Jacob pointed out that the choice is not between Mormonism and Orthodox Judaism, but rather between Mormonism and liberal Judaism, which means that a Jewish choice is far less countercultural than observant Mormonism. Liberal Judaism provides a better fit for the family's political views, and it also allows for more mainstream behaviors like drinking coffee and alcohol and having premarital sex. As a result, a Jewish choice would better match the progressive American tenor of their lives. Jennifer saw the children choosing Judaism in part for what it offers, but also because the liberal, feminist Mormonism in which she found strength was not the mainstream, institutionally available Mormonism to which the girls would have ready access. Jennifer pointed out that, in her view, it is the responsibility of the religious organizations to make themselves appealing enough to attract her children. It was not her job, or Jacob's, to make religious choices for their children, she said. If her daughters remain feminists, she believed they would be Jewish, because Judaism offered more progressive options.

While Jennifer acknowledged that it may be hard for her children not to see choosing a religion as siding with one parent over the other, she returned to Amelia's "Give and Do" song, saying that what was important to her about that song was the message that in the end, everything was okay. "There will be back and forth, and changing, but there is a loving context for this discovery. All children want to please their parents with their religious choices, that is inevitable, but what would be terrible would be for them to feel torn. And so if it kills me, I am going to keep telling them, you make a good choice and I will be proud of you." Jennifer continued, "I just don't think that my tradition offers them [enough]. . . . I won't be mad at them if they do not choose my tradition, because it is a hard place to be and be a girl." Jacob added, "And we always say that it is not a permanent choice anyway," a point that he articulated throughout the conversation—the girls would be able to move fluidly between their two religious positions.

By embracing a consumption-oriented understanding of religion, based both in Jacob's avowal that if he is paying a rabbi, the rabbi should bat mitzvah his kid and in Jennifer's argument that the religious organizations needed to attract members in a market economy, the family demonstrated elements of the modes of consumption shared by multicultural interfaith families. In addition, the switching that Amelia described to her mother, being Mormon with Mormon relatives and Jewish with Jewish ones, was in keeping with optional ethnicity. Multiculturalism, however, trades on equivalencies, in which practices become meaningful as symbols and constituents of identity, but it is not concerned with nuances of meaning. The Kimball-Gellers were very focused on meaning, though unconcerned about contradictions. For them, Mormonism and Judaism were not to be separated from self-reflective meta-conversations about meaning, God, and spirituality.

The Kimball-Geller home engaged selectively in both Mormon and Jewish religious practice and kept narratives from both traditions alive in their home. They cultivated a prayer life in their daughters, who saw their parents engaging with both religious communities. They believed that the best tools with which they could raise their daughters were a deep knowledge of their dual heritage and the skills to make thoughtful choices, in their faith lives and in the rest of life. They provided that religious literacy by maintaining relationships with both Mormon and Jewish religious communities. They aspired to leave their daughters no doubt that they are loved and supported, regardless of which choices they make. The emphasis, then, in this family, was on process rather than on product.

Years after our initial interactions, I reached out to Jennifer and Jacob to see how their family's path had continued to unfold. When we reconnected, Amelia was thirteen and had recently become a bat mitzvah, in a congregation that Jennifer describes as "a welcoming synagogue home that understands and respects the complexity of our choices and affords us some privacy in not questioning how we have raised them."[29] Jennifer wrote that Amelia wept when the Torah was placed in her arms. She is grateful that they have found a Jewish community that allowed her, the Mormon mother, to stand on the bimah with her daughter, so that she could "wipe the tears from my daughter's face and bless her."[30]

While Amelia has been welcomed into a Jewish community who accepts that she has a complex identity, she has not been as lucky in organized LDS communities. Jennifer wrote:

> Over the summer, [Amelia] had a very difficult conversation with a Mormon lay clergy leader during a routine interview before going to a summer camp. She shared with him her beautifully nuanced view of how parallel her paths were, and in how many places they intersected, and he rather bluntly and heavy-handedly told her she could not be "both," that her Jewish identity was opposed to her Mormon affiliation. I knew this conversation would happen some day but did not expect this conversation to happen when [Amelia] was just 12. She conducted herself with tremendous courage and dignity—held it together until we left the church building, and cried for a few hours at home insisting fiercely that he had no right to tell her she was not who she knew herself to be. I reached out to a Mormon feminist friend who practices our deeply traditional but forgotten/suppressed tradition of giving healing blessings—women to women—and she blessed [Amelia] in a very inspired way that she was exactly who God intended her to be and that she was meant to be a bridge between peoples.[31]

Amelia was not banished from Mormon community. Not only was Jennifer able to call on adult friends to support Amelia's Mormon identity, but when Amelia told a Mormon friend what had happened, the friend responded, "He's stupid, ignore him, come camping with us."[32] Amelia did go camping and had a spectacular time and many Mormons were present at her bat mitzvah, family friends who traveled from several states to be present as Amelia entered Jewish womanhood. They have what Jennifer calls "my Mormon community," feminist, left-leaning, and accepting, but the path in mainstream Mormonism has been, as the parents initially predicted, more complicated.

Simone, meanwhile, has wondered if she might be an atheist. At eleven, she felt strongly connected to her Jewish and Mormon heritages, but not necessarily to God. Her mother reflected, "That's fine. Her path will be complex as well, and she will have great strength and so many who love her to draw from as she walks it."[33] Atheism, however, did not get Simone out of Hebrew school. Simone's Mormon mother was clear. "Even protoatheistic 13 year olds have to bat mitzvah in our house."[34]

While, as young adolescents, the Kimball-Geller girls were growing into their own narratives, and experiencing complexities and sometimes pain in doing so, Jennifer did not think that their decision to actively participate in two communities had been a mistake. "I am so glad that we have always been open with our daughters about the complexity of our lives, their identities, and our spirituality," she wrote. "It has enriched them both immeasurably."

Writing to me in the early days of the Trump administration, after the extremely polarizing 2016 presidential campaign, Jennifer was particularly aware that by raising her daughters in Mormon community, she was raising potential bridge builders. "They have been able to see the good and the bad in both of the religious traditions they come from, to love Mormon people and appreciate their kindness, sweetness, good intentions, and hard work, even though they are both vocal young feminists and are politically different than the people they attend church with. In an increasingly polarized America, our daughters will know how to be a bridge between cultures, to see the good in others and enjoy them on their own terms." In Jennifer's words, one sees the hope that interfaith families and people who study them sometimes place in the next generation—the dream that, by knowing both worlds, the children of interfaith families might, somehow, create bridges. Whether or not the Amelia and Simone Kimball-Geller grow up to actively move between those worlds, Jennifer Kimball and David Geller hope that they will continue to be able to raise them with enough hope and support that meetings like the one Amelia had with her Mormon lay leader and the inflexibility that they may one day experience in the greater Jewish world do not erase the kindness they have met in both communities.

The Interfaith Family Project: Two Traditions in One Community

> Yes, we have chutzpah. We decided to politely ignore everyone who thinks my son is not Jewish because his Judaism is patrilineal. We decided to politely ignore everyone who thinks my son is not Jewish because he has been educated in both of his family religions—Judaism and Christianity. . . .
> We made our own decisions, and chose our own labels.
> —Susan Katz Miller, "My Interfaith Son: The Bar Mitzvah and Coming of Age," www.onbeingboth.wordpress.com

One May day, I arrived at a small, rented church for a bar mitzvah. Inside, a community was getting ready, the mother handing out programs by the door and directing people to a big basket of beautiful *kippot*. Recognizing me as the visiting ethnographer, Susan Katz Miller, interfaith blogger and proud mother, told me that one of the many ways that they were living out their values in the

FIGURE 7 Coming of age and bar mitzvah invitation. Image courtesy of Susan Katz Miller.

ceremony was by "springing for" those *kippot,* expensive because they were made in Guatemala and purchased through a fair-trade shop. I found a seat in the sanctuary, an octagonal room whose windows looked out on woods, and chatted with the former director of religious education for the family's religious community, the Interfaith Family Project (IFFP), while I waited for the ceremony to begin. IFFP was a community founded as a religious school that could educate children in both their Jewish and Christian heritages, but it had grown into a community with religious services and learning for adults as well.

While IFFP had long offered coming-of-age ceremonies to its youth, only some of their students choose a bar mitzvah, complete with chanting from the Torah. The family was very aware that they were making it up as they went along, figuring out how to braid together the strands of the bar mitzvah boy's heritage. In the end, they created a ceremony focused along themes of peace and environmental justice. Their ceremony mirrored IFFP's intention of weaving Christianity and Judaism together while keeping them distinct and was designed to be accessible to the many non-Jewish relatives and friends in attendance.

While much of the *shacharit* service, or traditional morning prayers, was omitted from the bar mitzvah, three central prayers were included: the *Sh'ma*, the *V'ahavta*, and the mourner's *Kaddish*.[35] The bar mitzvah boy read from the Torah, standing next to his Jewish grandfather, IFFP's rabbi, and the rabbi who served as his trope tutor, before carrying the community's Torah scroll around the room while the congregation sang.[36] Musical pieces were chosen for their connections to the bar mitzvah's themes of peace and environmentalism with the congregation singing "*Lo Yisa Goy*," "Morning Has Broken," and "For the Beauty of the Earth," Jewish and Protestant songs referencing peace and the beauty of the natural world, respectively. Again, as in a multicultural model, those practices both signaled the bar mitzvah boy's complex identity and their equivalence was highlighted with explanations of their similar orientations toward nature and peace.

Christianity was honored with inclusion of Christian hymns in an otherwise Jewish service, but the service participants also explicitly linked the two traditions. For instance, after the bar mitzvah boy led the congregation in the *Sh'ma* and the *V'ahavta*, central prayers of the Jewish liturgy, his uncle, an Episcopal seminarian, read from the Gospel of Mark 12:28–33. In this passage, one of the scribes asks Jesus what the first commandment is, and in his answer, Jesus paraphrases both the *Sh'ma* and the *V'ahavta*, centralizing their importance for Christianity, "Hear, O Israel; The Lord our God is one Lord: And thou shalt love the Lord thy God with all thy heart, and with all thy soul, and with all thy mind, and with all thy strength: this is the first commandment." Rabbi Harold White, the rabbi at the IFFP who was also newly retired as the rabbi of the Georgetown University Hillel, offered commentary on the importance of the prayers in Jewish contexts and their echoes within Christianity. (In fact, it was Rabbi White who had suggested including the reading from the Gospel of Mark.) Finally, IFFP's minister, the Reverend Julia Jarvis, ordained in the United Church of Christ and in the Disciples of Christ, Christian Church, presented the young man with a stone on which a blessing was written. The stone was passed around the room, so that each person could add his or her own blessing (in energy and prayer, not in writing) to the stone, giving him a tangible reminder of his community's support and love.

The ceremony ended with a laying-on of hands by the entire congregation. In the mode of ordination in Protestant traditions with congregational polity, the young man was surrounded by those assembled, who each laid a hand on him, or on someone who was touching him, so that the entire gathering was grouped around him. The practice, traditional in many Christian settings, was, in this ceremony, linked to Jewish antecedents. As Katz Miller later reflected on her blog, "In Genesis, Jacob lays hands on his grandsons as he blesses them, and Jewish parents bless their children on Shabbat, placing hands on their heads as they do so. . . . What may have seemed to some like a startling Christian element grafted on to a Bar Mitzvah, to us felt like a completely appropriate acknowledgement of the echoes and synergies in the sibling relationship between these two Abrahamic faiths."[37] This explanation, a version of which was presented at the bar mitzvah itself, underscored IFFP's central framing of Christianity as an outgrowth of Judaism such that Jewish thought and practice underscore much of Christian life. The community asserted these underpinnings as historical fact, rather than as theological interpretation, also supporting their sense of themselves as exploring the connections and tensions between two traditions rather than forging a new, third tradition.

The bar mitzvah was a particular moment in the life of a family that was explicitly dedicated to Christian-Jewish family life. Indeed, the mother, Susan Katz Miller, keeps an extensive blog entitled *On Being Both*, writes on interfaith family life for the Huffington Post, and is the author of a book entitled *Being Both: Embracing Two Religions in One Interfaith Family*, which surveys and reports on intentional interfaith family communities across the country.[38] Both the Miller family and IFFP rejected the idea that they were creating a new, third religion that blends Christianity and Judaism. Rather, they understood their religious lives as a way of "celebrat[ing], explor[ing], question[ing], and enjoy[ing] both traditions equally."[39]

IFFP was founded in 1995 by four women who were dedicated to educating their children in both Christianity and Judaism. The member-driven group grew to include approximately three hundred children and adults, to employ a part-time minister and rabbi, and expanded to include both a weekly "gathering for worship" and other adult programming. My conversations with IFFP members reflected a shifting sense of the community's purpose. Parents of younger children tended to explain their presence in terms of their children and were uncertain whether they would participate in IFFP as their children got older. Parents of teens tended to explain that they were in the community for themselves as much as for their children. Of course, these people were self-selected: I did not speak to parents of teens who had phased out of the program. There was, however, clearly a contingent of adults who considered IFFP their community, above and beyond its offerings for their children. The question of IFFP's ultimate purpose, as a permanent spiritual home or as a community to support families in raising interfaith children, remained a live issue in the community. The answer could have larger implications, should children raised in the community remain in the D.C. area. Over the near decade that I spent in conversation with IFFP members, two adult children of the community returned to the D.C. area and decided to teach in the religious education program. Two more returned to the community with their own spouses.

The day that I attended a Sunday morning service, IFFP's orientation toward children was particularly evident, because it focused on thanking the religious school teachers for the work that they did throughout the year. The primary ritual elements of the service were, however, intact, with the singing of hymns, the recitation of the Lord's Prayer, the *Sh'ma*, the *V'ahavta*, and the Mourner's *Kaddish*, prayers that were central to the community's gatherings. Afterward, the general ethos of the service, emphasizing the values strengthened by the traditions, and some of their common messages, seemed to me to be similar to that of the Unitarian Universalists. Because I knew that the former education director had moved on to serve as the minister of a UU congregation, I asked the Reverend Jarvis what she saw as the primary differences between IFFP and UUA-affiliated congregations. She quickly answered that their differences were primarily and very importantly liturgical. She said, "I do not think that in a Unitarian church, you would ever have people reciting both the Lord's Prayer and the *V'ahavta*—being Unitarian is really taking a third path, and here we are walking both paths together, in community."

The inclusion of Christian and Jewish prayers is, Reverend Jarvis explained, deeply important to many of the couples. Members tell her, "You cannot imagine what it means to me to have my Catholic husband stand next to me, reciting the *V'ahavta* in our shared community." She emphasized that some members were explicitly raising their children in one tradition or the other, but wanted them to have familiarity with both traditions. Many people, however, were taking the path that Katz Miller and her husband had chosen for their family: to educate their children in both traditions and to celebrate both traditions.

Katz Miller was very clear, both in our conversation and in her writing on her blog that she has consciously chosen to cultivate a dual identity for her children. This was, in part, in response to the choices that her parents made for her. Katz Miller, who was fifty when we spoke, was raised as a Reform Jew before the Reform movement came to formally accept patrilineal descent. While her mother was fully supportive of raising her children as Jews, she had not converted to Judaism. Throughout her life, people have questioned Katz Miller's Jewish status (coming as it does from her Jewish father), an experience reflected in the quote from her blog with which I opened: "We decided to politely ignore everyone who thinks my son is not Jewish because his Judaism is patrilineal."

Katz Miller also argued that there are real costs to asking a parent, usually the mother, to give up her own religious identity in the raising of her children. She respected her mother's choices, made before feminism's second wave changed many of the dynamics and ideals of modern marriage, but she could not choose to subsume her own religious identity into that of her Protestant husband. Nor was that a choice that she could ask him to make. Such a choice had costs in terms of feminism, but also in terms of traditions, wisdom, and family continuity lost. Katz Miller pointed out that her parents' decisions were informed by conventional wisdom of the 1960s, which suggested that raising children exclusively as Jewish would gain them acceptance in the Jewish community. Her own experience as the child of interfaith marriage, however, taught her that complete acceptance was not, in fact, possible. The tensions embedded within the Reform Jewish community around Jewish identity and interfaith marriage, particularly in their early attempts to navigate rising rates of interfaith marriage during Katz Miller's childhood and adolescence, made it clear to her that her Jewish identity would often be read as lesser because it was patrilineal. Therefore, why should other sacrifices be made for an unattainable goal?

One of the central tenets of IFFP, as articulated by Rabbi White, was that, because Christianity was born out of Judaism, Christians need a strong grounding in Jewish thought and traditions in order to completely appreciate and grow in their faith. He underscored that this is very different from the position of Messianic Judaism: in Rabbi White's view, Judaism is not made complete or even superseded by Christianity. Rather, he suggested that the traditions are deeply related and that knowledge of Judaism is how Christians can explore and come to understand the roots of their traditions. This argument, a variation of the one used in literature encouraging mono-religion families to select Judaism as the household religion, at IFFP becomes the argument for raising children in Judaism *and* Christianity without overt contradiction, because the practices, the holidays, and even the prayers work in thematic concert, creating space for a liturgical year intertwining both traditions.

The idea that Christianity was an outgrowth of Judaism does not, of course, address the figure of the Christ. Katz Miller's blog documents community exploration of the figure of Jesus, both as historical figure and as Savior. IFFP conversations envisioned Jesus as representing love, inclusion, egalitarianism, and nontribal religion. She even mentioned a community member exploring the idea of "Jesus envy," meaning "a sense that Jesus brought peace and inspired spirituality in a way that is inaccessible to Jews." At the same time, the community's conversations also addressed the fear and discomfort that Jesus can create for Jews "after two thousand years of some Christians labeling Jews as Christ-killers" or in contexts in which He is figured as a "weapon of exclusion." Katz Miller emphasized the process of wrestling with discomfort, not resolving differences in response to Jesus, and that the entire community can "share a common goal of presenting a Jesus who is not feared or forbidden, who preached on the subject of love, who inspires to this day." Such a message, she noted, does not require that IFFP families or individuals "aspire to or pretend to consistency within our families, or within our community, on the question of his divinity."[40]

In questions about Jesus, just as in conversations about the relationship between Christianity and Judaism, the community turned to a history that they framed as stripped of the inaccuracies created by theological bias. They taught the evidence of Jesus as a historical figure, be he divine or not, apart from Jesus as he has been figured in subsequent Christian (and Jewish) thought. The historical Jesus on whom the community agreed is itself historically located, privileging certain aspects of Jesus as he appears in biblical texts as well as claiming the Gospels as historical artifacts of Jesus' life. IFFP, then, raised certain biblical depictions of Jesus over later depictions of the Christ figure and emphasized an intellectual understanding of Jesus rather than an emotional relationship with him. In coming to the shared ground of the historical Jesus, the community also sacrificed some of the theological power of the Christ figure, but it has created a Jesus they could all agree to engage with in adult dialogue and in the education of children.

Neither Jarvis nor White knew much about the religious lives the children raised in the community retain in adulthood. Having been founded in 1995, the community was just beginning to have young adult religious school alumni. Will they affiliate, and if so, will they do so as Jews or as Christians, or will they find formal and informal groups of similarly religiously mixed people? Will those who remain in the D.C. area remain with the community, or, as parents, return to IFFP? What traditions will they carry forward into their own homes? Katz Miller raises similar questions about her own children. Her book documents the fact that while organizations like IFFP are growing in number, they are located in only a few U.S. cities. As a result, she could not guarantee that her children will be able to find communities similar to the one in which they were raised.

While not all IFFP participants expected to remain in the community beyond their child-rearing years, I spoke with one who found the community dissatisfying. Frank explained that IFFP had been wonderful to and for his family, but he found that the community's needs and interests did not match his. He suggested that the attempt to engage with both traditions prevented deep engagement with one tradition. As a result, he found that IFFP lacked spiritual depth. His Catholic wife found herself wanting to return to the rituals of Mass and prayer. Though he was the Jewish partner, he was drawn to the liturgy and prayers of the Catholic Church and had, when we talked, made the decision to convert to Catholicism. One of the only people with whom I spoke who drew a distinction between cultural and religious identity, he explained that he still felt himself to be culturally Jewish, and he wanted his children to have a sense of themselves as cultural Jews, but he also wanted them all to have the faith life that he found in the Catholic Church.

One of IFFP's primary strengths was that it offered a dynamic religious community, intentionally focused on the needs of interfaith families above all others. When I asked IFFP families about raising children in two traditions and in two religious communities, a pathway described in *Celebrating Our Differences: Living Two Faiths in One Marriage* and exemplified by the Kimball-Geller family, members pointed out that such a path means religion dominates family life.[41] IFFP created the possibility of a dual heritage that was less cumbersome—the two traditions required engagement in only one community. It was also potentially much less lonely—one had a community of people with a similar liturgical and holiday calendar, who also understood the joys and challenges of celebrating two religions. Rather than potentially being an outsider in two different religious communities, IFFP members could exist in a community that truly supports their endeavors.

It remains unclear whether the idea of dedicated interfaith family communities will spread beyond a few major cities. And what pathways will adult children take when raised this way? Will their children have what the Kimball-Gellers call the ability to make strong, grounded choices, but be likely to choose one identity or the other? Will they become what sociologists and journalists have taken to calling "religious nones"? Or potentially, despite their avowals that they are not creating a third way, is that exactly what they are doing? Will communities like IFFP find themselves expanding beyond serving the needs of families whose parents come from different traditions to include adults who were raised in interfaith communities, whether or not they are married or single, parents or childless? At the moment, these communities are constructed to meet the needs of interfaith families—it will be interesting to see whether and how they might meet the needs of their children as they grow to adulthood.

Some IFFP members' concerns about being viewed as creating a third path derived from two realities: first, the assumption that they were mixing religions drew fire from outsiders. These critics argued that inherent differences between the religions mean that no mixture could be consistent or true to the fundamentals of both Christianity and Judaism. Inherently, then, critics argued, such a third way would be less than the sum of its parts. Members of IFFP, of course, saw their intentional interfaith dialogue as more than the sum of its parts. Second, IFFP included many who are deeply connected to their own tradition and love and respect that connection in their spouses. They were not searching for something new, but rather for a way to share both of those heritages and systems of belief with their children.

IFFP created a community that integrated practices and prayers from both traditions into their worship, education, celebrations, and ethical conversations (if not into their belief systems). In doing so, they were, in fact, creating a new way of being in the world. Inherent in being an interfaith community was maintaining space for difference and dialogue, but IFFP also privileged certain narratives about the nature of and the relationship between Christianity and Judaism, searching for a shared historical understanding rather than faith claims to create common ground. The idea that this process is not a third way resonated with the parental generation, who have a sense of the independent tradition, but it may not have strong meaning for the children. One of those children, Eli Kane, age seventeen in 2011, was quoted in a Voice of America article about the community as saying, "To me interfaith is its own thing, and I identify with interfaith."[42] If "interfaith" in this context is its own form of finding meaning, making a religious identity in which multiple truth claims are held in tension, and the practices of multiple traditions can be woven together in ways that highlight their similarities and acknowledge their differences, then being the child of interfaith marriage and an inherently interfaith individual became a distinct way of being in the world, in which a worldview was drawn from the interplay of practices and intellectual histories. Individuals with these complexly layered identities have always existed—often because they were born into interfaith families and their experiences of extended families gave them intimate knowledge and memories of more than one tradition. IFFP, however, provided a space where such identities are celebrated and accepted, and it worked to provide language and space for such syncretic religious identities. More, perhaps, than any of the other examples explored in this chapter, then, the Interfaith Family Project, founded in 1996, in the midst of the multicultural movement, was theory put into practice, living out a multicultural ideology.

Conclusion

When the couples described in these families decided to marry and start families, they had different reactions to being from different backgrounds. For the Kaplan-Brewsters, their differing religious backgrounds were a nonissue. For the other three couples, they realized that there were challenges in their different backgrounds, and they sought solutions that honored what each of them brought to the table. For these families, the process of honoring both people and both families meant that a single-religion home was not possible. While the families have made different choices about how to create a home, there are some themes that run through all of their experiences.

While some of the parents valued their religious upbringings and others did not, none of them felt strong allegiance to their childhood religious institutions. Rather, they are interested in forging ways of life that incorporate practices and worldviews that matter to them. These families understand their religious homes as serving their needs: Kathy and Dan remain without a community because they have not found a good fit, and Audrey and James left the Jewish community for the Unitarian Universalist community because the UU congregation better addressed their needs. Susan Katz Miller and her family are active participants in creating a new religious conversation about interfaith religious communities that meets the needs of Christian-Jewish families. Jennifer Kimball and Jacob Geller maintained relationships and memberships with two distinct religious communities. They then articulated the belief that it was the job of the religious institutions to attract their children—it was not their job as parents to instill loyalty to the institutions in their children. While each family values the religious community that they have found and dedicates time and energy to that community (or regrets the absence of a community), they follow the trends outlined in chapter 5 and consider it perfectly acceptable to find a religious community that meets their needs or do without, rather than fitting themselves into a community.

Not only do the families exercise agency in finding religious community, but also they exercise and emphasize agency in their family religious cultures. Self-reliance is a central value of the homesteading lifestyle shared by the Kaplan-Brewsters and one of the key values that their daughter Hannah emphasized in her description of the family farming practices. Agency around religious choices is more overt for the other families: the Kimball-Gellers stress to their daughters that they can and must make strong and thoughtful choices about their religious identities. The Groffs have recast the meanings of both Christian and Jewish religious holidays, and the Millers have chosen to devote their energies to helping to grow a community specifically for interfaith families celebrating both religions. Individual agency is stressed in these family models—the ability to create, interpret, and combine one's own practices. While most of the families draw from both Christian and Jewish traditions, they do not do so thoughtlessly and therefore, while the juxtapositions are different in each household, each household has created a thoughtful narrative that holds the practices together.

While there are distinct differences in the approaches that the families took to the creation of their blended families, with the Groffs intentionally reinterpreting practices to offer shared meaning and the Kimball-Gellers and the Millers carefully holding differing religious narratives in tension, each of the families brought differing practices together to create expanded options for their children, who are comfortable with the practices drawn from Christianity and Judaism (even in the Kaplan-Brewster household, Rebecca and Hannah feel very comfortable with a limited range of Christian and Jewish practice), as well as the modes through which the family created their moral framework: homesteading in the case of the Kaplan-Brewsters, reinterpretation for the Groffs, meta-conversations and reflections for the Kimball-Gellers, and intentional interfaith dialogue for the Millers.

In addition, far from being without moral anchors, as critics of the dual-faith families feared, these families had strong and deeply intentional moral frameworks, which animate the choices that they have made about creating hybrid traditions. All four of the couples in this chapter are deeply committed to egalitarian marriages, with both men and women identifying as feminists. As a result, none of the couples really felt that it was viable, if they were going to have marriages in which both partners contributed equally, for one partner to give up his or her own religious traditions. It simply did not strike them as fair. Although I spoke with feminist, egalitarian couples that found other solutions, for these families, egalitarianism meant that they could not select a single tradition.[43]

Similarly, the families all valued the needs of the individual and the family above those of the religious groups. While they understood concerns of Jewish leaders about the impact of intermarriage on the life and size of Jewish communities and also understood the pain relatives felt at seeing children raised outside of particular religious traditions, each family felt that they had to make the choices that were best for them, as a family unit, and best for their children as individuals. Jennifer Kimball reflected this value system when she explained that it was not her or her husband's responsibility to shape their children into believing Mormons or Jews as neither of them hold strong commitments to the truth claims of their traditions of origin. Rather, it was their responsibility to provide their children with the skill sets needed to make powerful spiritual choices. It is, in her view, the job of religious groups, Mormon and Jewish, though also potentially another outside tradition, to then persuade her children that they will be best served, spiritually, by membership. Susan Katz Miller offered a similar focus on the individual when she pointed out that the Reform movement's willingness to accept children of interfaith marriage had, in her experience, been limited. If they could not promise full acceptance, in trade for giving up the celebrations and wisdom of half of one's heritage, then the bargain was, for the individual, a poor one. In the end, while the families acknowledge different levels of responsibility to religious institutions, they do not assume that what is best for the institutions is necessarily in line with what is best for the individuals, and as the heirs of the generation of religious seekers, they place individual needs ahead of religious institutional or communal ones.

These families have woven their interfaith identities together to create cohesive narratives, internalized for their own family identities. In the families where the children have grown, it is clear that those children have developed skills for creating their own morality-based worldviews and have explored what matters to them in religious practice and identity. Because each of the families is idiosyncratic in their practices and definitions, it remains unclear, and at times unlikely, that the children will be able to replicate their parents' religious practices in their lives as adults. That reality, however, does not set them apart or adrift in the contemporary American religious landscape.

For the Sake of the Children

Identity, Practice, and the Adult Children of Intermarriage

Interfaith families are increasingly part of the American landscape. Versions of their stories are told in our houses of worship, but perhaps more importantly on our televisions, in our movie theaters, in our newspapers, and on the shelves of our libraries and bookstores, where, in the past ten years, books aimed at Christian-Jewish families have been joined by books celebrating and trouble-shooting marriages across many "cultural" and "religious" divides. Amidst all the cultural production around interfaith families and their choices, families are attempting to make those choices and create meaningful lives, connections, and identities. Without understanding all of the different strains of cultural production and the values underpinning them, we cannot understand the landscape in which these families situate themselves. I map the wide range of material attempting to shape interfaith family life, asserting that families navigate the varied practices and rhetorics of interfaith life through strategic use of terms like "religion" and "culture" and through the logics of multiculturalism. These tactics allow them to negotiate, not just in the American Jewish landscape, but in the broader American landscape as well.

Interfaith Marriage and the American Religious Landscape

And interfaith marriage is most definitely an American story. On July 31, 2010, Chelsea Clinton, the daughter of former president Bill Clinton and then secretary of state Hillary Rodham Clinton, married Marc Mezvinsky in what both the *New York Times* and the *Huffington Post* described as an interfaith ceremony.[1] The leading picture for the story in the *New York Times* demonstrates the blended nature of the marriage (see figure 8). Chelsea is a practicing Methodist, whose religious background is nationally known because, as the daughter of both a former president and the Democratic nominee for president in 2016, her parents' religious affiliations became common knowledge for the entire country.[2] Her groom's attire, a *kippah* and a *tallit*, or prayer shawl, proclaimed his Judaism for any who viewed the few wedding pictures released to the public.

FIGURE 8 Chelsea Clinton and Mark Mezvinsky's wedding. Used with permission from Genevieve de Manio Photography.

Far beyond these facts of their upbringing, reports indicated that, in their ceremony, the couple blended both of their traditions. Rabbi James Ponet and the Rev. William Shillady conducted an interfaith ceremony, which, according to the *Times*, included both a reading of the seven blessings of a traditional Jewish wedding and the marriage vows from a traditional Protestant wedding.[3] Despite the history of debates about interfaith marriage, neither the couple nor the bride's influential parents indicated any sense that an interfaith marriage was at all unusual or inappropriate. The official announcement from the former president and the secretary of state referred to the ceremony as both "beautiful" and "interfaith."[4]

If interfaith marriages historically served as a chance to move into the dominant religious culture, it was not so for Mr. Mezvinsky, though Ms. Clinton is arguably as elite as they come. The couple married under a *chuppah*, or Jewish wedding canopy, with their elegantly calligraphied *ketubah*, or Jewish wedding contract, on an easel nearby.[5] This possibility—an interfaith wedding that is markedly Jewish, yet emphatically not Jewish alone—in which the couple's different religions can be treated (at least by the principals) as a footnote to their shared backgrounds and history, exists because of a particular historical trajectory. Without both an increasingly individualized approach to religious practice and without the impact of multiculturalism on the options available to interfaith couples, a wedding like the Clinton-Mezvinsky wedding would be hard to imagine.

The couple has since had children, but they have not formally announced the choices that they have made about their children's religion(s). As I have written elsewhere, however, more options are available to them, as an interfaith couple today, than were available to interfaith couples in their parents' generation.[6] Certainly, many Jewish publications have weighed in on what they will, or should, do.[7] In addition to the option of choosing one religion, be it his or hers, the couple can choose to move forward in their lives as they did in their wedding: actively blending and combining.

The fact that hybrid families exist and are beginning, as chapter 5 demonstrates, to find and create communities, does not mean that this path has eclipsed other options. The choices and concerns traced out in chapter 3 and 4 exist in tandem with the multicultural and blended realities of chapters 5 and 6. Chelsea Clinton's interfaith wedding was not without controversy caused by the couple's different religions. *Time Magazine* ran an article entitled "Did Chelsea Clinton's Wedding Threaten Jewish Identity?," which suggested that the "Jewish community" worried that "high-profile" interfaith marriages would lead others to intermarry, a concern echoed in the *New York Times*.[8] The *Times* noted that it was unlikely that Chelsea would convert.[9] "Chelsea Clinton Married a Jewish Man, But Will They Raise Their Children Jewish?" asked the *Palm Beach Post*.[10] The blogosphere and Internet chat rooms overflowed with opinions about whether the couple should marry and how they should raise their children, including posts entreating the bride to convert or at least allow her children to be raised as Jews.

The entreaties to Clinton to raise her children as Jews underscore an important aspect of the debates about interfaith marriage. The model of the multicultural interfaith family did not replace the model of the Jewish interfaith family. It added another compelling option, and support for that option, to the choices facing couples. The paths explored by families like the Millers or the Kimball-Gellers, analyzed in chapter 6, exist alongside the ideals detailed by Paul Cowan and Andrea King in chapter 3 and the Jewish family choices in chapter 4. Even as multicultural interfaith families have gained a public conversation and as Jewish interfaith families have contained aspects of hybridity, there remained multiple camps about what outcome would be best for the families, all located on a continuum between "strive to blend" or "strive not to."

The questions of interfaith marriage and families, either what they do or what Americans think that they should do, do not have simple answers. The responses that shapers of culture, be they religious leaders, television writers, or members of interfaith families themselves, provide depend on a number of factors: how they define religion and culture in relationship to each other, whether they aspire to an assimilationist world or a multicultural one, whether they are comfortable living with tension or whether they seek resolution, whether they are most concerned with communal needs or with individual needs.

Beyond Chrismukkah argues that all of these tendencies can only be understood in the context of a broader American religious narrative. The individual, as the primary unit of religious decision making, had long held sway in dominant strains of American Protestantism. In 1970s popular culture, that focus on the individual looked like assimilation—the marrying couple broke away from the communal norms to establish their own needs, based on their own values. Individualism did not, however, *have* to look like assimilation. If, in the 1970s, the Reform movement thought that interfaith marriage could be stemmed by withholding Jewish marriage, they soon realized that they were wrong. American Jews, like American Protestants and, increasingly, American Catholics, understood themselves as individual religious actors. As a result, Jewish outreach attempts to interfaith couples strove to convince them that they as individuals, their marriages, and their families would be happiest and most fulfilled if they lived Jewish lives. Individuals, however, do not make their decisions exclusively as individuals—they make their decisions in relationship, often privileging the family as the unit for which decisions are made. As a result, in interfaith families, parents—in particular mothers—are asked to set aside their own needs in the interest of what is best for relationships with spouses or children. Similarly, family practices coalesce in relationship and in negotiation, rather than purely as a manifestation of what suits the individual seeker.

It was in these relational, familial units that the interfaith families could draw from multiculturalism. Multiculturalism and optional ethnicity were both predicated on an understanding of the autonomous actor (or, at most, family unit), who could choose among the various ethnic or religious practices and products available in order to shape an identity. While that identity would not be cohesive according to more broadly held tropes (it might not be entirely Jewish, Episcopalian, Irish, or Italian), it would be authentic to the self who was doing the selecting. The very act of selecting, and of putting seemingly incongruous elements together, operated according to a moral logic—one that explicitly valued difference, as long as it could be turned into occasional practice. In this way, then, interfaith families are part of the contemporary American landscape, drawing from their surroundings, largely through their consumption, to make distinctly American and blended identities. Purely consumption-based models of multicultural identity formation, however, fail to capture one of the key elements of interfaith family life, developed in chapter 5. Much material for multicultural interfaith families assumes that these families exist without reference to religious organizations or beliefs. Chapter 6 argues that there are blended interfaith families who are deeply connected to religious narrative and community. These families took as fundamental their own ability and authority to decide what was best for themselves and for their families, but they did not necessarily do so by sidestepping tension or by existing exclusively in the realm of practice. They reshaped and reformed, sometimes creating new, blended forms of their traditions or shaping interfaith sensibilities, different from the sensibilities of their component religions.

The many ways of negotiating interfaith family life, then, are in part tied to the many ways of negotiating what it means to be an American individual, as well as to late twentieth century and early twenty-first century shifts in what that might mean. Does being an American individual mean being inherently Protestant or does it mean being multicultural? Does it mean choosing the best of the options available in the religious marketplace or does it mean finding the very terms of the market to be overly limiting and creating your own combinations and community? More and more interfaith families, and Americans more broadly, are choosing the latter, although those choices are not eclipsing previous models. Rather, debate between the models continues, with individual couples choosing how to shape their family lives, just as Chelsea Clinton and Marc Mezvinsky will do. While most couples will do so with less media attention, the choices they make will not necessarily be less hotly debated.

While not all families take the path of multiculturalism, the moral logic of multiculturalism helps to dispel the argument that families who choose to double their religious practices are, in effect, choosing to be "nothing," both in terms of their moral formation and in terms of their community life. Rather, families who actively nurture more than one religious heritage do not do so passively. Rather, in each choice, they enact their value system in the choices made and combinations that they create—or even, as the Kimball-Geller family highlighted in chapter 6 demonstrates—in replacing Christian and Jewish practices with another set altogether. Is that moral logic always a strong force in the actions of selecting practices? Likely not, but as practice theorists have long argued, practice exists apart from and beyond meaning. Acts of blending, intentional or not and ideologically informed or not, may not create the dispositions expected of a Christian or a Jew, but create dispositions they do. Those dispositions are part and parcel of the worlds that contemporary religious communities must navigate.

Increasingly, these blended identities shape the American landscape. First and foremost, as Pew's 2016 study tells us, 20 percent of American adults grew up in interfaith families.[11] Even more enter into them. Once a cultural minority, interfaith marriages and the families that they create are a full third of American families today. The needs and experiences of those families, and their perspectives, practices, and choices, increasingly structure how religious community, belief, and practice function in the United States; but they also increasingly shape how American culture views concepts such as religious difference and the degree of permeability between different traditions. Individuals shaped in these families will be inherently hybrid individuals, regardless of whether the families chose singular or plural religious identities. They will have blended extended families and deeply intimate connections across religious lines and are likely to have experience with multiple forms of religious practice. Some of these interfaith families and interfaith individuals will seek religious community. They will come to exist in a wide variety of locations. Religious communities that cater to interfaith families exist in multiple American cities and are worthy of further study in and of themselves. More traditional mono-faith communities, otherwise known as churches and synagogues (but also mosques and temples), have found themselves adapting to the presence of interfaith families in their midst. Increasingly, however, it may not be enough for churches and synagogues to tell interfaith families that they are welcome in the community if they follow the community's rules. Frequently, interfaith families want to participate in these communities, but want to do so, as Jennifer Thompson puts it, "on their own terms."[12] As standards and expectations around interfaith families change, the churches and synagogues will need to change with them if they wish to attract that clientele. That process will continue to play out over time and will shape what it means to religiously affiliate in the United States. Lastly, not all interfaith families and individuals will choose to join communities. They will become, as they have recently been labeled, "religious nones." Thinking about interfaith families and the people forged in interfaith families provides another window onto the world of the religious nones, allowing scholars to consider how tradition, heritage, and religious practice might live on, separate not only from affiliation, but also from identity.

Interfaith Families beyond Christian and Jewish

Christian-Jewish interfaith families are, of course, only one of the many kinds of interfaith families that make up the fabric of the United States. Near the end of my fieldwork, I attended a very informal Jewish-Muslim wedding on the banks of the Hudson River. As I approached, I could identify the location of the wedding by the folding chairs and the *chuppah* made out of a *tallis*. The groom, an atheist Ashkenazi Jew from the Midwest in a seersucker suit, met his guests as they gathered in the park. Once everyone was seated, the bride, a Bengali Muslim from suburban Washington, D.C., in a red and gold sari, processed in, escorted by her parents, her brother, and her sister-in-law.

The wedding was performed by a member of the Ethical Culture Society. The bride's mother read from the Qu'ran, then provided a translation in English. The groom's mother explained the seven blessings of a Jewish wedding. As in Jewish custom, the couple sipped from the same cup, but rather than wine, they drank white grape juice. Juice, in deference to the fact that the bride, an observant Muslim, did not drink alcohol. White, out of fear that someone would spill on the wedding finery. Much was made of small coincidences. The groom's mother noted that the *tallis* they had used for the *chuppah* was the groom's, given to him for his bar mitzvah. Just that morning, they had realized that it had been made in India.

That afternoon, when I walked into the reception, the mothers were leaning against a wall, laughing hysterically as servers circulated with appetizers. While they had remembered to make sure that half of the appetizers should be vegetarian, for the couple's lefty friends, they had not actually selected the appetizers. No one had mentioned to the catering staff that this was a Muslim-Jewish wedding, and the caterers had not realized that they should not serve asparagus wrapped in prosciutto at the Khan-Levine wedding.

I was at this wedding as a guest, not as a researcher, and any answer that I can give to the question of interfaith marriages beyond those between Jews and Christians is, by its very nature, speculative.[13] Along the way, however, I certainly did encounter people in other kinds of interfaith families, many of whom shared their stories with me. I also talked to interfaith family advocates, some of whom are intentionally expanding their scope to families outside of the Christian-Jewish dynamic.

Christianity and Judaism have a very historically particular relationship to each other that brings certain tensions to the fore. While many Jews have looked for ways to assimilate to American or European culture, many Jews and certainly many Jewish institutions have feared that the Jewish people will be lost to assimilation. Other Jews have resented being a minority in a Christianity-dominated society. As a result, American Jews have a particularly complex relationship with dominant Christianity, and one that tends to resist depicting holidays like Christmas and Easter as part of secular American life.

This contentious or complex relationship might well be mirrored in other kinds of interfaith marriages—certainly there were many historical moments when Protestant-Catholic marriages were particularly fraught, though that moment has largely passed in the United States. The historical (and contemporary) relationships between India, Pakistan, and Bangladesh, along with the rise of Hindu Nationalism and Islamic Fundamentalism, mean that Muslim-Hindu marriages can cause severe tensions in South Asian immigrant communities, though neither tradition has the status of a dominant religion in the United States. Tensions around Israel and Palestine, or around the United States' "War on Terror" can make marriages between Jews or Christians and Muslims particularly tense.

Many other groups, however, do not have long histories of tensions with each other. Hindu immigrant communities, at least in the early twenty-first century, have largely embraced Christmas as the secular American holiday that many post-Christian Americans see it to be. Hinduism is also a tradition that is frequently permeable in its borders and boundaries. As a result, marriages between Hindus and Christians avoid one of the purported primary stumbling blocks of Christian-Jewish marriages: the December dilemma. At one of my field-work sites, the rabbi invited a Hindu grandfather who was also a pundit to include some traditional Hindu coming-of-age elements into his grandson's bar mitzvah. While that same congregation worked hard to include Christian grandparents in b'nai mitzvah celebrations, and was often particularly sensitive to the feelings of grandparents who were Christian clergy, they did not allow them to incorporate Christian rituals in those ceremonies.

That said, just because two traditions do not have historically difficult relationships with each other, they may have specific traditions that cause conflict. For instance, in March 2015, a Hindu woman married to a Jewish man wrote to the *Forward*'s short-lived "Seesaw" column about whether or not she and her husband should circumcise their son. She found herself balancing Jewish law with a strong anticircumcision sentiment among Hindus.[14] A

Catholic-Hindu couple explained that they had two weddings, one Hindu and one Catholic. In order to be married in the Catholic Church, the Catholic wife needed to promise to raise the children Catholic, and the Hindu husband had to promise not to impede her in doing so. He did not, however, have to promise not to expose their children to Hindu rituals and she does not see participating in those rituals as problematic. Therefore, their children, ages three and six, have spent their childhoods observing Hindu holidays at home and sometimes at temples and also attending family-friendly Mass and celebrating Christian holidays. The older child is almost old enough to start catechism classes, at which point they will find out how the Catholic Church will respond to the role Hinduism is playing in the children's lives.

Sometimes, as with Christian-Jewish marriages, historical tensions coincide with incompatible laws or rituals. Kerry Olitzky, the executive director of Big Tent Judaism, notes that he is particularly interested in Muslim-Jewish marriages, in part because of tensions between Palestinians and Israelis but primarily because Judaism is matrilineal and Islam is patrilineal. As a result, the children of (heterosexual) Muslim-Jewish interfaith marriages formally belong, in his view, to either both religions or neither religion. He would like to see both Jewish and Muslim organizations develop resources for such couples and figure out how to welcome such families into their communities.[15] Susan Katz Miller, an interfaith family advocate, blogger, and author, says that she is tired of the current conversation that focuses on Christian-Jewish interfaith families and wants to see that conversation expand. She notes that, today, the most common form of interfaith family is between believer and nonbeliever, rather than between Christian and Jew.

Clearly, there are many kinds of interfaith marriages beyond the Christian-Jewish examples on which I have focused, and each kind is distinctive. At the same time, some of my findings from this project seem to hold true for how couples navigate other forms of interfaith marriages. As with Christian-Jewish interfaith families, people find a myriad of ways to combine their traditions, and sometimes they need, for personal or structural reasons, to privilege one tradition over another. When they do so, they tend to use some of the same tools that I identified among the Christian-Jewish families. Notably, they drew distinctions between religion and culture, they reinscribed practices to have broadly acceptable meanings, and they framed their traditions in terms of stories rather than truth claims.

Many interfaith family combinations strategically deployed distinctions between religion and culture to justify their decisions about which practices to take on or how to combine them. As with Christian-Jewish combinations, distinctions between religion and culture can cut both ways. For instance, when the Hindu woman wrote to "Seesaw" asking how to talk to her parents about circumcising the son she was having with her Jewish husband, she talked about Jewish law requiring circumcision versus Hindu cultural objections to the practice. In doing so, she created a hierarchy between religion (law) and culture, in which religion was understood to be more important. At the same time, when I asked the rabbi why he allowed Hindu elements into the bar mitzvah of a half-Indian Jewish child, he pointed to honoring the bar mitzvah boy's Indian heritage. Again, while Hinduism was clearly more comfortable than Christianity would have been in the same context, he deployed the same division between "religion" and "not-religion," in this case "heritage," that Christian-Jewish couples use to defend their combinations.

Just as the Unitarian Universalist Christian-Jewish couples and the families in the Interfaith Family Project sought commonalities in their traditions, other forms of interfaith couples do so as well. A Jewish-Hindu couple talked about bringing Israeli and Guajarati folk dancing to their wedding. My own Unitarian-Hindu parents liked to say that "all Unitarians are Hindus; sadly, all Hindus are not Unitarian." The child of a Buddhist-Christian couple talked about how, while her parents raised her in the Episcopal Church, they emphasized that Jesus exemplified the values and practices of Buddhism. As with the Jewish-Christian couples, other forms of religiously blended families downplayed theological, historical, and cultural differences in favor of drawing out similarities.

Lastly, many of these interfaith couples avoid issues of truth claims. Like Jennifer Kimball and Jacob Geller, who emphasize that they are providing their daughters with stories that root them in tradition and place, the Hindu-Catholic couple who are raising their children formally Catholic, but keeping Hinduism in their home, do not see the traditions as inherently incompatible. They see both traditions as ways of orienting people in the world. The Hindu father wants his children to have a connection to the stories and rituals that have mattered in their family, but he does not see those stories as advancing specific truth claims. While their Catholic mother wants them to understand the mysteries of the sacraments, and to be able to experience the sacraments, her Catholicism is also free from truth claims. These are stories and rituals that ground people in the world. The Muslim bride from the opening story made a similar point: she wants her children to have an orienting story in the world. She, like many Christian women married to Jewish men, realized that her secular Jewish husband would be more comfortable if those claims came from Judaism than from Islam. She, therefore, planned to follow the model of many Christian women raising Jewish children—she would ask her husband to be more Jewish than he would have been on his own and together they would have a Jewish home. For her, this was a compromise. They would be as religious as she wanted them to be, but they would draw from his tradition rather than her own.

While the historical particularities of these interfaith families are different than those of their Christian-Jewish counterparts, many of the strategies that they use to decide what traditions to include, or exclude, are similar. They, too, seem to operate in multicultural models, combining traditions as they see fit, largely through their participation in specific rituals and their avoidance of truth claims. They, too, tend to strategically deploy the concepts of religion and culture in order to set the parameters for acceptable and unacceptable combinations. Are Christian-Jewish interfaith marriages a perfect model for the increasing religious diversity of the United States? Clearly not, but they are a place that we can turn to start asking "How have people imagined their lives and families and how might they continue to do so?"

Identity, Practice, and the Adult Children of Intermarriage

> I managed to hammer out an intentional religious life, a Half/Life full of very particular choices but rooted in my haphazard beginnings. I had grown up with a Christmas tree, so in my adult life, I bought a Christmas tree. I stopped eating pork and shellfish, but didn't claim to keep kosher. I read Jewish novels and collected Catholic religious art. . . . I had found my own particular identity, made something from my muddled mishpochah.[16]

So Laurel Snyder writes in the introduction to a collection of essays that she edited, *Half/Life: Jew-ish Tales from Interfaith Homes*. Each essay is written by the adult child of interfaith marriage, and together they provide one set of answers to the question people have asked me the most when they learn that I research Christian-Jewish interfaith families: "What about the children?" Over the almost ten years that I have spent researching and writing *Beyond Chrismukkah*, people have often asked me variants of this question. They want to know—does one's upbringing ensure a particular kind of identity? How do the changes in the options available to interfaith families change the outcomes for interfaith families? Are the kids all right?

While I understand why these are the questions that animate and excite my interlocutors inside and outside of academia, in some ways they are also unanswerable questions. The first question is impossible to answer simply because people are deeply unpredictable. As the parents of intermarrying couples know all too well, the choices that parents make for their own homes are not always replicated in the homes of their children. This is perhaps especially true in this historical moment, when fully a third of Americans change their religion at some point over the course of their lifetimes.[17]

The second question cannot be answered simply because we do not yet have the data. The options of multiculturalism really only developed beginning in the 1990s. The people who were raised in interfaith families that could draw from a multicultural logic (in a Jewish, Christian, Unitarian, interfaith, or other setting) have only been able to do so since the 1990s. At the time of this writing, children raised in such settings are, at most, about twenty-five. Many of them are younger. And so, while we can know what they say about their religious identity now, in adolescence or early adulthood, it is too soon to say whether they will join religious communities as adults, whom they will marry, or how they will raise their children. As a result, any observations I might make about the children of interfaith marriage are, by definition, speculative. I can write about the experiences of people who grew up in the 1970s, 1980s, and 1990s and who are now adults, but those people were largely formed before the rise of multiculturalism, and so they do not tell us much about the choices of the people who are young adults now, and even less about the people who are children and adolescents now.

That said, I am happy to speculate and would like to do so by drawing on my conversations with adult children of interfaith marriage and on two books that explore the experience of children growing up in interfaith families, Snyder's book (quoted above) and *Being Both: Embracing Two Religions in One Interfaith Family* by Susan Katz Miller. In general, it is hard to say how a family's choices will shape their children's identities as Christians, Jews, both in some combination, or neither in favor of another path. What I can say, with some confidence, is that it is becoming much easier to be an interfaith family, and therefore to grow up in an interfaith family. It is easier because there are more people in interfaith families, and more resources available to interfaith families. Increasingly, those resources support a range of choices. Couples are more able to make the choice that makes the most sense for them and find support for that choice.

Half/Life and *Being Both* were published in 2006 and 2014, respectively. Less than a decade apart, they represent different moments in interfaith family life. Snyder was born in 1974, and the essays that she collected were written, with a few exceptions, by people who were born in the 1960s, 1970s, and 1980s. While their ages are not included in their essays, Snyder is fairly certain that her oldest author was born in 1955 and her youngest in 1982.[18] Miller's book combines memoir with journalistic accounts of other interfaith family lives and experiences, collected through both interviews and surveys. She contrasts her own experiences with those of people growing up in her children's generation, largely in their teens and early twenties. As a result, these books can actually give us a sense as to the changes in interfaith family life over the half-century that I consider.

Both Miller and Snyder were raised by parents who had decided that their children would be Jews, though both were patrilineally Jewish. Though Miller notes that when she was a week old her mother baptized her "in the kitchen sink of our walk-up apartment on Beacon Hill in Boston," and then her grandmother and an aunt also secretly did so, she was raised in Jewish community.[19] She reflects that she has "nothing but empathy and gratitude for [her] mother's brave but covert gesture."[20] She suggests that perhaps it was this secret baptism, combined with a Jewish upbringing, that led her to her life in an interfaith community, and as an advocate for that community and for raising children in all of their family heritages. At the same time, she makes it clear that she is being tongue in cheek—she has three siblings, all of whom were also raised Jewish, all of whom also had secret baptisms. One sibling is raising his children Catholic, another is raising hers Jewish. The third does not have children, but "prefers Buddhism."[21]

Miller believes that her parents made the best choice available to them as an interfaith couple, married and having children in the 1960s, and notes that her mother never took them to church and "threw herself into the project" of raising Jewish children, mastering the cooking, studying Hebrew, attending synagogue, and overseeing b'nai mitzvah for her children. At the same time, being a patrilineal child of interfaith marriage proved difficult. She writes that as she entered the adult world, she was repeatedly told she was not Jewish. Sometimes those comments were the result of appearance or cultural capital. Being from New England, she didn't "know the difference between a bagel and a bialy" and she has an "'Irish' nose."[22]

Most frequently, Miller faced the argument that Judaism is matrilineal. Miller was in college while the Reform movement was debating whether to consider people Jewish if they had Jewish fathers. Many people that Miller encountered in college, particularly in settings like Hillel, found these conversations threatening, because they so firmly inscribed the boundaries of matrilineal descent. Her mother was not Jewish: ergo, neither was she. She writes of repeated rejections by the Jewish community—by rabbis, by men she dated. These arguments made her feel like an outsider.[23]

Miller suggests that in some ways, the problem was heightened by Jewish embrace of difference in the 1980s. During her childhood, when American Jews were more "assimilationist" or "inclusivist," she argues that it was easier to be an interfaith family. While organized Judaism would suggest that Miller could have resolved this problem through conversion, she had been raised Jewish, in Jewish community, and she finds it offensive to argue that she needs to convert to an identity that she already has. The insult is compounded by the fact that, had she been raised Christian, but had a Jewish mother, no conversion would be necessary.[24]

Snyder's parents also decided that she would be raised Jewish, though at some point after her parents divorced her mother joined Corpus Christi, a vibrant Catholic Church in Baltimore. Snyder's classmate and best friend was also a member of her mother's church, so though she was Jewish, she spent a lot of time at the Catholic Church. She wrote that she "was love with the incense and the candles. I was in love with the Christmas tree and the smell of the soup kitchen. I played hide-and-seek with Susan in the church rectory and in the church itself, where I got tangled, literally, in the robes hanging inside a vestment closet, and felt at home."[25]

While Snyder loved the Catholic Church, she never felt confused about what religion was hers. She knew that she was Jewish. Partly that was because her father's Jewish community, the Bolton Street Synagogue, was every bit as much a home. It was a young and scrappy Jewish community, building itself from the ground up. Snyder was part of that process. She painted the bathrooms. She helped build the bima, "with [her] own two hands."[26] But Snyder also knew she was Jewish because, as involved as she was in the Catholic Church, no one ever asked her to choose between the traditions. "I had been bat mitzvahed, and I knew which prayers I was supposed to say. When I sat in a pew with Susan or my mother, I never took communion or said the creed. I never crossed myself. That wasn't me, or any part of what I expected."[27] In a talk at the Museum of Jewish Heritage, Snyder said that she even found comfort, when presented with the mysteries of the Catholic Church, that they were not her responsibility. She was Jewish. She did not need to understand them.[28] Snyder writes that her religious identity did not feel haphazard—she fused for herself the religion that she describes in the quote with which I opened this chapter. But she did point out that it was lonely—it was hers alone.

The essays that Snyder collected reflect many of the experiences that she and Miller write about when speaking about their individual experiences. One of the essayists, Margaret Schwartz, writes, "Half is to miss something you've never possessed. To call into question."[29] Deba Seidel writes about getting taken in by strangers when she gets lost on a bus trip in Israel. They asked her if she was Jewish. She said yes. They asked if she had grown up in a religious community. "Not at all," she responds. "I grew up with my mother but my mother's a Christian Scientist." Her hostess "looks at [her] puzzled. 'If your mother's not Jewish, then you are not a Jew. . . . Hasn't anybody ever told you that?' "[30] Seidel writes that she laid awake that night, thinking about the woman, telling her that she is not a Jew.

Not all of the essays that Snyder collects are sad—some of them are stories of blended lives. Katharine Weber's essay is a scene from her childhood, about driving into her father's old neighborhood in Brooklyn to get their Christmas tree, where the tree seller is a Satmar Hassid. He and her father haggle in Yiddish; they buy a hot knish for the ride home. Snyder's sister Emma writes her own account of their childhood, a story that proves Miller's point: children can be raised in the same family, subject to the same decisions made by their parents, but, because of any number of other factors, including their experiences of that family, end up with differing adult identities.

By and large, however, these essays written by people born between 1955 and 1982 talk about interfaith identities, not as inherently confusing, but as hard. Growing up in an interfaith family was lonely because, whether or not the person chose one identity, as Snyder did, it was a complex identity. Being the child of an interfaith marriage was hard because people's chosen identities were challenged by other people who wanted to explain that, if their mother was not Jewish, they were not Jewish, if they had a Christmas tree, they were not Jewish. Sometimes interfaith families meant moments of confusion, when one needed knowledge that was missing or when a ritual failed to provide comfort.

Being Both, however, is more than Miller's own story of an interfaith life. She interviewed and surveyed many interfaith families and dedicated a chapter of her book to the identities of children who grew up in families that located their interfaith lives in communities like the Interfaith Family Project. These children are of another generation. Miller interviewed them between 2010 and 2012. While some of the people she interviewed have settled on one religion, most of these teens and young adults (none of them older than twenty-five) continued to identify with both of their family traditions. They felt that their dual upbringings offered them choices and left them both free to believe as they saw fit. At the same time, they believed that their interfaith identities left them educated and grounded in both traditions. When she asked them about the disadvantages to being raised interfaith, one-third of her survey respondents did not see any. Others pointed to the difficulty of defending their identities to people who did not understand them. They did not find themselves to be confused by the messages of two religions or pressured by the need to choose between them. They did believe that their interfaith upbringing made them more tolerant of difference, more open-minded toward other worldviews. They felt that their interfaith worldviews made them more introspective.[31]

Miller's respondents are young. They are not yet fully independent of their parents, and they mostly have not yet begun to create their own homes. They may find that their viewpoint changes as they get older and, realistically, they are not old enough to have their experiences answer the question "but what about the kids?" Miller is also an advocate for raising children in two communities—for all her journalistic training, this is not a place in which she is an unbiased journalist, nor is she pretending to be one. She argues that raising children in two traditions is a good and viable option, especially given supportive communities. She makes a compelling case, but in the end she is not talking about adults, at least not in the world of an extended American adolescence.

My own interviews with adult children of interfaith marriage suggest that Miller's positive message is based in a changing American reality. When I interviewed adult children of interfaith marriages, they were similar in age to Miller, Snyder, and the authors of the essays that Snyder collected; that is, they were mostly born in the 1960s and 1970s. They had not been raised in the interfaith communities that Miller describes, because these didn't exist when they were growing up. Instead, they grew up in one of three settings: Unitarian Universalist churches, in entirely secular American settings, or in Jewish communities. It has not turned out to be the case, however, that a perfect overlap exists between how they were brought up and how they live as adults.

The Unitarian Universalist adults suggest that Lee Barker's arguments in chapter 6 were correct: most of the people who were raised UU either left the UU church to become secular Americans (possibly carrying some Jewish observance with them, possibly not), or they developed strong UU identities. In fact, two of the UU-raised children of intermarriage I spoke with are UU ministers, and they knew of at least two other UU ministers with interfaith parents. While they see Judaism as an important part of their heritage, they do not all agree on whether or not they themselves are Jewish. One of these ministers, Leah Hart-Landsberg, has served as president for the group UUs for Jewish Awareness and sees Judaism as an active part of her identity. The other commented, "I like the Reform movement's approach. Even though my mother is Jewish, I am not Jewish because I did not have a Jewish education. I have Jewish heritage. I am Unitarian Universalist."[32]

Those who were raised in secular homes were sometimes raised secular because their parents could not agree on a religious home. Other times, they were raised in nonaffiliated homes because the Jewish parent was uncomfortable with formal Christian religious community, but unwilling to ask his or her spouse to give up holidays like Christmas and Easter. Unless there was a synagogue that would welcome a Christmas-celebrating interfaith family (and there usually was not), they stayed home. Most of the time, however, the people who had been raised as religious nones were raised without formal affiliation because religion was just not that important to their families. Like the Kaplan-Brewster family, these families had strong senses of themselves. They were simply among the growing unaffiliated segment of the population.

Lastly, there were people who were raised in interfaith families that had affiliated with Judaism. Some of these people now think of themselves as secular Jews, or as one person of Ashkenazi-Jewish, Italian-Catholic heritage called herself, a "pizza bagel—it is definitely more a bagel than a pizza, but it has some interesting toppings."[33] It is hard to say whether these children of interfaith marriage are more likely to be unaffiliated than their counterparts with two Jewish parents. They are probably slightly more likely to put up Christmas trees, but most of them do not cite Christian parents as reasons for not joining a shul. Rather, they say what many unaffiliated Jews say: synagogues are expensive and do not speak to their needs. Their responses suggest that Kerry Olitzky of Big Tent Judaism is correct when he says that Jewish engagement should be more of a concern for organized Judaism than interfaith marriage.[34] These informants are secular Jews. They believe themselves to be Jewish. Jewish culture matters to them. Jewish institutions do not.

Finally, I spoke with many adult children of interfaith families who have chosen to raise their children in Jewish communities. Sometimes they were raised in Jewish communities. Other times they were raised in unaffiliated secular families. Sometimes they are in Jewish communities because they have married Jews. As one person, now a Jewish professional, put it: "I was raised to be neither, but I married Jewish, so I do Jewish and my children are Jewish. My sister married Quaker, she does Quaker. We grew up doing Christmas and Passover. Now I spend Jewish holidays with my Jewish in-laws, which means I can always go home for Christmas. My sister spends Christmas with her Christian in-laws. She can always go home for Passover. My parents are never alone for the holidays, and we spend two weeks together on Cape Cod in the summer."[35] People who "married Jewish" were in the minority, however, even among the children of interfaith marriage who chose to join synagogues.

Most children of interfaith marriage who joined synagogues also married people who had grown up Christian. Repeatedly, they talked about how different their experience of interfaith synagogue life was from that of their parents. In one community, a number of interfaith couples invite Jewish friends to join them in their homes for Christmas. "I grew up having to hide the fact that we had a Christmas tree from my Hebrew school teacher," reflected one interfaith child who had grown up to be an interfaith parent. "I was delighted to have my son's Hebrew school teacher at our table for Christmas dinner. She knows our kid is Jewish. She knows my wife is not."[36] For this Jewish dad, with interfaith parents and a Protestant wife, Jewish community is possible because his children do not have to lie about what happens in their homes, and his wife does not have to give up the celebrations that matter to her.

While the example of a Hebrew school teacher at Christmas dinner is unusual, certainly organized Judaism is increasingly flexible about how it approaches interfaith families. As interfaith families make up larger and larger percentages of synagogue membership, and as Jewish communities continue to grapple with how to welcome interfaith families, they are increasingly likely to listen to those families, rather than inform them of how they must live. As one Reform rabbi in Atlanta, Georgia, put it, "If a family is living a robust Jewish life, if they are involved in a synagogue or a *havurah*, if they have Jewish friends, if they have a Shabbat practice, if their children attend Hebrew school, I just don't think that it makes sense to demand that the Christian partner give up Christmas, or a Christmas tree. Do we really think that a strong Jewish identity is so weak that something lived 365 days a year can be hurt by one or two days of holiday, that fifty-two weeks of engagement a year can be wiped out by four weeks of decorations and music?"[37] A similar point was made by a Jewish Federation official in New York City, who made the same point more generally: "We have always reached out to non-Jewish spouses and said, 'Let us show you what Judaism can offer you.' Now, we are starting to understand that it is not enough to say, 'Judaism can be wonderful.' Instead, we need to say, 'You are not non-Jewish. You are Christian, you are Muslim, you are Hindu. You are Swedish, you are Irish, you are Somali, you are Indian. Let's see how your Jewish home and even your Jewish community can honor some of who you are.'"[38]

Not all Jewish communities take the approach reflected by these two Jewish professionals, but, increasingly, interfaith families who want to affiliate Jewishly can do so without excising all elements of Christianity from their homes. As a result, more complicated identities can flourish.

None of these people, not Snyder's essayists, nor Miller's teen informants, nor my adult informants, can tell us what the fate will be of the people growing up after the multicultural turn. What I can say, and say definitely, is that people make many different choices about how to make meaning and community out of their interfaith lives. They, like other American adults, do so with a sense of their individualism and as consumers in an American religious marketplace. Largely, they seem to have agency in their choices and if they are unhappy, it is not because their parents married across religious lines. In short, I cannot tell you what the children will do, but I can tell you that they are, by and large, all right.

Notes

Introduction

1. *Kendall v. Kendall*, 426 Mass. 238; 687 N.E.2d 1228; 1997 Mass. LEXIS 408 SJC-07427 (Supreme Judicial Court of Massachusetts 1997).

2. "At What Price Success? The Boston (Church of Christ) Movement," *Christian Research Institute*, accessed February 12, 2017, http://www.equip.org/article/at-what-price-success-the-boston-church-of-christ-movement/.

3. *Kendall v. Kendall*, 426 Mass. 238; 687 N.E.2d 1228; 1997 Mass. LEXIS 408 SJC-07427.

4. Ibid.

5. Ibid.

6. Ibid.

7. Pew Forum on Religion and Public Life, "One-in-Five U.S. Adults Were Raised in Interfaith Homes."

8. Pew Forum on Religion and Public Life, "US Religious Landscape Survey: Religious Affiliation Diverse and Dynamic," 5.

9. The exception to this trend would be the work of Anne Rose, whose treatment of interfaith marriage in the nineteenth century in *Beloved Strangers: Interfaith Families in Nineteenth Century America* addresses marriages between Protestants, Catholics, and Jews as an American phenomenon, examining them in terms of both gender and the role of the public citizen.

10. Bourdieu, *Outline of a Theory of Practice*; Bourdieu, *Logic of Practice*; Certeau, *Practice of Everyday Life*.

11. Schmidt, *Consumer Rites*; Heinze, *Adapting to Abundance*.

Chapter One

1. Marbach, Sobel, and Brink, *What about Interfaith Marriage?*

2. May, *Homeward Bound*.

3. Barclay, "Mixed Religion Marriage Called Difficult to Sustain."

4. May, *Homeward Bound*, 13–15.

5. Goldstein, *Price of Whiteness*, 3.

6. Marbach, Sobel, and Brink, *What About about Interfaith Marriage?*, 1966.

7. Ibid.

8. Berman, *Speaking of Jews*, 53–72.

9. Marbach, Sobel, and Brink, *What about Interfaith Marriage?*

10. Ibid.

11. A note on terminology: during this phase in religious life, both Catholic and Jewish traditions referred to marriages between members of two different religious traditions as mixed marriages rather than interfaith marriages. Indeed, at this stage, the Reform movement distinguished between mixed marriages, occurring between Jews and "non-Jews," and interfaith marriages, between ethnic Jews and converted Jews.

12. In Judaism, Responsa are legal opinions on specific contemporary questions, drawing from the authors' interpretations of previous iterations of Jewish law. Each movement of Judaism has produced (and continues to produce) its own response.

13. Massarik, *National Jewish Population Study*, 10.

14. Essrig, "Letter to Rabbi Jacob Shankman."

15. Ibid.

16. Blackman, Eichhorn, et al., "An Open Letter to the CCAR."

17. Ibid.

18. Ibid.

19. Ibid.

20. Berman, "Mission to America," 205–39.

21. Eichhorn, "Letter to the Reform Rabbinate."

22. Ibid., 5.

23. Ibid.

24. Ibid., 5.

25. Ibid., 2–3.

26. Schindler, "Address of Rabbi Alexander M. Schindler," 83.

27. "Alexander Schindler—Biography in Context," accessed August 8, 2016.

28. Schindler, "Address of Rabbi Alexander M. Schindler," 87.

29. Berman, "Mission to America," 220. Berman's article considers the missionary impulses of the Reform movement in the early to mid-twentieth century, offering a useful perspective of how porous some members of the CCAR considered the line between Jew and non-Jew to be.

30. Schindler, "Address of Rabbi Alexander M. Schindler," 85. Schindler wrote this in the 1970s, at a time when, because of both the Holocaust and the 1967 war, Jews, including American Jews, believed themselves to be constantly under threat of extinction, not just from intermarriage, but from external forces as well. To take on a Jewish identity, then, could be seen as deciding to take on the potential of that threat. For theologies addressing this aspect of Jewish thought, see the work of Richard Rudenstein, Irving Greenberg, and Emil Fachenheim.

31. Ibid., 87.

32. Ibid. Heinze notes that while many Catholics were interested in the question of the "authentic self" the primary contributors to the psychological and popular psychological literature were Jewish and Protestant.

33. Herberg, *Protestant, Catholic, Jew*; Dolan, *In Search of an American Catholicism*, 127–260; Morris, *American Catholic*, 196–227.

34. Marbach, Sobel, and Brink, *What about Interfaith Marriage?*

35. Before Vatican II, priests and devout Catholics were also concerned about specific practices that varied between Catholics and Protestants: for instance, Catholic leaders feared that if a Catholic man married a Protestant woman, she would serve him meat on Fridays or that a Protestant man would insist that his wife feed him meat on Friday night and would not support her in making the children join her in eating fish (or, worse yet, would forbid her to cook fish). Because Vatican II eliminated many of the differences in mandated practice between Catholics and Protestants, by the late 1960s, Catholic leaders raised fewer practice-based objections to mixed marriage.

36. Lehmann, *Mixed Marriages in the Catholic Church*, 1.

37. Felix, "Why: Mixed Marriages."

38. Ibid.

39. Ibid.

40. Ibid.

41. Ibid. Lehmann, *Mixed Marriages in the Catholic Church*, 1.

42. Noll, "New Law Relating to Mixed Marriage."

43. Lehmann, *Mixed Marriages in the Catholic Church*, 6–8.

44. Ibid.

45. Ibid.

46. As chapter 3 will demonstrate, forty years later, in the 1980s, the Reform movement explored similar questions, with similar concerns and results.

47. Lehmann, *Mixed Marriages in the Catholic Church*, 8.

48. Ibid.

49. Ibid.

50. This letter was in part the product of a Synod of Catholic Bishops, which occurred in 1967 to discuss the problem of mixed marriage. The conference was international in scope, demonstrating that for the Church, mixed marriage was a problem in North America and in much of secularized Europe, as Catholics and Protestants came into increased contact with each other and were less likely to find themselves interacting across a deep theological and practice-based divide.

51. Paul VI, "Apostolic Letter," 1.

52. Ibid.

53. Ibid.

54. Ibid., 2.

55. Ibid.

56. "Father Kueng Speaks on Mixed Marriages," 453.

57. Having read all of the reader responses collected at the archives of Notre Dame, including those from readers who requested anonymity should their letters be quoted, I am confident that the sample selected by *U.S. Catholic* was indeed representative.

58. Mould, March 1980.

59. Ibid.

60. Jakobsen, "Sex + Freedom = Regulation: Why?," 292.

61. Elizey, "Divorce Phenomenon," 424.

62. Brill, "Is Marriage Dying, Too?," 270.

63. "Marriage Laws Create Interfaith Conflict"; "Catholic-Protestant Marriages Still a Problem"; "Gracious Gesture or Insult"; "Ecumenical Curtsy."

64. Rousseau, "Vatican and Mixed Marriages"; "Father Kueng Speaks on Mixed Marriages"; "Cushing Wants Church Laws Liberalized"; "Boston Archdiocese Accents Positive Ecumenism in Mixed Marriages."

65. "Ecumenical Curtsy," 420.

66. Ibid.

67. Ibid., 419.

68. Ibid.

69. Lehmann, *Mixed Marriages in the Catholic Church.*

70. "Ecumenical Curtsy," 420.

71. Ibid.

72. Ibid.

73. "Rabbis Rebuke Toynbee," 733.

74. Ibid.

Chapter Two

1. In creating the concept of excess ethnicity, I draw on Laura Levitt's work on excess in her essay "Other Moderns, Other Jews." In the essay, Levitt posits that Judaism is acceptable in America as long as it takes the form of a privatized religion, that is to say, as long as it fits into a Protestant model. Jews who do not fit this model, either because they are atheists or otherwise not religious, but continue to consider themselves Jewish or because they are too religious—their Judaism extends beyond the "acceptable." While Levitt explores what Jewishness means, particularly in its secular forms, I am drawing on her concept of problematic excess to explore American stereotypes of a particular Eastern European identity.

2. The popular television show *Rhoda* also featured an interfaith romance and marriage (with Jewish Rhoda's marriage to Joe Girard becoming the most watched television episode, at the time of its airing). Their marriage would also ultimately fail. While Rhoda's Jewishness was a central part of her character as a sidekick on *The Mary Tyler Moore Show*, it was largely downplayed in the subsequent show *Rhoda* and the marriage was not addressed as explicitly interfaith.

3. Anderson, *Imagined Communities*; Fessenden, *Culture and Redemption.*

4. Orsi, *Between Heaven and Earth*, 178–79.

5. Orsi. "On Not Talking to the Press," 19, as quoted in Fessenden, *Culture and Redemption*, 1–2.

6. Jakobsen, "Sex + Freedom = Regulation: Why?," 294.

7. Coontz, *Marriage, a History*; Jakobsen, "Sex + Freedom = Regulation: Why?"

8. Rose, *Beloved Strangers.*

9. *Abie's Irish Rose* was not the only popular depiction of a highly assimilationist Catholic-Jewish couple whose marriage separated them from Old World families. In 1926, Universal Studios started a series of films about *The Kellys and the Cohens*, which

reversed the genders of the young couple, making the woman Jewish and the man Catholic, but otherwise based on such a similar premise to *Abie's Irish Rose* that it became the subject of a court case for copyright infringement. Both shows were commercial, if not critical, successes.

10. The term "ghetto girl" is drawn from Prell, *Fighting to Become Americans*. The term "shiksa goddess" is drawn from interviews with a Jewish woman who explained that as she was coming of age in the 1970s, she came to understand that Jewish men did not want to marry her or her Jewish friends, they wanted to marry "shiksa goddesses."

11. Prell, *Fighting to Become Americans*. See particularly chapter 5 on the devouring Jewish mother.

12. Johnson, *Heartland TV*, 112–46. Johnson argues that the Midwest in general stands, in popular culture, for a more authentic American experience, as opposed to the coasts with their immigrants or the South with its evident regionalism. In particular, she looks at Minnesota niceness as a source of iconic nostalgia, in *The Mary Tyler Moore Show* and *Newhart*.

13. Prell, *Fighting to Become Americans*.

14. Rose, *Beloved Strangers*.

15. Antler, *You Never Call! You Never Write!*, 75–77.

16. Ibid., 77–80.

17. Ibid.; Prell, *Fighting to Become Americans*, 142–76.

18. McDannell, *Spirit of Vatican II*, 58.

19. Bellah, *Beyond Belief*, 168–89; Herberg, *Protestant, Catholic, Jew*.

20. Prell, *Fighting to Become Americans*, 5.

21. Roof, Greer, and Johnson, *Generation of Seekers*; Bellah et al., *Habits of the Heart*.

22. Diner, *Jews of the United States*; Dolan, *In Search of an American Catholicism*; Glazer, "Multiculturalism, Religious Conservatism, and American Diversity"; Heinze, *Jews and the American Soul*; Herberg, *Protestant, Catholic, Jew*; Joselit, *Wonders of America*; Oppenheimer, *Knocking on Heaven's Door*; Sarna, *American Judaism*; Tentler, *Catholics and Contraception*.

23. Dolan, *In Search of an American Catholicism*, 191–256; Oppenheimer, *Knocking on Heaven's Door*, 62–73.

24. Bellah et al., *Habits of the Heart*; Roof, Greer, and Johnson, *Generation of Seekers*; Wuthnow, *After Heaven*.

25. "CBS Hears Complaints: Rabbis Don't Love Bridget," *Jewish Post and Opinion*, January 19, 1973.

26. "Television," 59.

27. Shales, "'Live from Bagdhad,'" C01; "CBS Hears Complaints: Rabbis Don't Love Bridget."

28. "*Bridget Loves Bernie* under Fire."

29. Ibid.

30. Ibid.; "CBS Hears Complaints"; "Protests Had No Influence?"; Ben-David, "When Bridget Loves Bernie."

31. Fiske, "Some Jews Are Mad at Bernie"; "CBS Hears Complaints"; "*Bridget Loves Bernie* under Fire."

32. Zurawik, *Jews of Prime Time*, 93.

33. "Judaism 101: Jewish Attitudes toward Non-Jews"; "Why Not Intermarry?"; "Real Reason Why Interfaith Marriages Fail."

34. Montgomery, *Target*, 40.

35. McDannell, *Material Christianity*, 1–14. Colleen McDannell defines material culture as artifacts, landscapes, architecture, and art, and she points out that paying attention to such aspects of the historical record allows scholars both to see ways in which the traditionally opposed categories of sacred and profane are, in fact, routinely scrambled in religious experience and to access the experiences of those often left out of the written historical record.

36. Daly, *Michael Landon*, 112–13.

37. Rose, *Beloved Strangers*. Later in the series, Nellie, Percival, and the children move back east to New York and Percival's family. At that point, however, they also leave the cast of *Little House on the Prairie*, leaving us without data as to how their religious differences are negotiated in that setting.

38. Ebert, "*The Way We Were* Movie Review."

39. Cagle and Daly, "Movie Trivia and More."

Chapter Three

1. Freedman, " 'Sex in the City' Celebrates Judaism." Certainly, in her willingness to become Jewish, Charlotte demonstrates a very different pattern of interfaith romance than is documented in chapter 2 or than David Zurawik traces out in *The Jews of Primetime*, in which the lines between Jew and non-Jew are sharply drawn and can be overcome, but not crossed.

2. For an in-depth study of the ways in which non-Jewish women are taking a leadership role in the raising of Jewish children in interfaith families, see Jennifer Thompson's ethnography of the Mother's Circle, *Jewish on Their Own Terms*.

3. Bourdieu, *Outline of a Theory of Practice*, 214.

4. Herberg, *Protestant, Catholic, Jew*.

5. Goldstein, *Price of Whiteness*, 209–39; Berman, *Speaking of Jews*, 143–67.

6. While there are many non-Ashkenazi Jews in the United States, the dominant Jewish culture is Ashkenazi or Eastern European. When interfaith families, converts, or Christian mothers are criticized for homes that feel "insufficiently Jewish," they are criticized for not being Ashkenazi enough.

7. Seltzer, "Letter from Sanford Seltzer to Alexander M. Schindler"; Glaser, "Letter from Joseph Glaser to Alexander Schindler."

8. Seltzer, "Intermarriage, Divorce, and the Jewish Status of Children." Seltzer cites the following for these statistics: Mayer, "A Cure for Intermarriage"; Beal, "Separation, Divorce and Single Parent Families," 241; Maller, "Jewish Gentile Divorce in California."

9. Ibid., 1.

10. Ibid., 1–2.

11. Ibid., 1.

12. Ibid., 2.

13. Ibid., 3.

14. Ibid.

15. Ibid.

16. Glaser, "Letter from Joseph Glaser to Alexander Schindler."

17. "Report of the Committee on Patrilineal Descent."

18. Scholars have documented a post–World War II shift from Judaism as a racial or ethnic group to Judaism as a religious group. This shift, which was necessary for full acceptance into American society, was at times organic and at times strategic. Thus, while focusing Jewish identity on the religious institution offered a clearly defined path to "Jewishness" for interfaith families, it was also emblematic of trends in mid-twentieth-century American Judaism. For more information, see Goldstein, *Price of Whiteness*, 189–208; Sarna, *American Judaism*, 272–374.

19. Matrilineal descent, the idea that the mother determines the child's status as a Jew, was implemented in the rabbinic period. According to Shaye J. D. Cohen, this change likely occurred as a compensation for the secondary status of women in Jewish law. He argues that "the matrilineal principle bespeaks [women's] inclusion and equality" and was set up as an internal check against the fact that Jewish women are not circumcised (which, for men, is the embodied symbol of the covenant between God and the Jewish people). Others have argued that matrilineal descent came to Jews through the Romans, who determined Roman citizenship matrilineally. Either way, it is important to note that matrilineal decent is of rabbinic, rather than of biblical origin. Cohen, *Why Aren't Jewish Women Circumcised?*, 141–42.

20. "Report of the Committee on Patrilineal Descent," 3.

21. Interfaith family advocates dislike talking about the "Jewish partner and the non-Jewish partner" or, conversely, the "Christian partner and the non-Christian partner," because, they argue, no one should be defined by an absence—the non-Jew or Christian has an identity that they bring to the table. In this case, however, the rabbinical concern is specifically with the Jewish status of a child's biological mother. From the halachic standpoint, it does not matter whether the mother is Christian, Muslim, or Buddhist, as long as she is not Jewish.

22. "Report of the Committee on Patrilineal Descent," 3.

23. Ibid., 4.

24. Roof, *Religious Pluralism and Civil Society*; Roof, Greer, and Johnson, *Generation of Seekers*; Jacobson, *Roots Too*.

25. First, they noted that the Reform movement has always tried to balance tradition with modernity. They also pointed to places where Jewish tradition historically and biblically did use patrilineal descent, such as when tracing the descendants of Abraham from father to son or passing the governance of Israel from David to Solomon. They also explored the rationale for matrilineal descent, assessing the ways in which it did not, in their view, apply to contemporary society.

26. "Report of the Committee on Patrilineal Descent," 3.

27. Interview with "Conservative Rabbi A."

28. The Reconstructionist movement is an American-based Jewish movement that came into existence in the first half of the twentieth century. It considers Judaism to be an "evolving civilization" and has accepted patrilineal descent since 1969.

29. Interview with "Alyssa Jackson."

30. Simon, "Forum on Intermarriage and Conversion."

31. Friedlander, "Letter to Alexander M. Schindler."

32. Purim is a Jewish festival that commemorates the events in the book of Esther. The celebration includes a telling of the story of the queen Esther, with much attention paid to the villain, Hamon, who wishes to have all of the Jewish people killed.

33. Cowan and Cowan, *Mixed Blessings*, 24.

34. Interview with Rachel Cowan.

35. Cowan and Cowan, *Mixed Blessings*, 26.

36. Ibid., 129.

37. Ibid., 19.

38. Ibid.

39. Ibid.

40. Ibid.

41. King, *If I'm Jewish and You're Christian, What Are the Kids?*, 3.

42. Ibid., 13.

43. Ibid.

44. Ibid., 47.

45. Ibid.

46. Ibid., 72–73.

47. Cowan and Cowan, *Mixed Blessings*, 32. In making this argument, Cowan drew heavily from the Reverend Ronald Osborne, an Episcopal priest and University of Iowa chaplain. Osborne's article appeared in the September 1985 issue of the Episcopal journal *Plumbline*. While for my analysis, Cowan's argument is more important, because it has been more widely read, it is valuable to note that some Christians shared the idea of cultural asymmetry between Christians and Jews and held that therefore interfaith couples should raise their children as Jews.

48. Osborne, quoted in ibid., 32.

49. Ibid., 33.

50. Ibid.

51. Ibid.

52. Ibid.

53. King, *If I'm Jewish and You're Christian, What Are the Kids?*, 3.

54. Ibid., 25.

55. Ibid., 27.

56. Ibid., 42.

57. Ibid., 25.

58. Ibid.

59. Seltzer, "Intermarriage, Divorce, and the Jewish Status of Children," 1.

60. Cowan and Cowan, *Mixed Blessings*, 33.

61. Ibid. Italics added for emphasis.

62. King, *If I'm Jewish and You're Christian, What Are the Kids?*, 43–44.

63. This framing of Christianity as rooted in belief combined with memories of Christian practice is not surprising, given a Protestant tendency to overlook practice in favor of belief, despite the presence of both in the lives of Protestants. Maffly-Kipp, Schmidt, and Valeri, *Practicing Protestants*; Hall, *Lived Religion in America*; McDannell, *Material Christianity*.

64. Bourdieu, *Outline of a Theory of Practice*; Bourdieu, *Logic of Practice*.

65. Portnoy, *Mommy Never Went to Hebrew School*; Cohen, *Papa Jethro*; Fisman, *Nonna's Hanukkah Surprise*.

66. "About Us," accessed February 14, 2017, http://www.karben.com/About-Us_ep_42-1.html.

67. Portnoy, *Mommy Never Went to Hebrew School*.

68. Ibid.

69. Karenfisman," *Karenfisman*, accessed February 14, 2017, http://www.karenfisman.com.

70. Gross, Rachel. "People of the Picture Book: PJ Library and American Jewish Religion," 177.

71. Ibid.

72. Sherwin et al., "People of the Book: An Evaluation of the PJ Library Program—Executive Summary," 2–3.

73. Ibid., 2; Gross, "People of the Picture Book," 185–86.

74. Gross, "People of the Picture Book," 185–87. Gross notes that the PJ Library's quest for inclusion has not always been seamless, noting that they are much more inclusive of racial diversity than they are of LGBTQ families.

75. Ibid., 183; "Bedtime Stories—Interfaith Family," accessed February 15, 2017, http://www.interfaithfamily.com/news_and_opinion/synagogues_and_the_jewish_community/Bedtime_Stories.shtml.

Chapter Four

1. Leventhal, "Letter from Mel Leventhal to Alice Walker."

2. Alice Walker was raised Methodist, but she rejected Christianity in favor of Buddhist practice and a more earth-based spirituality.

3. Fishman, *Double or Nothing?*; Thompson, *Jewish on Their Own Terms*; McGinity, *Marrying Out*; Kaplan, *Interfaith Families*.

4. Thompson, *Jewish on Their Own Terms*, 82–83.

5. McGinity, *Marrying Out*; McGinity, *Still Jewish*.

6. Ritual Well is a website created by Kolot: The Center for Jewish Women's and Gender Studies for the Reconstructionist Rabbinical College. It serves as a forum for "Jews by birth, Jews by choice, fellow travelers and seekers of all kinds" to "discover

and design rituals that . . . enhance Jewish life" by blending "tradition and innovation."

7. "Seeds of Change."

8. Rubel, "Feast at the End of the Fast"; Gross, "Draydel Salad"; Mehta, "'I Chose Judaism, but Christmas Cookies Chose Me'"; Harris-Shapiro, "Bloody Shankbones and Braided Bread"; Diner, *Hungering for America.*

9. McDannell, *Material Christianity*; Promey, *Sensational Religion*; Plate, *Key Terms in Material Religion*; Cash, "Kinship and Quilting"; Witzling, "Quilt Language."

10. Passing as white has a long and painful history in African-American communities, in part because when people presented themselves as white, they often lost touch with the families and communities whose continued existence could "out" them as African American. As part of undertaking what the historian Allyson Hobbs refers to as the "chosen exile" of passing, people would do their best to eradicate cultural traits, including foodways and speech traits that people associated with African-American culture. While this rupture was often extremely difficult for the person who decided to pass, the experience was also deeply painful for the communities and family members left behind.

11. Wilson and Wilson, initial interview, May 14, 2013.

12. Ferris, *Edible South.*

13. Wilson, Christmas celebrations, December 1, 2013.

14. Wilson and Wilson, William's bar mitzvah, November 3, 2013.

15. Cordero and Cordero, April 30, 2013.

16. Helen Wilson, "D'var Torah" sermon, September 16, 2015.

17. Ibid.

18. Ibid.

Chapter Five

1. "The Best Chrismukkah Ever," December 3, 2003.

2. "Year in Buzzwords."

3. McCarthy, "Have a Merry Little Chrismukkah."

4. Goldschmidt, *Race and Religion among the Chosen People of Crown Heights.*

5. Methodologically, I engage primarily with two bodies of literature in the study of American religion. Specifically, considering the role of material culture and American holidays, I draw from Leigh Eric Schmidt's *Consumer Rites* and Andrew Heinze's *Adapting to Abundance*, both of which explore the role of material and consumer culture in shaping American holidays and rituals. Marilyn Halter's work bridges ethnicity studies and consumerism studies, demonstrating that in the late twentieth century, patterns of consumption are central in enacting ethnic identity and particularly in fusing disparate identities. Matthew Frye Jacobson's *Roots, Too* explores the creation of white ethnic identity in the late twentieth century, providing a safe space for assimilation. Both of these authors flesh out an understanding of ethnic identity that illuminates the conditions and privileges of white engagement with multiculturalism.

6. Hecht, "Active versus Passive Pluralism"; Halter, *Shopping for Identity.*

7. Putnam and Campbell, *American Grace,* 151. Putnam and Campbell define intermarriage as marriages between members of the following groups: Catholic, Jewish, mainline Protestant, evangelical Protestant, and "other faiths." This means that a marriage between an Episcopalian and a Southern Baptist would count as intermarriage, but not one between a Reform Jew and an Orthodox Jew or an Episcopalian and a member of the United Church of Christ. As noted in the introduction, the Pew Foundation puts the number of interfaith marriages closer to 37 percent, though the Pew Foundation is asking what percentage of marriages are currently interfaith, and Putnam and Campbell are asking about the number of marriages that are interfaith at the moment that they are contracted.

8. Ibid., 156.

9. Goldschmidt, *Race and Religion among the Chosen People of Crown Heights,* 117.

10. Katz-Miller, "Ask Interfaith Mom."

11. Katz-Miller, "An Interfaith Child in the World."

12. Joshi, *New Roots in America's Sacred Ground*; Jacobson, *Roots, Too*; Halter, *Shopping for Identity*; Hecht, "Active Versus Passive Pluralism."

13. For examples of how multiculturalism has been applied in educational settings, see Banks, *Introduction to Multicultural Education*; Nieto, *Finding Joy in Teaching Students of Diverse Backgrounds.*

14. Halter, *Shopping for Identity,* 11.

15. Goldschmidt, *Race and Religion among the Chosen People of Crown Heights,* 131.

16. Ibid.

17. *Lynch v. Donnelly,* 465 U.S. 668 (1984)

18. Halter, *Shopping for Identity.*

19. Ibid., 189.

20. Lears, "From Salvation to Self-Realization," 8.

21. Ibid., 11.

22. Ibid., 16.

23. Heinze, *Jews and the American Soul,* 273.

24. Roof, Greer, and Johnson, *Generation of Seekers,* 250.

25. Bellah et al., *Habits of the Heart.*

26. Roof, Greer, and Johnson, *Generation of Seekers,* 250.

27. Bellah et al., *Habits of the Heart,* 219–49.

28. In Goldschmidt's own work, he points out that if one sees Jewish food as a set of cultural markers, such that one is Jewish because one eats kugel just as one is Jamaican because one eats jerk chicken, simply exchanging food and recipes is a mode of creating cultural diversity and getting along. If, instead, one sees food not as Jewish, but as kosher, which is to say adhering to a strict set of laws that must be followed because they were given by no less an authority than God, the entire playing field shifts. The foodways may or may not become more important, but they certainly cease to be simply ethnic markers. In his work, these different viewpoints on the function of food, cultural versus religious, is the point of miscommunication between the black community

and the Lubavitch community. It is important to note that while my interfaith families understand, and in fact use, the distinction that Goldschmidt depicts as existing within Crown Heights, both Jewish and Christian members of multicultural interfaith families adhere closely to the cultural model.

29. Laderman, *Sacred Matters*, xlv.

30. Orsi, *Between Heaven and Earth*, 3.

31. Pleck, *Celebrating the Family*, 238.

32. Hawxhurst, *Bubbe and Gram*.

33. This is particularly true of Effin Older's *My Two Grandmothers*.

34. Wolff, *Mozart Season*, 247.

35. In this case, sources addressing Christian-Jewish heritage and interfaith family life diverge sharply from much of the literature on biracial identity. Scholarship on biracial identity argues that language of "halfness" essentializes race, negatively impacting biracial people by excluding them from full participation in racial groups. Rather than seeing halfness as negative, many sources on interfaith families explicitly use the term to directly counter the idea of a belief-focused, in-or-out institutionally based definition of religion. While arguing that a child of interfaith marriage is in an inherently liminal position, these sources often also claim that through that very status, the "half-Jew" gains a valuable skill set. Among my interview subjects, some embraced the term "half-Jewish," as presented in the stories here. Others rejected the term, either on the grounds of Jewish law (which states that if your mother is Jewish, you are Jewish and if your mother is not Jewish, neither are you, but which does not allow for partial Jewish identities) or on the grounds that naming someone "half-Jewish" erases the non-Jewish half of the identity, be it framed in religious terms (Catholic, Episcopalian, Mormon, Hindu, Jain) or ethnic terms (Irish, Italian, Lebanese, WASP). The particular sources above, however, claim "half-Jewish" as a term and I, in keeping with my respect for the categories deployed by my sources, have chosen to replicate the term here.

36. Margaret gives God male pronouns.

37. Wolff, *Mozart Season*, 29.

38. Klein and Vuijst, *Half-Jewish Book*, xv.

39. Ibid., xvii.

40. Ibid., xix.

41. Ibid., 97.

42. Gompertz, *Chrismukkah*.

43. Ibid., 10.

44. Lofton, *Oprah*, 22. While Lofton points out that not all consumption offers the promise of shaping who you are, some does. The implication is that consumer choice is presented as holding potential for spiritual growth and formation.

45. "Mixed Families Set to Celebrate 'Chrismukkah'?"

46. Gompertz, *Chrismukkah*, 16.

47. "Mixed Families Set to Celebrate 'Chrismukkah'?"

48. Donohue and Potasnik, "Joint Statement on Chrismukkah."

49. Gompertz, *Chrismukkah*, 16.

50. Schmidt, *Consumer Rites*, 188.

51. Heinze, *Adapting to Abundance*, 79.

Chapter Six

1. Jennifer Kimball, who has written a memoir about her experience growing up Mormon, previously wrote a memoir focused on her interfaith marriage and on raising her children in both of their family traditions. During my interviews with her and Jacob Geller, they shared her rough drafts with me, what she calls her "fieldnotes on her marriage and children."

2. "Portrait of Jewish Americans." The Pew study does not include the religious identities (if any) of the non-Jewish spouses.

3. Ibid., 9.

4. Fishman, *Double or Nothing?*; Mayer, *Intermarriage and the Jewish Future*; Mayer, *Love and Tradition*; Mayer, *Imperatives of Jewish Outreach*; Mayer, *Children of Intermarriage*.

5. Katz Miller, *Being Both*.

6. Pew Forum on Religion and Public Life, "US Religious Landscape Survey," 7.

7. Ibid., 37.

8. Ibid., 25. If movement within Protestant denominations is counted as "switching religious traditions," this number increases by 16 percent.

9. Pew Forum on Religion and Public Life, "Many Americans Mix Multiple Faiths," 2–5.

10. Ibid., 7.

11. Ibid., 8.

12. Gould, *At Home in Nature*.

13. Ibid., xvii.

14. Ibid., 2.

15. My conversations with the Kaplan-Brewster family were colored by the fact that they took place less than a year after the death of Kathy's father, a retired minister and seminary professor. The family remembered the Reverend Brewster as a strong and abiding presence in their lives. While I do not doubt that he was such an influence, I must acknowledge that the timing of our conversations may have heightened the role his influence was given in the family narrative.

16. Interview with Kathy Brewster, November 21, 2009.

17. See Tillich, *Dynamics of Faith*.

18. Fishman, *Double or Nothing?*

19. A *havurah* (plural, *havurot*) is a small group of like-minded Jews who gather for prayer services, life-cycle events, and/or Jewish learning.

20. "Our Unitarian Universalist Principles," http://www.uua.org/beliefs/principles/. In 1961, the merging American Unitarian Association and the Universalist Church of America created a list of six guiding principles: to strengthen one another in a free and disciplined search for truth as the foundation of our religious fellowship; to cherish

and spread the universal truths taught by the great prophets and teachers of humanity in every age and tradition, immemorially summarized in the Judeo-Christian heritage as love to God and love to man; to affirm, defend and promote the supreme worth of every human personality, the dignity of man, and the use of the democratic method in human relationships; to implement our vision of one world by striving for a world community founded on ideals of brotherhood, justice, and peace; to serve the needs of member churches and fellowships, to organize new churches and fellowships, and to extend and strengthen liberal religion; and to encourage cooperation with men of goodwill in every land. In 1984, the purposes and principles were adapted at the Unitarian Universalist General Assembly, rewriting the above principles with nonsexist language; adding a seventh principle acknowledging the "interdependent web of all existence of which we are a part," and separating out the sources of the principles into a separate list. In that separate list, Judeo-Christian heritage was replaced by Christian and Jewish teachings. While the Groffs were uncertain about precisely when in the early 1980s they joined their congregation, one of these two sets of principles would have been in place when they began attending. See Ross, "Shared Values"; Skinner, "Time to Review the Principles."

21. Conversation with Lee Barker, Boston, MA, October 19, 2009.

22. Both Unitarians and Universalists historically identified as liberal Christians, though most contemporary UUs no longer see themselves as Christian. As early as the nineteenth century, both denominations, but in particular the Unitarians, were interested in exploring wisdom from other world traditions, particularly Hinduism and Buddhism, incorporating aspects of their philosophies and practices into Unitarian life and thought. For more information on early UU interactions with other religious traditions, see Tweed, *American Encounter with Buddhism*; Schmidt, *Restless Souls*. In the twentieth century, as both Unitarians and Universalists moved in the direction, post–World War II, of an atheist humanism, congregations attracted occasional Jewish members, some of whom approached the tradition with an interest in cultural assimilation and others of whom brought elements of their Jewish heritage with them, occasionally into their congregational life. UU clergy and congregations interpret the reference to Jewish heritage in the UU principles (see the previous note) in a variety of ways. Some see it as a politically correct reference to biblical texts and as an acknowledgment of the UUA's long-standing working relationship with liberal Judaism. Others see it as permission to draw from Jewish thought, liturgy, and practice. Still others consider it a mandate to do so. Regardless, whether or not individual congregations draw from Jewish sources or whether individual clergy and congregants are comfortable with including Jewish holidays and rituals in congregational life, the highest articulated ideals of the Unitarian Universalist movement allow space for including aspects of Jewish identity.

23. Hart-Landsberg, conversation with Hannah Hart-Landsberg, president, Unitarian Universalists for Jewish Awareness, May 28, 2012.

24. For more on the idea that food is intimately connected to Protestant religious and cultural experiences, much as it is conventionally understood to be part of Jewish

religious and cultural experiences, see Sack, *Whitebread Protestants*. For more on the ways that foodways function specifically in the lives of interfaith families, see Mehta, " 'I Chose Judaism, but Christmas Cookies Chose Me.' "

25. While Mormonism is distinctive enough from other forms of Christianity that I have been asked many times whether their differences shape my analysis, I focus on the process of combining traditions rather than the actual theological or practical details of their combination. As a result, the distinctive features of Mormonism matter only in that their differences from Judaism need to be addressed, but its differences from other forms of Christianity are not highly relevant.

26. Jack Mormons are lapsed or inactive members of the LDS church, who often live lives that are not in keeping with Mormon religious practices, but who also maintain a loose identification with the LDS church, rather than rejecting it outright. They might not feel comfortable (or bother about) attending church because of lifestyle choices, particularly with overtones of alcohol consumption—hence, the "jack" (as in apple jack); they might, especially in the past (1950s and earlier), have attended or still attend church but drink.

27. Because the Reconstructionist and Reform movements accept patrilineal descent, the girls did not need to be converted in order to have b'nai mitzvah celebrations unless the Mormon baptism posed a problem.

28. http://onbeingboth.wordpress.com/2011/01/10/interfaith-child-the-bar-mitzvah-plan/.

29. Kimball, personal communication, February 17, 2017.

30. Ibid.

31. Ibid.

32. Ibid.

33. Ibid.

34. Ibid.

35. The *Sh'ma* is the central prayer of the morning and evening prayer services. The *V'ahavta* is a prayer commanding the Jewish people to love God, and it enjoins them to remember the commandments. The Mourner's *Kaddish* is said at all services. Its text serves primarily to glorify God and its recitation is part of a year-long process and ritual of mourning for the death of an immediate relative.

36. Trope refers to the melody used when the Torah is chanted in synagogue. A trope tutor teaches b'nai mitzvah students (or others) the melodies, but also sometimes how to read both the Hebrew and the cantillation marks.

37. http://onbeingboth.wordpress.com/2011/05/26/my-interfaith-son-the-bar-mitzvah-and-coming-of-age/.

38. Katz Miller, *Being Both*.

39. http://iffp.net/about/index.html.

40. http://onbeingboth.wordpress.com/2010/10/24/interfaith-families-wrestling-with-jesus/.

41. Rosenbaum and Rosenbaum, *Celebrating Our Differences*.

42. Socolovsky, "US Religious Diversity Prompts Increase in Interfaith Marriage."

43. Other families, for instance, raised the children as Jewish but let the non-Jewish parent determine much of the content of the family's Judaism. Some families treated religion and language as equivalents, raising the children in the religion of the American parent while working extremely hard to ensure that the children spoke and were connected to an immigrant parent's language, a process that involved German school commitments that were as or more extensive than Hebrew school commitments or the decision to raise Jewish children and to speak Spanish exclusively within the home. Lastly, multiple families created compromises in which non-Jewish men agreed to raise children as Jews and the woman agreed to either change her name or to give the children their father's last name. Each of these families saw themselves as balancing out the compromises in marriage, as they strove for egalitarian marriages.

Conclusion

1. Seelye and Haughney, "As Chelsea Clinton Celebrates Her Wedding,"; "Chelsea Clinton and Marc Mezvinsky Married."

2. Stolberg and Schweber, "On the Trail of Chelsea Clinton's Wedding." Bill Clinton was raised as a Southern Baptist. During his time in Washington, the Clinton family attended a Methodist church, Hillary Rodham Clinton's religion since birth.

3. Seelye and Haughney, "As Chelsea Clinton Celebrates Her Wedding."

4. "Chelsea Clinton and Marc Mezvinsky Married."

5. Ibid.

6. Mehta, "Does Chelsea Clinton's Baby Look Jewish?"

7. Many people have weighed in about whether or not Chelsea Clinton's children will (or should be) Jewish. See "Chelsea Clinton Married a Jewish Man, but Will They Raise Their Child Jewish"; "Charlotte Clinton Mezvinsky: Jew or Not Jew?"; "Chelsea Clinton Gives Birth to (Non-Jewish) Baby Girl."

8. Townsend, "Did Chelsea Clinton's Wedding Threaten Jewish Identity?"; Berger, "Interfaith Marriages, Like Chelsea Clinton's, Stir Conflicting Feelings."

9. Stolberg and Schweber, "On the Trail of Chelsea Clinton's Wedding."

10. "Chelsea Clinton Married a Jewish Man, but Will They Raise Their Child Jewish."

11. 1615 L. Street et al., "One-in-Five U.S. Adults Were Raised in Interfaith Homes," *Pew Research Center Religion and Public Life Project*, October 26, 2016, http://www.pewforum.org/2016/10/26/one-in-five-u-s-adults-were-raised-in-interfaith-homes/.

12. Thompson, *Jewish on Their Own Terms.*

13. That said, I provided the bride and groom with my Institutional Review Board paperwork, got their permission to write about their wedding, and have given them pseudonyms. The bride pulled me aside between the wedding and the reception to make sure I knew that they had used white grape juice and to see if I had any other questions about what I had witnessed.

14. Padula, "No Circumcision, Please—We're Hindu."

15. Conversation with Kerry Olitzky, executive director of Big Tent Judaism, March 17, 2015.

16. Snyder, *Half/Life*, 4.

17. Pew Forum on Religion and Public Life, "US Religious Landscape Survey."

18. Conversation with Laurel Snyder, "Half/Life Follow-Up," October 14, 2016.

19. Katz Miller, *Being Both*, 1.

20. Ibid.

21. Ibid., 2.

22. Ibid., 9.

23. Ibid., 9–11.

24. Ibid., 16.

25. Snyder, *Half/Life*, 4.

26. Ibid., 3.

27. Ibid., 4.

28. Snyder, "Interfaith Families Today."

29. Schwartz, "Question in the Shape of Your Body," 9.

30. Seidel, "My Father's Hebrew Name," 31.

31. Katz Miller, *Being Both*, 178–203.

32. Anonymous interview with a UU minister with interfaith parents, June 13, 2009.

33. Anonymous interview, June 20, 2010.

34. Olitzky conversation.

35. Anonymous interview, October 18, 2014.

36. Anonymous interview, October 13, 2012.

37. Anonymous interview with Reform rabbi, September 8, 2009.

38. Anonymous interview with an NYC Federation employee, May 17, 2015.

Bibliography

Archival Collections

Cincinnati, OH

American Jewish Archives

Blackman, Murray, David Max Eichhorn, et al.
"An Open Letter to the CCAR," SC-1699, April 25, 1973.

"*Bridget Loves Bernie* under Fire: Rabbis Upset, Some Call for Boycott of Show's Sponsors." *Jewish Post and Opinion*, December 8, 1972, Intermarriage Nearprint Box 1.

Eichhorn, David Max. "Letter to the Reform Rabbinate." Intermarriage Nearprint Box 4, November 22, 1971.

Essrig, Harry. "Letter to Rabbi Jacob Shankman, Chair Ethics Committee CCAR." SC-1695, February 28, 1973.

Friedlander, Barbara. "Letter to Alexander M. Schindler." Mss Co 630, Box 10, Folder 11, September 9, 1992.

Glaser, Joseph, "Letter from Joseph Glaser to Alexander Schindler." Mss Co 630, Box 10, Folder 5, April 12, 1982.

"Protests Had No Influence? Network Says Bridget-Bernie Going Off the Air for Good." *Jewish Week*, April 5, 1973. Intermarriage Nearprint Box 1.

"Report of the Committee on Patrilineal Descent on the Status of Children of Mixed Marriages Adopted by the Central Conference of American Rabbis at Its 94th Annual Convention." Mss Co 739 Box 8, Folder 13, March 15, 1983.

Schindler, Alexander. "Address of Rabbi Alexander M. Schindler, President Union of American Hebrew Congregations to the Board of Trustees." Houston, TX, December 2, 1978, 83, Alexander M. Schindler Mss Co 630, Box 11, Folder 11.

Seltzer, Sanford. "Intermarriage, Divorce, and the Jewish Status of Children." Horizon Institute, Union of American Hebrew Congregations, August 1981, Mss Co 630, Box 10, Folder 5.

Seltzer, Sanford. "Letter from Sanford Seltzer to Alexander M. Schindler." Mss Co 630, Box 10, Folder 5, February 4, 1982.

Simon, Leslie. "Forum on Intermarriage and Conversion: Preconference Planning." Mss Co 630, Box 10, Folder 10, December 14, 1981.

Atlanta, GA

Stuart A. Rose Manuscript, Archive, and Rare Book Library of Emory University
Leventhal, Mel. "Letter from Mel Leventhal to Alice Walker." 1967, Alice Walker Papers MSS Co 1061 2/4.

Notre Dame, IN
> The Archive of the University of Notre Dame
>> Mould, Daphne Pochin article and artical notes. March 1980. US Catholic
>> Records. CUSC 11/01.
>> Noll, John Francis. "The New Law Relating to Mixed Marriage," 1932, PNOL
>> Box 1, Folder 34.
>> VI, Paul. "An Apostolic Letter Issued 'Motu Proprio' Determining Norms for
>> Mixed Marriages." 1970, 1, PMRH Box 74, Folder 32.

Interviews

The majority of interviews took place as conversations during participant observation
conducted between 2007 and 2014. In addition, I conducted the following formal interviews.

> Anonymous, October 18, 2014.
> Anonymous interview with a Reform rabbi, September 8, 2009.
> Anonymous interview with a UU minister with interfaith parents, June 13, 2009.
> Anonymous interview with an NYC Federation employee, May 17, 2015.
> Anonymous interview, October 13, 2012.
> Anonymous interview, June 20, 2010.
> Conversation with Lee Barker. Boston, MA. October 19, 2009.
> Conversation with Leah Hart-Landsberg. President, Unitarian Universalists for
> Jewish Awareness, May 28, 2012.
> Conversation with Kerry Olitzky. Executive director of Big Tent Judaism, March 17,
> 2015.
> Interview with "Alyssa Jackson." May 11, 2011.
> Interview with "Conservative Rabbi A." April 15, 2009.
> Interview with "Kathy Brewster." November 21, 2009.
> Shabbaton with Rachel Cowan. Congregation Bet Haverim, Atlanta, GA. Fall 2007.

Primary Sources

Barbara Zeitler Kendall v. Jeffery P. Kendall, 426 Mass. 238; 687 N.E.2d 1228 (1997)
Mass. LEXIS 408 SJC-07427. Supreme Judicial Court of Massachusetts, 1997.
Barclay, Dorothy. "Mixed Religion Marriage Called Difficult to Sustain." *New York
Times*, April 2, 1957.
Ben-David, Calev. "When Bridget Loves Bernie." *Jerusalem Report*, accessed April 21, 2010.
Berger, Joseph. "Interfaith Marriages, Like Chelsea Clinton's, Stir Conflicting
Feelings." *New York Times*, August 4, 2010, http://www.nytimes.com/2010/08/04
/us/04interfaith.html.
"Boston Archdiocese Accents Positive Ecumenism in Mixed Marriages." *Christian
Century*, June 4, 1969, 86, no. 23.
Brill, Earl H. "Is Marriage Dying, Too?" *Christian Century*, March 1, 1967, 84, no. 9.

Brooks, Joanna. *The Book of Mormon Girl: A Memoir of an American Faith*. Original edition. New York: Free Press, 2012.

Cagle, Jess, and Steve Daly. "Movie Trivia and More," *Entertainment Weekly*, accessed November 3, 2015, http://www.ew.com/article/1991/05/10/movie-trivia-and -more.

"Catholic-Protestant Marriages Still a Problem." *Christian Century*, July 7, 1965, 82, no. 27.

"Charlotte Clinton Mezvinsky: Jew or Not Jew?" *Haaretz*, September 28, 2014.

"Chelsea Clinton and Marc Mezvinsky Married." *Huffington Post*, July 31, 2010, http://www.huffingtonpost.com/2010/07/31/chelsea-clinton-wedding p_n _666338.html#s121283.

"Chelsea Clinton Gives Birth to (Non-Jewish) Baby Girl." *Jewish Press*, September 27, 2014, http://www.jewishpress.com/news/breaking-news/chelsea-clinton-gives -birth-to-non-jewish-baby-girl/2014/09/27/.

"Chelsea Clinton Married a Jewish Man, but Will They Raise Their Child Jewish?" Accessed August 26, 2012, http://www.palmbeachpost.com/news/news/chelsea -clinton-married-a-jewish-man-but-will-they/nL8yF/.

Cohen, Deborah Bodin. *Papa Jethro*. Minneapolis: Kar-Ben Publishing, 2007.

Cowan, Paul, and Rachel Cowan. *Mixed Blessings: Overcoming the Stumbling Blocks in an Interfaith Marriage*. New York: Penguin, 1988.

"Cushing Wants Church Laws Liberalized." *Christian Century*, June 26, 1963, 80, no. 26: 820–21.

Donohue, William, and Joseph Potasnik. "Joint Statement on Chrismukkah: Catholic League and New York Board of Rabbis." Catholic League, December 6, 2004, http: //www.catholicleague.org/joint-statement-on-chrismukkah-catholic-league-and -new-york-board-of-rabbis/.

Ebert, Roger. "*The Way We Were* Movie Review and Film Summary (1973)." Accessed June 1, 2016, http://www.rogerebert.com/reviews/the-way-we-were-1973.

"An Ecumenical Curtsy." *Christian Century*, April 6, 1966, 83, no. 14: 419–20.

Elizey, W Clark. "The Divorce Phenomenon." *Christian Century*, April 3, 1963, 80, no. 14: 424.

"Father Kueng Speaks on Mixed Marriages." *Christian Century*, April 10, 1963, 80, no. 15.

Felix, Abbot Richard. "Why: Mixed Marriages." *Our Faith Press*, n.d. (but prior to 1956, PNOL Box 2 Folder 150), University of Notre Dame Archives, Notre Dame, Indiana.

Fiske, Edward B. "Some Jews Are Mad at Bernie." *New York Times*, February 11, 1973.

Fisman, Karen. *Nonna's Hanukkah Surprise*. Minneapolis: Kar-Ben Publishing, 2015.

Freedman, Samuel G. " 'Sex in the City' Celebrates Judaism." *USA Today*, July 17, 2003.

Gompertz, Ron. *Chrismukkah: Everything You Need to Know to Celebrate the Hybrid Holiday*. New York: Stewart, Tabori and Chang, 2006.

"Gracious Gesture or Insult." *Christian Century*, June 15, 1966, 83, no. 24.

"Judaism 101: Jewish Attitudes toward Non-Jews." Accessed March 26, 2016, http://www.jewfaq.org/gentiles.htm.

Hawxhurst, *Bubbe and Gram: My Two Grandmothers.* Boston, Kentucky: Dovetail Publishing, Inc, 1997.

Kaplan, Jane. *Interfaith Families: Personal Stories of Jewish-Christian Intermarriage.* Seabury Books, 2005.

Katz Miller, Susan. "An Interfaith Child in the World: Rise Up Joyful." In *On Being Both: Interfaith Parent, Interfaith Child: Life with Two Religions*, August 24, 2012, http://onbeingboth.wordpress.com/tag/interfaith-identity/.

———. "Ask Interfaith Mom: Is It OK for Interfaith Parents to Adopt Interfaith Identity?" In *On Being Both: Interfaith Parent, Interfaith Child: Life with Two Religions*, June 27, 2013. onbeingboth.wordpress.com/tag/interfaith-identity/.

———. *Being Both: Embracing Two Religions in One Interfaith Family.* Boston: Beacon, 2014.

King, Andrea. *If I'm Jewish and You're Christian, What Are the Kids? A Parenting Guide for Interfaith Families.* New York: Urj Press, 1993.

Klein, Daniel, and Freke Vuijst. *The Half-Jewish Book: A Celebration.* New York: Villard, 2000.

Lehmann, L. H. *Mixed Marriages in the Catholic Church.* New York: Agora Publishing, 1941.

Marbach, Joseph F., Samuel Sobel, and Fredrick W. Brink. *What about Interfaith Marriage?* Washington, DC: General Commission on Chaplains and Armed Forces Personnel, 1966.

"Marriage Laws Create Interfaith Conflict." *Christian Century*, March 14, 1962, 79, no. 11: 318.

Mayer, Egon. *Children of Intermarriage: A Study in Patterns of Identification and Family Life.* New York: American Jewish Committee, Institute of Human Relations, 1983.

———. "A Cure for Intermarriage." *Moment Magazine* (June 1979): 3–4.

———. *The Imperatives of Jewish Outreach: Responding to Intermarriage in the 1990s and Beyond.* New York: Jewish Outreach Institute, 1991.

———. *Intermarriage and the Jewish Future: A National Study in Summary.* New York: American Jewish Committee, Institute of Human Relations, 1979.

———. *Love and Tradition.* New York: Schocken, 1987.

"Mixed Families Set to Celebrate 'Chrismukkah.'" NPR.org, December 15, 2006, http://www.npr.org/templates/story/story.php?storyId=6630803.

Moorman, Margaret. *Light The Lights! A Story about Celebrating Hanukkah and Christmas.* New York: Cartwheel, 1999.

"No Circumcision, Please—We're Hindu." *Forward*, March 21, 2015, accessed October 6, 2016, http://forward.com/articles/217186/no-circumcision-please-were-hindu/.

Older, Effin. *My Two Grandmothers.* San Diego, CA: Harcourt Children's Books, 2000.

Portnoy, Mindy Avra. *Mommy Never Went to Hebrew School.* Minneapolis: Kar-Ben Publishing, 1989.

"Rabbis Rebuke Toynbee." *Christian Century,* June 14, 1961, 78, no. 24: 733.

"The Real Reason Why Interfaith Marriages Fail." *Haaretz,* March 15, 2012, http://www.haaretz.com/jewish/the-real-reason-why-interfaith-marriages-fail-1.418812.

Rosenbaum, Mary Helene, and Stanley Ned Rosenbaum. *Celebrating Our Differences: Living Two Faiths in One Marriage.* Revised ed. New York: Ragged Edge Press, 1998.

Ross, Warren. "Shared Values: How the UUA's Purposes and Principles Were Shaped and How They've Shaped Unitarian Universalism." *UU World,* December 2000.

Rousseau, Richard W. "The Vatican and Mixed Marriages." *Christian Century,* August 1970, 87, no. 32: 963–70.

Schwartz, Margaret. "A Question in the Shape of Your Body." In *Half/Life: Jew-ish Tales from Interfaith Homes.* Brooklyn, NY: Soft Skull Press, 2006.

"Seeds of Change." Ritualwell, accessed October 10, 2015, http://www.ritualwell.org/blog/seeds-change.

Seelye, Katharine Q., and Christine Haughney. "As Chelsea Clinton Celebrates Her Wedding, Town of Rhinebeck, N.Y., Elbows Its Way In." *New York Times,* July 31, 2010, http://www.nytimes.com/2010/08/01/nyregion/01chelsea.html.

Seidel, Dena. "My Father's Hebrew Name." In *Half/Life: Jew-ish Tales from Interfaith Homes.* Brooklyn, NY: Soft Skull Press, 2006.

Shales, Tom. " 'Live from Bagdhad': The Cameras of War; Timely Tale of CNN's Defining Moment." *Washington Post,* December 7, 2002, Final edition, sec. Style, C01.

Sherwin, Jay et al. "People of the Book: An Evaluation of the PJ Library Program—Executive Summary." Berkeley, CA: Informing Change, 2013.

Skinner, Donald. "Time to Review the Principles." *UU World,* Spring 2006.

Snyder, Laurel. *Half/Life: Jew-ish Tales from Interfaith Homes.* Brooklyn, NY: Soft Skull Press, 2006.

———. "Interfaith Families Today." March 25, 2015. New York: Museum of Jewish Heritage.

Socolovsky, Jerome. "US Religious Diversity Prompts Increase in Interfaith Marriage." *Voice of America,* October 5, 2011, http://www.voanews.com/a/us-religious-diversity-prompts-increase-in-interfaith-marriage--131178068/162759.html.

Stolberg, Sheryl Gay, and Nate Schweber. "On the Trail of Chelsea Clinton's Wedding." *New York Times,* July 16, 2010, http://www.nytimes.com/2010/07/18/fashion/18CHELSEA.html.

"Television." *New York Times,* September 16, 1972.

Townsend, Allie. "Did Chelsea Clinton's Wedding Threaten Jewish Identity?" *Time,* n.d., http://newsfeed.time.com/2010/08/05/did-chelsea-clintons-wedding-threaten-jewish-identity/.

Unitarian Universalist Association. "Our Unitarian Universalist Principles." http://www.uua.org/beliefs/principles/.

"Why Not Intermarry?" *Aishcom*, accessed March 26, 2016, http://www.aish.com/jw/s/48969651.html.

Wolff, Virginia Euwer. *The Mozart Season*. New York: Square Fish, 2007.

"The Year in Buzzwords." *Time Magazine*, December 20, 2004.

Secondary Sources

"Alexander Schindler—Biography in Context." Accessed August 8, 2016, http://ic.galegroup.com/ic/bic1/BiographiesDetailsPage/BiographiesDetailsWindow?disableHighlighting=false&displayGroupName=Biographies&currPage=&scanId=&query=&source=&prodId=BIC1&search_within_results=&p=BIC1&mode=view&catId=&u=loc_main&limiter=&display-query=&displayGroups=&contentModules=&action=e&sortBy=&documentId=GALE%7CK2874900273&windowstate=normal&activityType=&failOverType=&commentary=.

Anderson, Benedict. *Imagined Communities: Reflections on the Origin and Spread of Nationalism*. Revised ed. Brooklyn: Verso, 2016.

Antler, Joyce. *You Never Call! You Never Write! A History of the Jewish Mother*. New York: Oxford University Press, 2008.

Banks, James A. *An Introduction to Multicultural Education*. 5th ed. Boston: Pearson, 2013.

Beal, Edward W. "Separation, Divorce and Single Parent Families." In *The Family Life Cycle*, edited by Elizabeth A. Carter and Monica McGoldrick. New York: Gardner Press, 1980.

Bellah, Robert N. *Beyond Belief: Essays on Religion in a Post-Traditionalist World*. Berkeley: University of California Press, 1991.

Bellah, Robert N., Richard Madsen, William M. Sullivan, et al. *Habits of the Heart: Individualism and Commitment in American Life*. 3rd ed. Berkeley: University of California Press, 2007.

Berman, Lila Corwin. "Mission to America: The Reform Movement's Missionary Experiments, 1919–1960." *Religion and American Culture* 13, no. 2 (Summer 2003).

———. *Speaking of Jews: Rabbis, Intellectuals, and the Creation of an American Public Identity*. Berkeley: University of California Press, 2009.

Bourdieu, Pierre. *The Logic of Practice*. Trans. Richard Nice. Stanford, CA: Stanford University Press, 1990.

———. *Outline of a Theory of Practice*. Trans. Richard Nice. Cambridge, UK: Cambridge University Press, 1977.

Cash, Floris Barnett. "Kinship and Quilting: An Examination of an African-American Tradition." *Journal of Negro History* 80, no. 1 (Winter 1995): 30–41.

Certeau, Michel de. *The Practice of Everyday Life*. 2nd ed. Berkeley: University of California Press, 2002.

Cohen, Shaye J. D. *Why Aren't Jewish Women Circumcised? Gender and Covenant in Judaism*. Berkeley: University of California Press, 2005.

Coontz, Stephanie. *Marriage, a History: How Love Conquered Marriage.* New York: Penguin, 2006.

Daly, Marsha. *Michael Landon: A Biography.* New York: St. Martin's Press, 1987.

Diner, Hasia R. *Hungering for America: Italian, Irish, and Jewish Foodways in the Age of Migration.* Cambridge, MA: Harvard University Press, 2003.

———. *The Jews of the United States, 1654 to 2000.* Berkeley: University of California Press, 2006.

Dolan, Jay P. *In Search of an American Catholicism: A History of Religion and Culture in Tension, Trade.* New York: Oxford University Press, 2003.

Eichler-Levine, Jodi. *Suffer the Little Children: Uses of the Past in Jewish and African American Children's Literature.* New York: New York University Press, 2013.

Ferris, Marcie Cohen. *The Edible South: The Power of Food and the Making of an American Region.* Chapel Hill: University of North Carolina Press, 2014.

Fessenden, Tracy. *Culture and Redemption: Religion, the Secular, and American Literature.* Princeton, NJ: Princeton University Press, 2013.

Fishman, Sylvia Barack. *Double or Nothing? Jewish Families and Mixed Marriage.* Waltham, MA: Brandeis University Press, 2004.

Glazer, Nathan. "Multiculuralism, Religious Conservatism, and American Diversity." In *Religion, Ethnicity, and Self-Identity: Nations in Turmoil.* Session 316, Salzburg Global Reports. Salzburg, 1997.

Goldschmidt, Henry. *Race and Religion among the Chosen People of Crown Heights.* New Brunswick, NJ: Rutgers University Press, 2006.

Goldstein, Eric L. *The Price of Whiteness: Jews, Race, and American Identity.* Princeton, NJ: Princeton University Press, 2007.

Gould, Rebecca Kneale. *At Home in Nature: Modern Homesteading and Spiritual Practice in America.* Berkeley: University of California Press, 2005.

Gross, Rachel. "Draydel Salad: The Serious Business of Jewish Food and Fun in the 1950s." In *Religion, Food, and Eating in North America,* edited by Benjamin E. Zeller et al. New York: Columbia University Press, 2014. 91–113.

Gross, Rachel. "People of the Picture Book: PJ Library and American Jewish Religion." In *Religion and Popular Culture in America,* 3rd edition, edited by Bruce David Forbes and Jeffrey H. Mahan, 2016.

Hall, David D. *Lived Religion in America: Toward A History of Practice.* Princeton, NJ: Princeton University Press, 1997.

Halter, Marilyn. *Shopping for Identity: The Marketing of Ethnicity.* New York: Schocken, 2000.

Harris-Shapiro, Carol. "Bloody Shankbones and Braided Bread: The Food Voice and the Fashioning of American Jewish Identities." *Food and Foodways: History and Culture of Human Nourishment* 14, no. 2 (April 2006): 67–90. doi:10.1080/07409710600691907.

Hecht, Richard. "Active versus Passive Pluralism: A Changing Style of Civil Religion." In *Religious Pluralism and Civil Society,* vol. 612, *Annals of the American Academy of Political and Social Science.* Los Angeles: Sage, 2007. 133–51.

Heinze, Andrew R. *Adapting to Abundance.* New York: Columbia University Press, 1992.

———. *Jews and the American Soul: Human Nature in the Twentieth Century.* Princeton, NJ: Princeton University Press, 2006.

Herberg, Will. *Protestant, Catholic, Jew: An Essay in American Religious Sociology.* New York: Anchor, 1960.

Jacobson, Matthew Frye. *Roots, Too: White Ethnic Revival in Post–Civil Rights America.* Cambridge, MA: Harvard University Press, 2008.

Jakobsen, Janet. "Sex + Freedom = Regulation: Why?" *Social Text* 23, no. 3–4 (Fall–Winter 2005): 285–308.

Johnson, Victoria. *Heartland TV: Prime Time Television and the Struggle for U.S. Identity.* New York: New York University Press, 2008.

Joselit, Jenna Weissman. *The Wonders of America: Reinventing Jewish Culture 1880–1950.* London: Picador, 2002.

Joshi, Khyati. *New Roots in America's Sacred Ground.* New Brunswick, NJ: Rutgers University Press, 2006.

Laderman, Gary. *Sacred Matters: Celebrity Worship, Sexual Ecstasies, the Living Dead and Other Signs of Religious Life in the United States.* New York: New Press, 2009.

Lears, T. J. Jackson. "From Salvation to Self-Realization: Advertising and the Therapeutic Roots of the Consumer Culture, 1880–1930." In *The Culture of Consumption: Critical Essays in American History 1880–1980,* Richard Wrightman Fox and TJJ Lears, editors. New York: Pantheon, 1983.

Levitt, Laura. "Other Moderns, Other Jews: Revisiting Jewish Secularism in America." In *Secularisms.* Durham, NC: Duke University Press, 2008. 108–38.

Lofton, Kathryn. *Oprah: The Gospel of an Icon.* Berkeley: University of California Press, 2011.

Maffly-Kipp, Laurie F., Leigh E. Schmidt, and Mark Valeri. *Practicing Protestants: Histories of Christian Life in America, 1630–1965.* Baltimore, MD: Johns Hopkins University Press, 2006.

Maller, Allen. "Jewish Gentile Divorce in California." *Jewish Social Studies* 37, no. 3–4 (1975): 280–90.

Massarik, Fred. *National Jewish Population Study: Intermarriage, Facts for Planning.* New York: Council of Jewish Federations and Welfare Funds, 1971.

May, Elaine Tyler. *Homeward Bound: American Families in the Cold War Era.* Revised ed. New York: Basic Books, 2008.

McCarthy, Michael. "Have a Merry Little Chrismukkah." *USA Today,* 16 December 2004.

McDannell, Colleen. *Material Christianity: Religion and Popular Culture in America.* New Haven, CT: Yale University Press, 1995.

———. *The Spirit of Vatican II: A History of Catholic Reform in America.* New York: Basic Books, 2011.

McGinity, Keren R. *Marrying Out: Jewish Men, Intermarriage, and Fatherhood.* Bloomington: Indiana University Press, 2014.

————. *Still Jewish: A History of Women and Intermarriage in America*. New York: New York University Press, 2009.

Mehta, Samira K. "Does Chelsea Clinton's Baby Look Jewish?" *Religion in American History*, accessed October 6, 2016, http://usreligion.blogspot.com/2014/10/does -chelsea-clintons-baby-look-jewish.html.

————. " 'I Chose Judaism, but Christmas Cookies Chose Me': Food, Identity, and Familial Religious Practice in Christian/Jewish Blended Families." In *Religion, Food, and Eating in North America*, edited by Benjamin E. Zeller et al. New York: Columbia University Press, 2014. 154–74.

Montgomery, Kathryn C. *Target: Prime Time Advocacy Groups and the Struggle over Entertainment Television*. New York: Oxford University Press, 1989.

Morris, Charles. *American Catholic: The Saints and Sinners Who Built America's Most Powerful Church*. New York: Vintage, 1998.

Nieto, Sonia. *Finding Joy in Teaching Students of Diverse Backgrounds: Culturally Responsive and Socially Just Practices in U.S. Classrooms*. Portsmouth, NH: Heinemann, 2013.

Oppenheimer, Mark. *Knocking on Heaven's Door: American Religion in the Age of Counterculture*. New Haven, CT: Yale University Press, 2003.

Orsi, Robert A. *Between Heaven and Earth: The Religious Worlds People Make and the Scholars Who Study Them*. Princeton, NJ: Princeton University Press, 2006.

Pew Forum on Religion and Public Life. "Many Americans Mix Multiple Faiths: Easter, New Age Beliefs Widespread." Washington, DC: Pew Research Center, December 2009.

————. "US Religious Landscape Survey: Religious Affiliation Diverse and Dynamic." Washington, DC: Pew Research Center, February 2008.

Plate, Brent, ed. *Key Terms in Material Religion*. New York: Bloomsbury Academic, 2015.

"A Portrait of Jewish Americans." Pew Research Center Religion and Public Life Project, October 1, 2013, http://www.pewforum.org/2013/10/01/jewish-american -beliefs-attitudes-culture-survey/.

Pleck, Elizabeth. *Celebrating the Family: Ethnicity, Consumer Culture, and Family Rituals*. Cambridge: Harvard University Press, 2000.

Prell, Riv-Ellen. *Fighting to Become Americans: Assimilation and the Trouble between Jewish Women and Jewish Men*. Boston: Beacon, 2000.

Promey, Sally M., ed. *Sensational Religion: Sensory Cultures in Material Practice*. New Haven, CT: Yale University Press, 2014.

Putnam, Robert D., and David E. Campbell. *American Grace: How Religion Divides and Unites Us*. New York: Simon and Schuster, 2012.

Roof, Wade Clark. *Religious Pluralism and Civil Society*. Los Angeles: Sage, 2007.

Roof, Wade Clark, Bruce Greer, and Mary Johnson. *A Generation of Seekers: The Spiritual Journeys of the Baby Boom Generation*. San Francisco: Harper, 1994.

Rose, Anne C. *Beloved Strangers: Interfaith Families in Nineteenth Century America*. Cambridge, MA: Harvard University Press, 2001.

Rubel, Nora L. "The Feast at the End of the Fast: The Evolution of an American Jewish Ritual." In *Religion, Food, and Eating in North America,* edited by Benjamin E. Zeller et al. New York: Columbia University Press, 2014. 234–52.

Sack, Daniel. *Whitebread Protestants: Food and Religion in American Culture.* Illustrated ed. New York: Palgrave Macmillan, 2001.

Sarna, Jonathan D. *American Judaism: A History.* New Haven, CT: Yale University Press, 2005.

Schmidt, Leigh Eric. *Consumer Rites: The Buying and Selling of American Holidays.* Princeton, NJ: Princeton University Press, 1997.

Schmidt, Leigh Eric. *Restless Souls: The Making of American Spirituality.* Berkeley: University of California Press, 2012.

Seamon, Erica B. "A Leap of Faith: Interreligious Marriage in the United States." Washington, DC: Berkley Center for Religion, Peace, and World Affairs at Georgetown University, 2008.

Tentler, Leslie Woodcock. *Catholics and Contraception: An American History.* Ithaca, NY: Cornell University Press, 2009.

Thompson, Jennifer. *Jewish on Their Own Terms: How Intermarried Couples Are Changing American Judaism.* New Brunswick, NJ: Rutgers University Press, 2014.

Tillich, Paul. *Dynamics of Faith.* New York: HarperOne, 2001.

Tweed, Thomas. *The American Encounter with Buddhism, 1844–1912: Victorian Culture and the Limits of Dissent.* Chapel Hill: University of North Carolina Press, 2000.

Witzling, Mara. "Quilt Language: Towards a Poetics of Quilting." *Women's History Review* 18, no. 4 (n.d.): 619–37.

Wuthnow, Robert. *After Heaven: Spirituality in America since the 1950s.* Berkeley: University of California Press, 2000.

Zurawik, David. *The Jews of Prime Time.* Brandeis Series in American Jewish History, Culture, and Life. Hanover, NH: Brandeis University Press, 2003.

Index

Abie's Irish Rose, 55–56, 224–25n9

Adaptation, of mono-faith communities (churches, synagogues, mosques, temples) to interfaith families, 206

Adult children of interfaith families, 201–19; as creating meaningful lives, 201; siblings with different adult identities, 215; speculations about, 212

Advice manuals, 7, 13, 48, 50, 53, 81, 93, 94–106, 108–10, 161, 174

African-American Jews, 112, 120–28; and accommodation of black traditions, 123–25, 133; and biblical history of slavery, 120; and foodways, 120, 124–25; and legacy of "passing," 124, 230n10; and racism inside Jewish community, 66, 120, 127

Allen, Woody, 74–76

All in the Family, 67

American family: as central to American nation-state, 16; as weapon against communism, 15

American individual: choosing in the religious marketplace, 205; as creating one's one combinations and community, 205; as multicultural, 205; as Protestant, 205

American interfaith experience: change in, 215–19; institutions "honoring some of who you are," 219

American Jewish Committee, 95

American Jews, proportion of population, 3

American mainstream: as embodying modernity, 52; as the white Protestant norm, 52; assimilation to and marital happiness, 52; as Protestant Christian, 59; relative positions of Catholics and Jews to, 66

American myths: of classless society, 67; princess and pauper stories, 67

American religious history, 10

American religious landscape, 201; as changing, 215–19

Americans, religiously unaffiliated, 116–17

American therapeutic culture, 141–42

American values, as shared by Protestants, Catholics, and Jews, 82

Annie Hall, 74, 75–77; alternative titles for, 76

Apostolic Letter, of Pope Paul VI, 37–38, 223n50; and increased Protestant-Catholic tensions, 37; as same position on interfaith marriage as institutional Judaism, 37

Are You There, God? It's Me, Margaret, 26, 149

Assimilation: and achievement of higher social standing, 58; as all gain and no loss, 58; and avoidance of discrimination, 70; as desirable and inevitable, 58; and language, 65; and loss of Jewish peoplehood, 208; and popular culture emphasis on individualism, 204; and relationship to Judaism, 72. *See also* Marriage, interfaith in America

Atheism, 188

Autonomous self and decision-making, 204–05

Baptism, 101, 103; as bringing Protestants and Catholics together in communion, 37; secret, 213

Bar and bat mitzvah ceremonies. *See* B'nai mitzvah ceremonies

Barker, Lee, 174

Being Both: Embracing Two Religions in One Interfaith Family, 212, 215

Beliefs, blended, from multiple religious systems, 163–64

Berman, Lila Corwin, 222n29

Big Tent Judaism, 209, 217

Black and Jewish. *See* African-American Jews

Blume, Judy, 149–50

B'nai mitzvah ceremonies, 91, 114, 116, 120, 125–27, 130, 134, 184–92, 208, 210, 213–14

Bolton Street Synagogue, 214

Bridget Loves Bernie, 51–52, 59–69, 77; and class as greater difference than religion, 67; depicting post-Camelot Catholics, 64; humor based in difference between generations, 59; lack of Catholic objections, 68–69; message about humanity beyond race and religion, 66; Nielsen ratings, 67, 69; and post–World War II generation, 65; public criticism of, 67–69; as remake of *Abie's Irish Rose*, 60; showing primary importance of couple over upbringings, 61; signals of Catholic ethnicity, 64; as threat to Jewish continuity, 68

Brink, Fredrick W., 41–43

Campbell, David, 2, 138

Catholic Church, Post–Vatican II: as American religion, 31, 35; anger at, 115; concern about intermarriage with Protestants, 31; and concern with sacrament of marriage, 19; concerns of, expressed to American public, 31;

Corpus Christi, 214; Jewish child's experience of, 214; leadership of, 155; not considering Protestant marriages valid, 45

Catholic-Hindu wedding, 209

Catholic-Jewish intermarriage, and relative social status of white, Christian Catholics and more recently immigrated Jews, 66. See also *Bridget Loves Bernie*

Catholic laity: as having different concerns than their leadership, 49; and support of allowing mixed marriage, 38

Catholic League, 155

Catholic-Protestant intermarriage, 32–41

CBS, 51, 59, 67–69

Central Conference of American Rabbis (CCAR), 6, 48–49, 84–88, 89

Children of interfaith marriages: and access to Christian popular culture, 117–18; adding Hindu elements to bar mitzvah, 208; bedtime prayers of, 179–80; as casualties of interfaith marriage, 26; and children's books, 106–09; coming-of-age ceremonies for, 184–85, 187, 190, 208; and concept of half a religion, 96, 148–52; and confusion, 181–82; and formal Jewish education, 26, 82, 88–90, 95–96, 110, 112, 128, 143, 162; as Jewish partner in their own interfaith marriages, 118; one answer to outcome questions, 219; and parental responsibility to provide skills to make spiritual choices, 200; as primed for empathy, resisting intolerance, 139, 189; psychological health of, 30; psychologists' opinion of psychic damage to, 26; questions about outcome as adults, 211, 219; and self-esteem, 98; six-year-old's perspective, 183–84; and status in synagogue life, 22; traditions in opposition, 188; use of stories with, 182–83

Children's books, 106–10; emphasizing family connections, 148; showing differences in beliefs, 147; showing mutual respect across religious boundaries, 148

Chrismukkah, 136–38; as equally offensive to both religious institutions, 155; framed as "cultural," 136, 153–60; holiday cards, 156–69; and materialistic components to Christmas and Hanukkah, 155–56; as move away from theologically oriented holidays, 155; and *The OC*, 136; as adopted in popular culture, 136–37

Chrismukkah: Everything You Need to Know to Celebrate the Hybrid Holiday, 153–60

Christ. *See* Jesus Christ

Christianity: as based in personal belief, 80, 100, 102, 110; as culture, 4; as religion, 4, 95. *See also* Identity, Christian

Christian-Jewish marriage: with alternative lifestyle, 165–72; as model for interfaith marriages, 211

Christian marriage, definition of, among Catholics and Protestants after the Reformation, 54

Christian women raising Jewish children, 81, 101–06, 226n2

Christmas, 101, 103–06, 176–77, 181, 217–18; conflict with Hanukkah, 177; embraced as secular American holiday by immigrant Hindu community, 208; and excluding Christmas tree, 11, 119; with homesteading values, 168; as *other*, 106, 125–26, 130–31; and purchasing tree from Satmar Hassid in Brooklyn, 215

Church of Latter Day Saints (LDS), 180, 188. *See also* Mormon-Jewish family

Circumcision, Jewish law requiring versus Hindu cultural objections to, 208–10

Civil courts, US. *See* United States legal system

Classless society, American myth of, 67

Clinton, Bill, 201

Clinton, Chelsea, 201, 205

Clinton, Hillary Rodham, 201

Clinton-Mezvinsky children: and religious choices—his, hers, or both, 203; public entreaties to raise as Jews, 203

Clinton-Mezvinsky wedding, 201–03; as blended ceremony, 202; as interfaith, Methodist-Jewish, 201; as not without controversy, 203; perceived as normal by parents, guests, media, 202

Commission on Reform Jewish Outreach, 112

Communal religious life, Jewish: and concerns about assimilation, 51; as ethnic enclaves, 92; non-Jews entering, 92; patrollable boundaries of, 50

Community censure, fear of, and religiously endogamous couples staying married, 44

Comparisons, of Christianity and Judaism, 100–06

Conversion: conditions of, 25; as depicted in children's books, 106–07; and gender imbalance and expectations, 79; and giving up Christian practice and customs, 78–79, 173, 194; as insulting to patrilineal Jews, 214; as invalidated by Orthodox rabbis, 86; and Jewish laws and customs, 78; from Judaism to Catholicism, 196; as legally binding, 86; for non-Jewish spouse, 22–23; and patrilineal descent, 88–92; for Protestant spouse, 34, 96–97; and religious without ethnic assimilation, 82; reason for, 97; in *Sex and the City*, 78. *See also* Christmas; Gender; Jewish community

Converts: becoming more definitionally Jewish, 94; fervor of, 109; Jewish attitudes toward, 28; as second-class Jews, 25; as sincere Christians, 25

Cordero family (pseudonym), 128–33. *See also* Latin American Jews

Court cases, divorce, 84–87; and conversion certificate as legally binding contract, 86; and custodial parent determining religious affiliation of children, 85; and enforcement of premarital promises about religious education of children, 84; and individual religious freedom, 84; as revealing religious policy and practice in interfaith families, 84

Cowan, Paul, 81, 94–98

Cultural heritage, influence of, 97

Cultural rigidity, of older generation, 71, 73

Culture: American secular, 77; asymmetry of, between Christianity and Judaism, 101; definition of, 110–11; as distinct from religion, 3, 4; as ethnicity, 201; and equivalency of practice, 137, 140; popular, 3; in relationship to religion, 204; as strategic term, 3. *See also* Religion

Definition of terms, 111, 112

Degrees of faith and community, views on of Jews and Catholics, 39

Discrimination: avoidance of through assimilation, 70; in the Jewish community, 28, 92–93

Dispensations from Rome: becoming commonplace, 49; as demonstrations of desire to create new Catholics, 34; as expressed in nomenclature of contract law, 34; requirements for, 34

Diversity in the Jewish community. *See* African-American Jews; Latin American Jews

Divorce, 83–88; and child custody, 83; as a psychologically healthy choice, 44; reasons for, 44

Divorce rate: concerns about, 42; increase in, 16; Protestant dismissal of influence by intermarriage, 43

Dovetail Institute, 147

Easter, 1–2, 76, 103, 114, 119, 124–25, 127, 140, 147, 154, 175, 177, 181, 208, 217

Ecumenicism and commonalities among Christians, 49

Eichhorn, David Max, 24–25; and Jewish continuity, 25

Endogamy, Jewish, defense of, 20

Essrig, Harry, 22

Ethical Culture Society, 207

Ethnicity: as culture, 102; definition of, 110; and Jewish, and "New Jews," 91–94. *See also* Identity, formation of; Identity, Jewish

Ethnicity, optional, 175; and appropriation concerns, 196

Ethno-therapy, 97–98

Faith, as Christian perspective on religious identity, 11

Families, interfaith: as characterized in the American imagination, 10, 14; defined, 11; Jewish-Hindu and circumcision, 208; nonreligious, 154, 159–60; other than Jewish-Christian using similar strategies, 209–11; in popular media, 10; raising children with both Christian and Jewish practice, 13, 189–200; Reform Jewish Leadership and, 81; religious practices of, 10; welcoming children into, 70. *See also* Marriage, interfaith in America; Marriage, mixed

Families, racially diverse: multicultural, 154; and religiously complex practice, 9. *See also* African-American Jews; Latin American Jews

Felix, Abbot Richard, and worthiness to receive Sacrament, 33
Feminism, 10, 16, 29, 43, 48, 161, 168, 170, 172, 179, 180, 184–89 passim, 194, 199
Foodways, 10, 71, 145–46, 150, 178–79; African-American, 120, 124–25; Ashkenazi, 62; differences in, 61–62; and family identity, 146–47; Jewish mother trope and, 63–65; Latino, 131; matrilineal transfer of, 145; spoofing of, 154; as tradition, 146
Friedlander, Barbara, 93

Gay marriage, 7
Gender: and conversion expectations, 70, 104; and navigating an interfaith home, 114–19
Gendered stereotypes: and sexual encounters, 57; illustrating impediments to assimilation, 57. *See also* Ghetto girl; Shiksa goddess
General Commission on Chaplains and Armed Forces Personnel, 15
Gentile-free spaces, synagogues as, 93
Ghetto girl: as gendered stereotype of archetypal Jewish woman, 56; as grasping and crass stereotype, 56, 225n10
Gittleson, Roland, 22–23
Gittleson-Polish amendment, 23–24
Glaser, Joseph, 84; and children of interfaith divorce, 84–86
Gluckman, Donald, 87
Goldschmidt, Henry, 8, 137, 143
Gompertz, Ron, 136, 153–56
Gould, Rebecca Kneald, 166
Grandparents, 92, 105–07, 109–10, 120–21, 123, 126–28, 131, 148, 182, 208; in children's books, 145–50; in popular culture, 66, 70, 72–73
Groff family (pseudonym), 9, 172–79, 199, 234
Gross, Rachel, 108

The Half-Jewish Book: A Celebration, 151
Half/Life: Jew-ish Tales from Interfaith Homes, 211–12
Harms, Judge Christina, 1, 2
Hart-Landsberg, Leah, 176, 217
Hawxhurst, Joan C., 147
The Heartbreak Kid, 56–59, 74, 76; as depicting interfaith marriage as desirable, 56
Heinze, Andrew, 11, 137, 156
Hillel, 24, 191, 213
Hindu Nationalism, rise of, 208
Home: as private space, 6, 53; of custodial parent after divorce, 87–88; as a place of religious development, 21; as a place of sanctuary, 21
Home, dual-religion: as committed to egalitarian marriages, 199; contradictory truth claims, 100; and development intentional moral frameworks, 199; level of religious engagement of, 99–100; as not confusing to children, 2, 26, 41, 72–73, 88, 95–96, 119, 152, 154, 164, 181–83, 214–16; as religiously blended, 144; as valuing individual and family needs over those of religious groups, 199–200
Home, single-religion, 95–100; argument for, 194; but bicultural, 151; as desirable, 101–08; level of religious engagement of, 99–100; and sacrifice of one partner's childhood religion, 101–06, 173
Homesteading, interfaith, 165–72; emphasis on feminist, nonviolent moral and psychological development for children, 168; as escape from consumption-oriented culture, 165; ethical commitments of the adult children, 170; lack of compatible religious communities, 167; as prioritizing, not shifting, values, 165; sustainability and self-sufficiency as values, 169

Household, single-faith, 79–80
Humanist psychology, 142

Identity, Christian: as distinct from
cultural identity, 100; as resting in
personal belief, 80; undefined by, as
adults, 115–16
Identity, cultural, 2; Christian as more
than creed, 12; as different from
religious, 99; hybrid, 13, 14; as
intersected with consumer-based
identity formation, 137; as requiring
protection, 4; as tied to practices and
consumption, 141
Identity, ethnic: acquisition of, 109; as a
marginalized people, 101
Identity, Jewish: and absence of
Christian practice, 110; as culturally
Jewish, 172; half-Jewish, 148–52; and
influence of non-Jewish extended
family, 91; inhabiting versus enacting
Jewish observance, 80; and Jewish
home, 20; and Jewish spouse, 20; as
life experience, 114; as "looking
Jewish," 171; and matrilineal descent,
213–14; and patrilineal descent, 88–92,
213; as resting in belief and culture, 80.
See also Identity, cultural; Identity,
ethnic
Identity, religious, 2, 212; for children,
94–100; Christian, in creedal terms, 4;
and commitment involved for
families, 132; and confusion about and
dysfunction, 26, 181–82; as cultural, 93;
as different from cultural, 99;
fragmented, 96; Jewish as compared
to ethnic identity, 4; Jewish, definition
of, 82; Jewish, as limited to aspects
under rabbinic control, 82; as plural,
4; plural as lonely, 214; and relationship with practice, 80; requiring
protection, 4; as separable from other
forms of identity, 26; and transmitting

family recipes, 10; Unitarian Universalist, 173
Identity formation of, authentic, 31;
multicultural, 205; and upbringing,
211
Immigration Act of 1924, 56
Immigration and Nationality Act of 1965,
139
Individual conscience: as autonomous
moral unit, 50; sacredness of, 46
Individualism: and Protestantism, 41;
and religion, 67
Interfaith dating: and politics, 74–75; and
style of social interaction, 75; and
unintended pregnancy, 74
Interfaith Family Project (IFFP), 9,
189–98; founding of, 192; community
purpose, 192–93; as dual heritage
under one roof, 196; as dual religious
community or a third way, 197; as
impediment to engaging deeply with
one tradition, 196; as living, multicultural ideology, 198; orientation toward
children, 193; and religious lives of
children in adulthood, 195, 197;
17-year-old's perspective, 197; use of
Jewish and Christian liturgical sources
and practices, 191–92
Interfaith marriage. *See* Marriage,
interfaith in America
Interfaith marriage combining other
religions, other ethnicities: Catholic-
Hindu, 209; Jewish-Hindu, 208;
Jewish-Muslim, 207
Interfaith weddings. *See* Weddings,
interfaith
Intermarried. *See* Marriage, interfaith;
Marriage, mixed
Islamic fundamentalism, rise of, 208

Jackson, Alyssa Wolin (pseudonym),
117–18
Jarvis, Reverend Julia, 191, 193, 195

Jesuit education, 128–30
Jesus Christ, 1, 29, 55, 100, 102, 105, 118, 122, 147, 181–82, 184, 191, 210; divinity of, 195; historical, 195
Jewish Board of Rabbis, 155
Jewish community: and accommodating interfaith marriages, 93; and discouraging Christian practices, 119; and involvement in, 114–19; preservation of, 18; and racism within, 127; as religious belief and culture, 100; and minority status of, 101–02, 119; as religious, rather than racial group, 20
Jewish education, 26, 82, 88–90, 95–96, 110, 112, 128, 143, 162, 217; and children with patrilineal descent, 89–90, 194; and locus of Jewish self-understanding, 88
Jewish home: after divorce, 87–88; choosing over Christian home, 100–06, 194; Christian women creating, 79; and Reform movement, 79
Jewish law: and b'nai mitzvah, 91; and conversion, 78; kosher rules of, 71; and patrilineal descent, 88–92; and practice in reference, but not adherence, to, 121; and Responsa, 222n12
Jewish mother, trope of, 62–64
Jewishness, defining, 81–82, 91; and being challenged about, 213, 215; from four-year-old's perspective, 180; as hereditary identity, 92; and patrilineal descent, 88–92; of in religious manuals, 94–95, 98. *See also* Identity, Jewish
Jewish Outreach Institute, 27
Judaism: as an American religion, 21; as Christianity without Christ, 100; as culture, 4, 110; and ethical principles of the home, 20; as ethnic identity versus observance practices, 31, 80, 110; framing of, in creedal terms, 82; as more progressive choice, 186–89;

Reform movement in, 6; as religion, 4, 79; as "universal religion," 29. *See also* Judaism, Reform movement
Judaism, institutional, in accordance on interfaith marriage with Catholicism, 37
Judaism, Messianic, 194
Judaism, Modern Orthodoxy movement, 177
Judaism, Reform movement, 6, 17; and accepting of children of interfaith families, 200; and patrilineal descent, 193, 213; and policies on performing interfaith wedding ceremonies, 19, 173, 204

Kane, Eli, 197
Kaplan-Brewster family (pseudonym), 165–72, 198–99, 217, 233n15
Katz Miller, Susan, 139, 162, 186, 189–95, 198–200, 209, 212
Keaton, Diane, 76
Kendall, Jeffery, 1
Kendall divorce, 1–2, 5
Kennedy, John F., Catholicism and presidential campaign of, 31, 64
Khan-Levine wedding (pseudonym), 207
Kimball-Geller family (pseudonym), 9, 183–89 (passim), 196, 199, 203, 205
King, Andrea, 81, 94–95, 98–100, 102–05, 203
Klein, Daniel, 151–52
Kueng, Father Hans, 38

Landon, Michael, 69–70
Language: and assimilation, 65; as ethnic marker, 74, 131; for interfaith way of being, 197–98; and marking distinctions, 105; as metaphor for having two religions, 139; and offering religious choices, 184–89; understanding of, 178

Latin American Jews, 113, 126, 128–33; choosing to raise children as Jews, 129; and foodways, 131; Latin identity as choice, not default, 132–33

Lears, T. J. Jackson, 141

Leventhal, Mel, 112

Light the Lights!, 145, 147

Little House on the Prairie, 69–73, 77, 226n37; and women's rights, 69; and disability rights, 69; and religious material culture, 71; and foodways, 71; Shabbat dinner, 71; Sunday dinner, 71

Lived religion, 6, 70, 104, 162; and consumption, 11; and family ritual, 73; of Jewishly affiliated interfaith families, 13, 84; and rates of interfaith marriage, 82

Loving v. Virginia, 139

Lynch v. Donnelly, 140

Manuals, religious, 94–95; and delineation of cultural and religious, 94. *See also* Advice manuals

Marbach, Monsignor Joseph, concerns about interfaith marriage, 31–32

Marriage: as bedrock of American life, 21; change in structure of, 97; negotiating styles within, 97–98; social relevance of, 44

Marriage, as contract: binding couple to Catholic Church, 33; versus as Sacrament of the Life, 33; enforcement of by Archbishop, 34; Catholic Church concerns about enforcement of, 35

Marriage, endogamous, 21, 31; and Protestants, 48; as stable, 20, 44; as strengthened by social change, 44; versus assimilationist mixed marriages, 20

Marriage, interfaith in America: and American military, 15, 32; and assimilation, 13; children of, 13, 30–31,

166–72, 178–79; Christian-Jewish, 2, 8; Christian-Jewish as archetypal, 3; Christian, Jewish, and multiracial, 13, 108, 120–28; as contrary to the tradition of Jewish religion, 22; and conversion, 17; creating Jewish families from, 13; as dangerous to marital bond, 15; definition of, 2, 3; effect on Jewish communal life, 161–62; as difficult and unwise, 43; and egalitarian couples, 199; and generational tensions, 64–65; and impact on Jewish community, 8; and Jewish fears of extinction, 47; multiple paths for, 203; objections to, 13, 15, 21, 32, 33, 37, 95; as path into American secular, 52–54; and patrilineal descent, 88–92; prevention of, 17, 22–30, 33–34; and primetime television, 69–70; Protestant position on, 7, 44; raising children in, 13, 70; rates of, 2, 12, 47, 162–64; and sacramental theology of marriage, 49; and trends in U.S. history, 8; and *U.S. Catholic* survey about, 39–40. *See also* Marriage, mixed; Multiracial interfaith families

Marriage, mixed, use of term, 11, 222n11. *See also* Marriage, interfaith in America

Marriage, popular understandings of, 54; as embedded in liberal Protestant ideals, 54

Mary Tyler Moore Show, 67

Material culture, 142, 156; definition of, 226n35; and Protestant culture, 70–71

Maude and Catholic objections to abortion, 69

McGinity, Keren, 115

Media, popular: as depicting failure of interfaith marriage as failure of assimilation, 53; depiction of stereotypes in, 53; emphasizing ethnic stereotypes and class differences, 18;

and ethnicity as excess, 53, 224n1; and promotion of interfaith marriage as a social good, 18

Mezvinsky, Marc, 201, 205

Minnesota, as popular symbol of all-American charm, 58, 225n12

Mono-faith communities (churches, synagogues, mosques, temples), adaptation of, to interfaith families, 206

Moorman, Margaret, 145

Moral life in absence of religious identity, 171–72

Mormon-Jewish family, 179–89; "Jack" (unorthodox) Mormon lifestyle, 180; blended wedding ceremony of, 181; Mormon baptism and b'nai mitzvah, 184–86; influence of feminist philosophy, 186–87

Mould, Daphne, 38–40; survey of lay support of interfaith marriages, 39–40

The Mozart Season, 148–52, 172

Multiculturalism, 5, 13, 136–44, 204; and Clinton-Mezvinsky wedding, 203; impact changing over time, 149; and interfaith holiday celebration, 138; and material consumption of practice and objects, 137, 185–86; moral logics of, 201, 205; and optional ethnicity, 204, 212; and potential impermanence of choice of religion, 187; and ultimate religious authority, 185

Multiracial interfaith families, 13, 112–35, 198; and heightened awareness of differences between childhood cultures, 134

Museum of Jewish Heritage, 215

Muslim-Hindu marriages, 208. *See also* Interfaith marriages combining other religions, other ethnicities

Muslim-Jewish marriages, 209; as patrilineal and matrilineal descent, respectively, 209

My Two Grandmothers, 145–48

Native American cultural insights, 182–83

Needs of the Jewish community, as outweighing the needs of a couple, 27

Neubauer Family Foundation, 162

New York Board of Rabbis, 1973 resolution on performing mixed marriages, 22

1960s, and values of individualism and spiritual seeking, 65

Nonfaithful and differently faithful, views on of Jews and Catholics, 39

Non-Jewish extended family, influence of on children, 91

The OC, 136, 156

Older, Effin, 145

Olitzky, Kerry, 209, 217

Optional ethnicity, 13, 187, 204

Orsi, Robert, 144

Orthodox movement: and challenging legitimacy of Reform conversions, 86; as outlier in religious choices, 186

Patrilineal descent, 29–30; and Israel, 91; and Jewish upbringing, 90

Pew Foundation, 161–64, 206

Pew Research Center for Religion and Public Life, 161–62

PJ Library, 108

Pleck, Elizabeth, 147

Pluralism, and a Protestant norm, 5–6

Polish, David, 22–23

Political movement: American Indian Movement, 139; Black Pride, 139; influence of, 139

Popular culture, 77; interfaith marriage in, 51. *See also* Media, popular

Portnoy, Mindy Avra, 106–07

Princess and pauper stories, American love of, 67

Protestant-Catholic intermarriage, 32–41; historically more fraught, 208; statistics regarding, 36

Protestant culture: material culture of, 70; as not neutral, 70; set of valued practices, 70

Protestant-inflected secularism: as ethnically neutral, 52; familial culture of, 70; as permeating American imagination, 53

Protestantism: ecumenicism and, 7; as individualistic, 41; public voice of, 6–7; religious beliefs, 70; as social neutral, 70. *See also* Protestant culture

Protestant Mainline: defense of the individual, 41; and Jewish concerns about intermarriage, 47; as lesser Christians (than Catholics), 48; and nature of marriage, 41–42; and nurturing of children by both parents, 42; objections to Catholic position on interfaith marriage, 45–46; response to interfaith marriage, 41–48; support for individual rights of marrying couple, 43; supportive of intermarried couples, 43

Protestants, American: as less threatened by intermarriage, 19; regarded as heretics or schismatics by Catholic Church, 37

Protestant theology, and the primacy of the individual, 17

Putnam, Robert, 138

Rabbinical Council of Greater Washington (RCGW), 68

Rabbis: and performing interfaith marriage ceremonies, 21–22

Rabbi's Manual, 89

Race, and power dynamics, 120, 138

Redford, Robert, 74

Reform Jewish leadership, 81–94; and patrilineal descent, 88–92

Reform movement, 5, 6; and defining Jewish identity, 82; and determining who is a Jew, 30; as most liberal, 1; and patrilineal descent, 88–92; and relationship to Jewish law, 30; and understandings of identity, 80–81; and welcoming interfaith families, 28

Religion: and culture, 2; as defined by religious leaders, 17; as distinct from culture, 3, 4; and identity, 2; as strategic term, 3; as community over individual, 67; as holiday celebrations, practices, community, and morality, 95; institutional, 6; rate of persons changing religious affiliations, 212; in relationship to culture, 204; "seeker" mode of, 137, 137–38, 142; as spiritual engagement outside institutions, 142. *See also* Culture

Religious communities: Christian, Jewish, Unitarian Universalist, 9; connection to, 9; of intentionally blended Jewish-Christian families, 9

Religious decision-making: individual as primary unit of in American Protestantism, 204; in relationship with community and family, 204

Religious dispositions: as created by acts of blending, 206; and religious communities, 206

Religious education of children: biblical stories and, 177; use of stories and, 182–83

Religious iconography, display of, 1, 32

Religious leaders, focus on religious affiliation, 18

Religious nones, 196, 206, 217

Religious practice: combining multiple, 4, 8; depictions of in *Bridget Loves Bernie*, 61; as existing apart from meaning, 206; in the home, 3; family rituals, 11, 73; hybrid, 137, 143–44, 152–60; Jewish dietary laws, 63; and the logic of the marketplace, 5; and relationship with religious identity, 80

Rose, Anne, 221n9

Sacrament of the Life, and freedom from sin, 33

Sacraments, Catholic: and interfaith marriage, 18; Sacrament of Marriage as Sacrament of the Life, 33

Salvation. *See* Truth claims

Schindler, Alexander, 27–30, 92, 222n30; and children of interfaith divorce, 84–86; and converting the "unchurched," 28–29; and patrilineal descent, 29–30

Schmidt, Leigh Eric, 137

Second Vatican Council: influence on intermarriage guidelines, 19, 31, 32, 36–38, 47, 49, 223n35; erasing practices separating Catholics and Protestants, 65; moved from Old World to modernity, 65

Secular citizen ideal, American, as rooted in Protestant history, 53

Seltzer, Sanford, and children of interfaith divorce, 84–86

Sex in the City, 78–80, 226n1

Shiksa goddess, as gendered stereotype of Gentile woman, 56, 58, 225n10

Snyder, Laurel, 211–19 passim

Sobel, Samuel, 19–21, 30

Speech patterns. *See* Language

Spertus College, interfaith marriage workshops of, 92

Steinem, Gloria, 152

Stereotypes: of African-Americans and Jews regarding education, 121; culture- or personality-based, 98; of Episcopalian WASPs, 78; of Gentile women, 56, 58; of Jewishness, 76; of Latinos, 132; of Midwestern WASPs, 76; of New York Jews, 76

Stories, use of, 209; princess and pauper, American love of, 67

Streisand, Barbra, 74

Supreme Court of Massachusetts ruling on religious training of children, 1

Swafford, Thomas, 67–68

Synagogue Council of America (SCA), 67–68

Television, primetime, and interfaith marriage, 69–70, 224n2

Thompson, Jennifer, 8, 114, 119, 206, 226n2

Tolerance, 151, 157, 160, 165

Toynbee, Arnold J., 47

Traditions, blended, 122; from multiple religious systems, 163–64; and story quilt chuppah, 122

Training, religious, of children, 1, 174

Tri-faith America (Catholic, Protestant, Jew): as homogenous "Judeo-Christian" American identity, 16, 29, 39; as prescriptive language, 16

Truth claims: addressing of, 141, 143, 147–48; avoidance of, 102–03, 210–11; commitments to, 200; contradictory, 9, 100, 137, 152; and salvation, 102–03; threats to, 39; multiple, 197; nonbelief in, 153; and public square, 1, 6, 99; as replaced by stories, 209; and resigning doctrinal certainty, 181–82; and traditions in opposition, 188. *See also* Native American cultural insights

Union of American Hebrew Congregations (UAHC), 6, 84–88, 92

Unitarian Universalism, 174, 216–17; and chalice lighting, 178; compared with IFFP, 193; as compromise, 174; and description as a church, 196; Jewish holidays within, 175–78; meaning-driven practice, 195; and metaphoric meaning of holidays, 176–77; variety of practice, 196

Unitarian Universalists for Jewish Awareness (UUJA), 172–79

United States legal system: and protection of prenuptial religious contracts, 35; and separation of church and state, 35

Vatican II. *See* Second Vatican Council
Vuijst, Freke, 151–52

Walker, Alice, 112
The Way We Were, 73–75, 77

Weber, Katharine, 215
Weddings, interfaith, officiating at, 19, 22–23
White, Rabbi Harold, 191, 194
Wilson family (pseudonym), 120–28

Yiddish, use of, 62, 74, 82, 93, 165, 215

Zeitler, Barbara, 1